A New Tomorrow

Tricia Frestel

A catalogue record for this book is available from the National Library of Australia

Copyright © 2019 Patricia Cole
All rights reserved.

ISBN: 1 876922834
ISBN-13: 9781876922832

Linellen Press
265 Boomerang Road,
Oldbury, W.A. 6121
www.linellenpress.com.au

Dedication

This book is dedicated
to my two granddaughters,
Kirsty and Jennifer,
who both enjoy books and have a thirst
for the knowledge found within the pages.

Contents

Dedication iii
Contents v
Acknowledgments vii
1   The Beginning is the most important 1
2   It is an intolerable fact 2
3   Small children accept without question 10
4   Cry "Havoc" 16
5   Childhood is measured 21
6   "Eat your Ice Cream before it Melts" 26
7   "I will have it done, so I order it done." 32
8   Education has produced a vast population 44
9   Parents can learn a lot from their children 55
10   I began to believe nothing of what I heard 63
11   A child becomes an adult e right to be wrong. 70
12   What we have to learn, we learn by doing. 78
13   In the fell clutch of circumstance, ... 90
14   The wisdom of age 105
15   The stupid neither forget, nor forgive, ... 111
INTERLUDE 123
16   If a man points to the moon, ... 125
17   Woe to the man who has not learned, ... 139
18   Oh the days gone by, ... 152
19   I do not know whether there are Gods, ... 162
20   The selfsame well from which our laughter rises, ... 168
21   Home is the sailor home from the sea, ... 175
22   Behind the veil of tears. 183
23   Lord, what fools these mortals be! 188
24   You can, because you must. 200

25	There are very few mistakes in life	204
26	Select a pup	209
27	This only is denied to God:	215
28	And I wonder do I dare,	225
29	There is no armour against fate.	228
30	He who knows others is wise,	241
31	Now is the way clear,	245
32	It is a part of probability	255
33	One crowded hour of glorious life	262
34	Footfalls echo in the memory,	266
35	Reflections	268
36	A Backward Look: Grandfathers.	270
ABOUT THE AUTHOR		278

Acknowledgments

I would like to express grateful thanks to:
Budding Authors of Claremont for their staunch support.
Eversley, who performed a labour of love on the very first proof.
Lena, for putting me on the right path when I doubted.
Louise, for doing all the legwork that makes a book a Book.
And Heather Travers, who had unfailing faith in my ability to make it all happen.
Last, but certainly not the least, Helen Iles, Linellen Press, without whom this book might never have reached the printing stage.
You are ALL the stars in my firmament.

A NEW TOMORROW

1

*The Beginning is the most
important part of the work.*
         Plato 428-347 BC

The Beginning.

When dealing with an unpredictable, basically immoral, manipulative woman with whom he had become inextricably entwined, my father was quite unable to cope. Neither was I. The control over me was so absolute that I grew to fear her.

It had not always been so. I had been loved once, but I could not remember it. My mother, once she had walked away with her lover, became like a wraith, a shadow, hovering somewhere in the past, to be replaced by an imperious autocrat who found it difficult to love, and as a result could not be loved.

My father was a gentle man, kind, intelligent, a product of a good education, well read — but totally wrong. His edict when dealing with hysterical outbursts was that a soft tongue turneth away wrath. It worked for him, hiding behind a newspaper or with his nose in a book, but when I tried, it was dumb insolence. If I retaliated, it was the same thing, only vocal.

Here was I, stuck between a man who knew too much, and a woman who knew almost nothing. Yet I managed to write it all down, and stay sane — or did I?

2

*It is an intolerable fact that some people
do not deserve children.*
Author unknown.

He stood, golden red in the dappled light, pink tongue lolling and dribbling from one side of his mouth, eyes bright and alert in a proud head. The tail of this graceful creature was held parallel to the ground, and blonde wisps hung downward like stalactic hairy icicles. The dog sniffed, then pointed. Nothing moved. The stillness was almost palpable as the warm light from the dying sun breathed through the autumn leaves above. Then the nose, black and shiny, quivered once. Shocking in the silence, a single shot rang out. The collapse was instant and final: the dog lay still.

One of my first memories is of Rusty, the dog. It was some time later when I missed him, that his absence was explained. Like any small child I accepted whatever reason was given. It was my first brush with remembered sorrow. I was just three years old. We found the grave, my brother and I, when the ground was still damp and the grass wilting and withering. Neat little squares of yellow. A patchwork for jumping upon. We leapt up and down delighted to find something new and different, not knowing what lay beneath, or indeed that anything did. The gardener found us, and angrily chased us away. He was a very tall man with piercing blue eyes and a stern face. I didn't know him, but had seen him around the garden snipping and mowing. It is his wife I remember. She was tubby and beautiful in my eyes. They lived in a small cottage somewhere in the grounds, and she would sit me on the front step, and feed me homemade scones smothered in cream and raspberries, some of which she would let me pick from her little side garden.

At this time we lived in Fareham, Hampshire, which lies between Portsmouth and Southampton. The house stood in spacious grounds, which boasted a small wood where Rusty had found his last resting place, and through which roamed a couple of noisy peacocks. One had a beautiful tail, but my how they screeched. There was a rolling green lawn cut by the gardener with what to me looked like a huge green monster upon which he sat. He frightened me which is probably why I didn't like the poor man. I liked to sit on the grass at the feet of my young nanny while she sat in a chair knitting, occasionally using a knitting needle to poke out the marrow from bones filched from the kitchen. This she would carefully place on my fingers, and Rusty would lick it off causing me to giggle helplessly. It was my favourite pastime — Rusty's too I suspect. So much for the garden, happily remembered, and the nanny who imbued in me a fearless lifetime love of dogs. Nannies came and went in that household, but it is she whom above all others I most remember, for her kindness, and her care.

It was not a big house, as houses go. Just large enough to require the services of a cook, a nanny and a maid. A yellow gravel drive wound briefly up to the front door before curving around the side of the building, and disappearing. At the rear, the house overlooked a small courtyard which, in turn, was faced by old stables. These had been converted into garages. One of these was home to a shiny black car which had a little window-hole in the roof. Frustrating for me for I could never quite reach to open it. Above this garage was a lofty room. I was once, and only once, taken into this mystery room, and allowed to play with a beautiful dolls house. I did not know to whom it belonged, but I pretended it was mine. There were numerous boxes lying around which seemed to be overflowing with yellow stuff, which must have been sawdust.

My jolly marrow picking nanny was replaced by a woman named Miss Cross. She not only lived up to her name, but tormented me by such thoughtless acts as sticking cotton wool over my festering boils, or telling me the daddy-long-legs that flapped against the night curtain would disappear when the light was switched off, which even I knew they wouldn't. Worst of all was when she dropped me in the Public Swimming Pool, hoping, no doubt, that I would paddle, doglike. Granted it was the shallow end, but not that shallow. I neither paddled nor floated, but simply sank. Consequently I have never been able to swim, paddle or even float. At least she gave me a lasting respect for deep water. I once hid in the lavatory to get away from her, locked the door, and couldn't unlock it. Mass hysteria all round, but exit Miss Cross.

Mama owned another house, in Southsea, facing a park. Across this was a walk known as The Ladies Mile. From this tall red brick house, attached to several other tall red brick houses, was a view over the park, and across the Solent to the Isle of Wight. Within walking distance was the Canoe Lake, a small man-made body of water of perhaps a metre in depth upon which floated several small boats, some shaped like a swan. My brother nearly tipped me head first into this when he was allowed to push my pram, with me in it, down a slope where he suffered a speed wobble and couldn't stop. The two front wheels ended up in the water before the exciting journey was abruptly stopped. I recall the nanny of that time taking me out in her arms one evening to point out a group of stars in the night sky that looked like two sparkling Scottish terriers, saying I would remember them forever. I have. In later years I took a day bus trip to Southsea, (when I was working in Winchester) and stood on the same street corner, looked up into the same sky, this time in daylight, and remembered. And there are still boats that look like swans on the Canoe Lake.

My brother was two years my senior. He was called Roger which name is shown on his birth certificate along with Rodney and Antony. I was called Sally, which appears absolutely nowhere on my certificate which reads Patricia Shirley Rodney. Why this should be so I have not the least notion, but there it is. Roger was a strange child. We were not often in the same company, me being with Nanny and he being who knows where. He enjoyed horrible occupations like catching flies from the windowpanes in the nursery, and removing their wings to see what they would do. Nobody can tell me that little boys are prone to such deeds because I don't believe they are. He would stalk Rusty with a toy bow and arrow, but I don't think an arrow ever found its mark. Poor Rusty. Years later I learned that the dog had bitten him, and I remember a bandaged arm so no doubt the story was true. That could have been the ultimate cause of Rusty's demise. My brother had his kinder moments, and once made me a potato doll to put in a dilapidated dolls pram he had discovered in the loft.

I didn't really see very much of Mama. She must have been in the offing in order to deal with the constantly changing nannies, and she was there when I lay in a darkened room while a strange man peered at my chest. Most of the time we really only saw her after our nursery tea, before we were put to bed by the Nanny. She was not, however, really important in these early recollections, except perhaps by her very absence. We looked, and were, perfectly well cared for. By all accounts she was a spoilt child of wealthy parents who had doted upon her. When they died they left behind not only a daughter, but also a son, an adopted son, and a great deal of money. Mama depleted her portion rather rapidly and the remainder, still substantial, was tied up in a Trust Fund. Mentioned here because many years later the existence of this Fund was cunningly introduced to me.

Charles Dickens might have described Eileen, my mother, as 'ineddicated' for she had never attended a school but had been taught at home. Supposedly by a governess as opposed to a tutor. Of what possible use was a broad education to a woman of her ilk? As long as she could pour tea behind a silver tea service, and sparkle with wit at a dinner table, nothing else was required of her. She was beautiful, wilful and wayward, as well as capricious and downright naughty. All this acceptable in an age when flappers and flibbertigibbets were fashionable. She sparkled her way into my father's faint heart.

I have spoken hardly at all of my father. The reason is simple enough: he was seldom there. He was born in Swindon, Wiltshire in 1906 and educated at Christ's Hospital, Horsham. In due course, he became a law student in London, but later shocked his widowed mother by burning if not his books, then certainly his boats, and became a student pilot at Cranwell, joining that band of men who 'slipped the surly bonds of earth and danced the skies on laughter silvered wings.'* Thus was his career in the Royal Air Force established. He was of the same era as Douglas Bader, author of Reach for the Sky,* but was four years senior to Bader. When I read the book as a teenager, I gushed with enthusiasm over the man's heroic actions, but my father simply grunted!

Although Daddy was stationed elsewhere, he came sometimes to Fareham. Once he took my brother and I out for a drive in a car. The same car with the window in the roof that I could not reach. He bought us each an ice-cream cone and mine was so pretty, white with cascades of dripping pink. I held it with both hands and gazed at it with admiration. I had no wish to spoil it by licking, and in the end the dripping mess self-destructed. Surely no ice cream had a more brilliant moment of glory? On the same trip we became stuck in a traffic jam and watched an enormous fire engulf an entire house. All very exciting. It never entered my small head that there might have been loss of life. I was to learn that sort of tragedy a year or so later, after the terrible German bombing of Belfast where we were then living, in 1940.

It follows therefore that, by the very nature of his career, he was seldom in one place for very long. It was however, long enough for him, charismatic, and handsome in his R.A.F. uniform with wings a-splendour, to charm with his beautiful modulated speaking voice, the inconstant Eileen. They married. No doubt their life was idyllic for a time. My father was posted to India, and there, as young newly-weds, they began their life together. During a leave of absence in England, their first child was born, my brother, in Portsmouth, in 1931. Returning to India an amah was duly employed, and Eileen no doubt performed her duties as the young wife of a serving officer with, I am sure, great aplomb.

My father was flying in those early years, and I understand that while in India he damaged his back badly. Whether from flying or falling from a horse, I do not know. (My stepmother once tried to sue the R.A.F. for damages, without success!) The back damage put an end to his flying, but not to the end of his career. Although he no longer flew, he played his part, (remembering John Milton's* words on his disability: 'They also serve who only stand and wait,' and was instrumental in turning a great many young men into competent flyers. All would-be pilots begin their training on the ground, and this is what my father excelled in, teaching and training young minds into whippet smart men who knew how to fly almost before they left the ground. Whether the back accident precipitated his return to England, or whether it was my imminent arrival I do not know, but in due course I was born at Bisterne Close, near Burley, in the New Forest on the 14th January 1934. In those days Bisterne Close was a house on the edge of a 'forest close' (an area where wild ponies were temporarily enclosed in order to count and brand them). Over the years the house has been modernised and become absorbed within a lovely residential area.

It must have been about this time that he made the decision to retire from the R.A.F. albeit temporarily. His profession on my birth certificate reads Flight Lieutenant R.A.F. (retired). Perhaps he thought that by being at home more often he might make a better success of his marriage. He tried his hand at tomato farming somewhere near Arundel, but the brief respite did not work because he returned to his chosen career. In our Fareham days he was always in uniform. Once a pilot, always a pilot, even on the ground.

Once again in uniform, history repeated itself and he was soon posted away from home. With my father being up north, so to speak, and Mama being down south, well able to live comfortably in one or another of her homes, a situation brewed that could not last, and would inevitably explode. Living in a naval area she could hardly avoid meeting a Lieutenant Commander in the Royal Navy. I saw him at the house once and thought him rather fat with a lot of blonde hair, but then most men looked good in a uniform and let's face it, the naval officers' uniform was much smarter than the air force! In the event, they fell hopelessly in love. He became her one great joy at the expense of all else. Whether they were right or wrong, who am I to judge? Much of this paragraph is conjecture, but I have tried to weave the threads together to make a pattern from the snippets I have heard. The words in a way serve to illustrate how an unlikely pairing could affect the offspring of such a union. Here I am given pause to wonder which pairing I mean, that of my father and mother, or that of my mother and her lover.

As that summer of 1938 drew to its close two events occurred which, although totally unrelated, would change the course of my life forever. Firstly the dark cloud that peeped hesitantly above the clear English horizon that season, very slowly gathered gloomier cumulus, relieved temporarily during later months by Neville Chamberlain's pretty, paper-clutching speech of "peace in our time". The year following would herald the greatest war in the history of mankind. Millions of lives would be re-directed or totally lost. Few, if any, would remain unscathed. Closer to me, and long before the autumn leaves had completed their golden shower, came the second event, immediate and devastating. Mama took us to a railway station in London, and with the words to my father, "Here are your children" left us. Then, with a flick of her fur foxtails, she was gone from our childhood forever.

3

Small children accept without question whatever life deals them. The past does not exist, the future not even dreamed of. They live only in the present.

Myself

Here we were, two little children, unaware that anything was wrong. We were not abandoned in the true sense of the word, because we were met by my father. I have absolutely no memory of Mama leaving us on that railway station. No, we were not abandoned, we were simply dropped off, like a cotton thread flicked from a coat and haphazardly dropped. In hindsight, it's a bit like losing a limb, losing a mother for no other reason than she wanted to be lost, not through death, not through sickness, not through mental illness, but simply because she no longer had time for us. Some might give the excuse that she was utterly in love, but no love is great enough to give up your children, never knowing when, or if, you would see them again. No, carnal love, or any other love, is not enough. Such an act is criminal. But this is only one side of the story and, in all humanity, there must be another. However, there isn't.

The tale continues that Mama had informed my father that either he collected the children or she would send them to his mother. I don't think he believed she would carry out the threat, but either way, and for whatever reason, here we were and away we went. So began my first train ride. Another first was coming up: I would soon meet my grandmother, and my aunt. They knew me, but I did not know them.

In those days trains were steam driven and a carriage which boasted a corridor was a rarity. Mostly there was a door each side of a compartment seating four or five people facing each other. I had a window seat opposite my father. As the train had not started the door remained open until it was time for the porter on the platform to walk the length of his particular carriage, slamming all the doors shut prior to the train's departure. I wriggled myself forward by hanging onto the crack between the door and the side of the train, the better to peer outside, and at that precise moment the door was slammed, and we began to inch forward, while my fingers remained in the door. Daddy, as I shall from henceforth call him, leapt up and somehow managed to extricate me. How, I do not know. He thrust my fingers into his mouth where the warmth soon took away the pain. I must have had very pliable fingers for there were no side effects but I have had slightly crooked fingers ever since.

My paternal grandmother, Christina Amy Part, to whom we were duly delivered by Daddy, was in her middle fifties. She was still an attractive woman living contentedly, augmenting her income by letting out the ground floor of her home, and teaching at a local school. She had learned to accept her only real personal tragedy, that of losing her seafaring husband who gone down with his ship during the First World War. She lived with her daughter, my Aunt Renée, in a red brick, free-standing house three storeys high, set in a small garden in a row of similar houses, all tall and narrow, ringed with evergreen hedges, in Southsea, within walking distance of the Canoe Lake, into which my brother had almost tipped me. Here she had lived and completed the upbringing of her two children in quiet acceptance of her fate, getting on with her life in what amounted to an orderly fashion, and encountering only one or two minor hiccups along the way, mostly caused by her two otherwise malleable children.

Aunt Renée, my father's sister, was a slightly built pretty woman in her twenties. She had made the mistake some years earlier of falling in love with the son of a Middle Eastern potentate. The love had been returned but such sons, however remote the crown, were not permitted to marry commoners, and certainly not foreign ones, no matter how gentle the birth. Thus it was that she and my grandmother lived together in amicable harmony along with a Scottish terrier named Jean.

My brother and I were absorbed into this peaceful existence without any apparent disruptions. There was not even a ripple of disquiet. Such was my dear grandmother's nature, compassion, and love.

We were housed on the top floor where a small playroom had been created and a little gate installed at the top of the stairs. We hardly ever used this, and the gate was never closed. Most of our free time, of which there was not a lot for we were always busy learning new things, was spent playing ships at sea in the two enormous square chairs with high sides which sat against one wall in the dining room, or crawling under one or the other of the bear skin rugs – one brown, one white, with glassy eyes and yellow teeth – which lay on the floor in the main lounge. For the first time in our lives we ate at the highly polished table in the dining room. Here we were first taught correct table manners with backs kept straighter than the backs of the chairs upon which we sat. This was where I discovered that drops of liquid spilt on the table formed little round circles which could be encouraged to slide, with the help of a small finger, along the polished wood until they disappeared over the edge!

Granny taught at a local junior school a short distance away. It was my somewhat questionable honour, at four years old, to stand in front of the class and read to them. This endeared me to none. Granny did not often make mistakes, but it was unpardonable of her to restrict me to the teacher's rest room at break-time when I wanted so badly to be haring around the concrete playground with the boys and girls who were all a little older than me but whom I considered admirable. My brother could, why not I? I do not remember how I came to be reading at such an early age, but I do recall picking out words from a soft-backed children's book one by one, when all of a sudden they all came together and made sense. Granny never insisted on anything, she merely encouraged: she might well have had the same effect on me as a Jesuit upon a young boy from whom originated the saying "give me a child until he is seven and I will give you the man". Certainly Granny was a strict and old-fashioned teacher who created in me, at so young an age, a desire to learn. I have never forgotten her.

Aunt Renée was always around. She would take me for walks and always bathed me at the end of the day. I cannot remember the name of the Nanny who came to stay. She was more like a friend of the family for she was treated as such. She had come from 'St John's Nursing Profession', I think it was called, and would generally just help all round. I will call her Sister here for want of a better name.

Once we all went on holiday and spent it somewhere on the South Downs, beside the sea, in a caravan park. Still only four, I walked across the park to a small shop and asked if they sold anything for nothing. So taken were they with this odd child that I was given a thin slab of chocolate which I quickly demolished before anyone changed their mind. By the time I got back to the caravan I was covered in chocolate. The three ladies there had been frantically searching the cliff tops for me, and were so relieved admonishment was forgone, but I was dragged unceremoniously back on tired little legs to apologise.

A couple more instances well remembered: being allowed to travel around the block with the milkman on his horse drawn cart – oh such joy! Aunt Renée would wait at the garden gate for my return. Being taken to the Sound to watch a huge Flying Boat land on the Solent Water – I was certain it would sink. Much worse, watching an Air Show some distance away when an aeroplane ploughed into the ground and burst into flames. Then before we knew it Christmas came, the first I can remember. Daddy visited us on a few occasions, and that Christmas was one of them. We had a few toys to open, but the only one I remember was the dolls' cradle given to me by Sister for which she had made all the coverings by hand. It was the most beautiful thing I had ever received. Regrettably, it 'drowned' in the basement when the house was damaged by floods during an air raid. And then it was 1939 and I was five years old at last.

The year that had begun with such disaster had ended in peaceful, happy and contented harmony, surrounded by the love of good people. Perhaps because he was two years older, my brother was allowed a great deal more licence than I. Also, he was a boy. I didn't seem to do very much with him in those Southsea days, and he was much too old to have so many women around him. I didn't much miss him. Each day I had to stand at Granny's side, and read to her from an Enid Blyton comic book which she purchased by the week, and she was teaching me to knit. I was very bad at that. I always had to pull it out and start again.

In May 1939, the newly crowned George VI, with his queen, arrived in Portsmouth en route to visit America. The streets were lined with Royal Marines and hundreds of people all waving miniature Union Jacks, including me. They returned just three months before World War Two was declared. In retrospect I can't but wonder at the equanimity of the man in the street that nearly always battled to make ends meet, but would nevertheless dress carefully in honour of the royal family. This was his heritage, his tradition, which had been handed down through the centuries. Ordinary people, living ordinary lives, doing dull things, on dull days, whose loyalty and pride was absolute.

On another day in this most important of years we were taken to Portsmouth and visited Horatio Nelson's flagship *HMS Victory*, cared for there in Dry Dock. During the war her masts were dismantled and she was carefully protected. Even then, she nearly met with total disaster when an enemy bomb narrowly missed her.

Then came the day when we were called into the lounge at teatime in order to say goodbye to Sister. She was returning to St. Johns, and Aunt Renée was to be leaving as well. We had a little tea party with brown buttered bread and little fairy cakes. Granny had tears in her eyes and we couldn't understand why she would cry at our first party. That was the last night Aunt Renée tucked me into bed.

Very soon after that day we were fitted with gas masks at school and told they were to protect us from funny smells. To small children they were the most terrifying facemasks although they were supposed to look like Mickey Mouse. I had no idea who Mickey Mouse was. The gas mask was kept in a square box on a long strap which had to be carried on every occasion when outside. It became like a second limb and none of us gave it the slightest attention. Sometimes the older children would take them out and play monsters, but I never once opened the box. That was fortunate!

The day after that we began our Big Adventure.

4

'Cry "Havoc" and let slip the dogs of war.'
Marc Anthony – Julius Caesar,
Wm. Shakespeare.

On the 1st September 1939, Southsea Junior School with the Headmistress, staff members, four helpers and 57 children, including Granny, Antony, which was the name that my brother Roger had now been given, and myself, were evacuated and sent to the Isle of Wight. The Government in their wisdom had decided it was a safe place to be. It was uncomfortably close to the Portsmouth Dockyards. To get there necessitated a ferry-crossing over the Solent – that strip of water which divides the mainland from the island – to Ryde and thence by train to Shanklin where we were to find shelter. The Solent curves a little to sneak between the shipyards in the east and the vast greenness of the New Forest to the west. It is wide and deep, dotted with craft, and curves a very short distance north to Southampton. Both Portsmouth and Southampton were heavily bombarded by enemy aircraft during WW 2.

Worthy of historical note here, for those that like this sort of thing, like me, is that Henry VIII's pride and joy, the great flagship *Mary Rose* sank before his eyes in the Solent waters in 1536. She was salvaged at enormous expense in 1982, and the recovery is of immeasurable value.

We disembarked at Ryde and then entrained for Shanklin, a little further along the coast. By the time we reached this little town, the entire convoy of children must have been pretty well exhausted, but the journey was not complete. A crocodile of children was formed and, with the adults, we walked from door to door knocking and dropping off one or two children along the way. It must have been pre-planned, and assistance provided, for how else would it have worked. We were just one school. There were so many others from London and all along the most vulnerable areas of the coastline, children literally torn from their mothers, travelling by train, bus and boat to reach places of safety, away from home to strange and unknown places with unfamiliar people. My brother and I were fortunate for we had Granny. And what an enormous debt is owed to those guardians who cared and loved these sometimes inadequately clothed little children, tried to keep them warm and keep away the hunger.

A young scout carried me on his back along the way and I fell asleep there, only waking up in a church hall at the end of the day. A few children remained and we all sat in a circle and sang a couple of songs. We were fed sandwiches and hot milk, and I promptly fell asleep again. The next day the door knocking continued until there were no children left. Granny, Antony and I, plus three or four other ladies unknown to me, were billeted in a small private hotel.

The following day World War Two was declared: 3rd September 1939.

We remained in this rather nice hotel for a few days and then moved to a smaller boarding house where the three of us shared a room. Every day we walked to the local school and for the very first time I was at last placed in a class with everybody else, and I loved it.

One occasion stands out vividly in my mind: it must have been when all the children that had evacuated together met. There was a very pretty garden area with walks that led down to a sandy beach. Here we all gathered to play games and picnic. I remember digging in the sand with our hands to build a castle when suddenly Granny somehow fell on top of me and was holding another child against her chest. We heard a great stuttering noise and much screaming. It was an enemy aircraft, probably returning to home base, flying low over the beach and using up ammunition on perfect targets. So much for the safe haven of Shanklin.

How did Granny manage with all this? I can only imagine it all with a sense of dismay for what she had to go through all alone. I give her my greatest gratitude and admiration. In my latest research I have her full name: Christina Amy Part, born Hulbert, Swindon 1883, died Portsmouth 1955. Her I salute, with great respect and love.

Did letters go back and forth to my father, or to my mother? Did Mother look for us but been refused visitations? Could she have found us if she wished? – I would have thought so had she really tried. Were Granny and Daddy keeping us hidden for revenge? Surely not? It couldn't have been easy for Granny. I will never really know. In later years I was only told what they thought I ought to know. These were only vague facts and one-sided at that.

Once I was out shopping with Granny when I spied a Stuart Tartan Skirt with masses of tiny pleats and a silver pin. I fell in love with it and wanted it so very badly. I poked my head beneath the skirt and tried to become one with the garment. However, all to no avail. Granny was adamant in her rebuke, and I was dragged from beneath its glorious folds. No tears, but I thought it was worth a try – only mentioned here because the incident has as future bearing.

One day, halfway up the stairs, or halfway down, whichever way you look at it, Granny stopped with a letter in her hand and spoke to the lady coming down. I was not in the habit of taking notice of adult conversation, and sat on the next step to wait for it to finish. Suddenly Granny bent down to me.

"Would you like a new Mummy?" she asked me.

"Oh yes, yes. That would be lovely," was my reply.

Granny rose and turned to the other lady. "See?" she exclaimed, "that's children for you." But I had taken no more notice, and thought even less of the subject. And that, certainly, is children for you.

Some days later Daddy arrived with a woman on his arm to be presented to Granny, and to us, as Winifred, and we were to call her Auntie, instead of Nanny, which we did willingly enough. She was very ordinary looking, with yellow hair, straight on top, but curled around the ends where it met her neck. Antony and I were taken for a walk to the beach, and on our return journey stopped at a shop where Winifred purchased, not a tartan skirt for me, but a vest. She said mine had a hole in it. Ungrateful? Indeed, I was!

Thus did the handmaiden of the Greek goddess, Ate, who led even the ancient gods to rash and ill-considered folly, a goddess of impulse and delusion, enter our lives.

Somewhat hastily, it seemed to me, we left Shanklin, and the kindest lady in the world, for other pastures, no greener – in fact somewhat sparse in genuine affection – and travelled up to Ilkley in Yorkshire. We had been protected from sad goodbyes with Granny. All I can recall of that departure was crying in the train tunnel between Shanklin and Ryde.

In Ilkley, Daddy left us in the care of his landlady for a few days while he went about his business. Too much was exploding around me, and happening to us both that it is hard to remember much of that period. There were long roads with bright lights; railway stations with dim lights and noisy engines belching smoke; there were frightening black tunnels to travel through, and huge city centres with gardens to sit in and wait beneath looming great statues of long forgotten princes in black armour. Finally, we boarded a ferry, not unlike the one we crossed the Solent on, but larger. We had a cabin below the water line, and I could see fish on the other side of the round glass porthole, and was frightened again, both of the fish and the water in case the glass broke. Finally, I slept.

5

Childhood is measured out by sound,
 smell and sight, before the dark
  hour of Reason grows.
                John Benjamin.

The little rabbit flicked his left ear, while his right remained still. His nose twitched. The brown dog, of indeterminate pedigree, grinned evilly, as some small dogs can, and bounded clumsily forward down the slope, reaching breakneck speed before he stumbled and tripped just feet from his target. The round fluffy tail disappeared in a tumble of bracken. The little brown dog was Nell. She attached herself to our home in Northern Ireland and I loved her.

So it was that we came to the village of Greenisland, a small hamlet of houses alongside the Loch several kilometres from Belfast in Northern Ireland. I daresay it has grown somewhat since then, seventy-five years has that effect. Our accommodation was a little way along the Loch from the village and was called The Lodge, attached as it was to the gardens of a large house behind, quite near the town of Carrick Fergus.

Previously we had stayed in a house in Belfast itself and had attended a school, however briefly, nearby. It's like a wisp in my memory before we left to settle in The Lodge. This was a very pretty little house, having a kitchen and dining room downstairs, and the remainder of the rooms upstairs, including a large lounge at the front of the house. My brother and I shared a room, so perhaps there were only two bedrooms.

My father was stationed in Belfast, and Winifred presumably became what is now known as his de facto wife. (I'm quite certain it was terribly 'non-u' in those days. Here we are today, when de facto is practically the done thing. Certainly no one frowns upon it.) Neither my brother nor I were particularly enamoured with her, but at our respective ages we simply accepted the inevitable; indeed there was little else for it.

We had been in Belfast for only a short while when one day Winifred promised us each a new shiny penny if, the next time Daddy arrived home, we would call her Mummy! A new penny! Riches indeed. We could hardly wait for him to arrive, but when he did neither of us could think of anything to say except hello. Antony eventually spoke first. Not to be outshone my own voice piped up too, except I said 'Auntie Mummy' which was not quite right. Daddy said absolutely nothing. That was how we came to call Winifred Mummy, and did so for the remainder of our life together. However, as I have been unable to do so for many years now, I will not call her Mummy for the remainder of this book, and will refer to her as Winifred.

My brother and I walked to and from the local village school, quite a long walk – about three kilometres each way – carrying our satchels on our backs, with gas masks bobbing along on our hips. I liked the school, where I was known as 'the foreign new girl' which I didn't mind a bit. I remember everyone as being very friendly and was quickly invited home with one of the girls, who, living so near to the school, was able to pop home at lunchtime. I gawked rudely at her grandmother who was dressed all in black, sitting on a stool outside the front door of the cottage smoking a long-stemmed pipe. Something to gawk at for a six-year-old foreigner. We were each given a slice of homemade bread, straight from a big black oven; more gawking, nothing smeared across it, just bread. No bread has ever tasted as good since.

Antony and I were thrown much into each other's company during our time in Ireland. When not in school we took long skip, hops and jumps in the country. It could not be considered walking, more like two colts gambolling. We took Nell with us and often went as far as Carrick Fergus. We learnt that if we gathered a few wildflowers on the return journey we would not incur the wrath of Winifred if we were late. Antony had become friendly with two brothers at school, and we frequently went to their big house on the hill where we would play in the large grounds. If it rained, we would play inside. I remember one occasion when the four of us, draped beneath one sheet, barrelled sideways down the wide staircase and knocked over the knights armour that stood at the bottom. Much hilarity while we untangled ourselves which brought the parents who were not at all upset, except for my safety, being a girl. I loved that house and decided that I would marry seven-year-old David Rankin, who always took my side.

It was around this time that I received my first good hiding, or what would pass for one. I had dropped a jar of jam in the kitchen, and the maid, a young Irish lass, had cleared the best of the jam up and put it into a dish. Regrettably, she included some of the glass! I shudder to think what might have happened had anyone swallowed some. Daddy was the one who found it in his mouth as he took a bite of toast. Winifred insisted my father should put me over his knee for a slipper spanking. He turned me over his knees and I heard Winifred say "You bloody fool," (she was always particularly fond of the word bloody and used it in most sentences) "you're crying. Well if you don't do it, I will." But the slipper never fell.

The Great Bombing Blitz of Belfast took place in the Spring of 1941. Unannounced, on Easter Tuesday that April, 200 enemy bombers – that's a lot of bombers – approached at dusk and proceeded to lambaste the Belfast Docks across the Loch from us. That raid resulted in the greatest loss of life in ANY night raid. Nine hundred people died and fifteen hundred were injured. From our upstairs lounge window, we had a clear view of the bombing which looked like fireworks to me. I have hated fireworks ever since. Remember it was dusk, and unexpected. We were banished to a temporary bed under the dining room table which was pushed under the staircase for whatever safety it might afford. There we slept for some nights to come.

A day or so after that dreadful raid, I was taken into the city by bus. We passed a row of bombed buildings, still smouldering. I could see stretchers with bodies on them being carried out from the rubble, and people digging in the dusty mounds, but then we were passed and I could see no more. Winifred took me to a hotel where we had tea in the lounge, and I performed a task similar to those that I would learn to carry out in future years with great aplomb and think nothing of: she sent me across the almost empty room to ask a gentleman if he had a box of matches with which to light her cigarette. The gentleman, I heard her tell later was Sir Anthony Eden, Lord Avon, a future Prime Minister of England. Ignorance is bliss and my ignorance was utilised quite often. I think she might have hoped the gentleman would get up and cross the room to light the cigarette, but he did not. Instead he said, "Is that your Mother? Tell her she may keep the matches with pleasure."

It must have been later that year that we left Northern Ireland. We were entrained outside Manchester in Lancashire for about 36 hours. Antony and I shared a bunk in the private compartment of a senior army officer while Winifred and Daddy were either in the corridor outside or in another compartment. Manchester was being consistently bombed and the train shuddered in its stationary position on the tracks several times, but other than that all appeared to be well, if a bit frightening. We travelled down to Shanklin again and I know Nell, our little brown dog was somehow with us though how that was contrived is beyond me. I wonder now if perhaps I was given some kind of medication for the next thing I recall is of being in a small bed and breakfast house in Shanklin. I neither saw nor heard of Granny. I remember being in trouble for refusing to eat the whitish looking wobbly pudding and was told to turn my chair away from the table. When I was allowed to turn back someone had put the entire remains of the serving dish of pudding on my plate. I took one look and vomited over the entirety. That was white blancmange – not on my shopping list these days. The next thing I knew we were sitting on another train with the window open prior to departure from Shanklin, and Winifred said, "Listen. You can hear Nell crying from here." We had left our little dog behind. Oh my!

More tears in the same black tunnel, but I was not crying through fear.

To this day I can think of no reason why we went to Shanklin at that time. What were my father's reasons? Neither Antony nor I saw Granny.

6

"Eat your Ice Cream before it Melts"
  My philosophy on Life. Aged 7.

We travelled north again but not quite so far, then west, and this time ended up in Wales in the middle of the night. There was a military car to meet us at the station. En route to our destination the running boards of the car were taken up with airmen standing on them and hanging on to the half-open windows, cadging a lift to the airbase. Accommodation at the Base must have been at a minimum for we were placed in a cottage on the outskirts of the village of Cowbridge, near Cardiff. It was great. At least, my brother and I thought so.

In the main kitchen-cum-living room, the only room downstairs, hung a large tin bath tub on the wall. What fun! But it was not long before the novelty wore off when we found it was our job to not only fill, but also empty it. The man who owned the cottage lived in the one to which ours was attached, and he was the village ice cream man. That is to say, he made ice cream in a large wooden barrel outside. It was a very special treat for us on a couple of occasions to help him by poking a stick through a hole in the top of the barrel and stirring vigorously.

When the stick was removed we were allowed to lick it. Heaven had arrived at our back door.

One day I climbed the hill behind the cottage and noticed a man in uniform ambling along with another very much older man using a stick. What a great idea, thought I, they were bound to know where they were going so if I followed I would not get lost. Thus we walked for ten minutes or so and then they decided to turn around and walk back. That was a bit tricky because there was I, behind them. Obviously they must have known I was there, but I had not thought of that, so I was trapped. However, they were very kind and invited me to join them when they discovered where I lived, and in no time I was chatting merrily away, and probably related my life story. It seemed no time before we could see the two little cottages below the hill and we said our goodbyes.

That would have been that, and the end of my great adventure, except that the same gentleman in the same uniform with the same elderly man came calling the following day and asked Winifred if I could go walking with them. Well, I'm not sure how they asked, but you can imagine the reply they received. Winifred exploded with wrath and I was severely reprimanded for taking up with strange men, and banished to the bedroom until my father's return. It turned out that he already knew as the culprit was the Commanding Officer of the army base nearby. Bush telegraph even in Wales!

Antony and I attended the village school and were in the same class, he at the back and me in the front row. The lessons were all in Welsh, except for the English lesson, and sums are sums wherever you are, so we managed to balance things out – no pun intended.

The road through Cowbridge curved around a grass covered cliff on the top of which several animals grazed. It was remarked upon by Winifred that it was surprising no cows fell off, and the words were no sooner out of her mouth when one did. Splat, right in front of us, poor cow. It was history in the making for apparently it had never happened before, and no doubt it has not occurred since.

The suitcases were packed once again. Antony was sent to pedal as fast as he could on a bicycle, borrowed from the ice cream man, to hold up the village train as we were running late. This could only happen in Wales, or perhaps in Ireland too, and maybe even England in some more remote areas where trains were still something of a novelty. Well, I expect they must have been: this one certainly was. It waited for us anyway, wooden seats and all. Before we realised it we were on our way again, this time to Shrewsbury.

Christmas must have come and gone, along with birthdays, but no one seemed to take much notice of either. Certainly I have no memory of anything festive, but there was a war on as we were constantly reminded. Growing up is hard, but growing up in wartime is very much harder.

Shrewsbury is a very historic town. Here, on the banks of the River Severn, our lives took another turn. It was a torturous route and began with my father's overseas posting. We were in a small rented house when the letter arrived. We did not know where he was going, only when. No doubt some frantic decisions must have been made pretty quickly. Antony and I were told nothing. The day arrived and we said goodbye, not being particularly concerned. Perhaps Antony, being older, might have had some feeling, but to me it meant very little. He would be back in due course. What I did not realise was that the bulwark between Winifred and us was removed.

We moved from the little rented house to a small boarding house where there were two girls about our age. The house was against a railway line, and the four of us would climb over the railway wall and pick up the bits of coal that fell from the trains for use in the boarding house fires – not only against the law, but also extremely dangerous. Winifred, rightly so, nearly had a fit, and after a serious argument with the landlady we moved again. This time to a house almost facing the river. She rented a front room, the use of a kitchen and the use of a bathroom, and one upstairs room. Winifred and I shared a double bed and Antony slept on a single. The lady's name was Mrs. Shakeshaft, and she was tubby, and funny. The pots in her kitchen were old food tins with nails stuck through the sides which acted as handles. None too sanitary so Winifred had to make alternative arrangements. Mr. Shakeshaft came into our front room at the end of each week to listen to the ancient radio giving out the football results. I looked forward to these visits because his front teeth fascinated me: all long and fangy and stained brown.

By this time Winifred had taken our name and become Mrs. Part. With my father posted abroad one would suppose they had married. At least one could assume that some sort of arrangement was made by the War Office, or whatever, for the provision and succour of his children. Perhaps Winifred was his wife, and therefore our stepmother, or maybe she really was just a Nanny. None of us could live on bread alone, and even bread was rationed so we all needed not only money but ration cards too.

We walked down the road, through a park, across the bridge, and along the river path to school. Perhaps Winifred thought the river would be safer than the railway line. Returning home from school one day, bundled up with scarves and Wellington boots, we pulled icicles from the bridge for a sword fight. When we reached the park some small boys our age began teasing us, and pushed us both into the nettles alongside the path. They punched my brother, and he began to cry as he was hurt, but I was furious and hit one of them with my clenched fist right in the middle of his nose. There was blood mixed up with his snot. I was so angry I turned to the next culprit, but he fled.

That night Winifred tried to teach Antony to fight by knocking him on his head with one hand then belting him in the chest with the other, but that, needless to say, made matters worse.

It seemed I had a problem when I slept, for instead of snoring like a normal person might, I clicked from the back of my throat. Click, breath, click, breath etc. Must have been very annoying. One night I awoke flaying my arms and thumping my heels on the bed with Winifred's hand firmly clenched across my nose and mouth. I was awake. Hurrah! She cradled me, and said she was sorry, and I must promise not to tell anyone. It was nice to be cradled, and I was soon asleep again. Later I was taken to a doctor, and it was decided I should have my tonsils and adenoids removed.

This was done in the Shrewsbury Hospital. There was a little trouble with the anaesthetic as they couldn't wake me for some time. When I did wake up I screamed and screamed because all I could see was a huge red cross. This was emblazoned over the front of the uniform of the nurse who was working over me. Winifred was there and her very presence soothed me. There were times when I actually loved her, and other times when I was afraid of her. When I was in the hospital I met Winifred's mother whom I was to call Nanna. She had arrived from Leeds presumably to find out what the hell was going on. She gave me a chocolate with a hole in the middle of it, and a colouring book. What a treat the chocolate was, and what a shame that I lost it. Nanna was a wonderfully motherly lady and I loved her dearly until the day she died.

One day, while we were in Shrewsbury, we were visited by a gentleman who was connected in some way to Granny. He had obviously been sent to check up upon the two of us now that Daddy had gone. We were sent for a walk, and have no idea what was said, but nothing more was heard, by us anyway, about our situation. This little visit had taken place when we were still playing on the railway lines!

Shrewsbury was a good town to live in, safe and secure, tucked away on the Welsh Marches, but for some reason Winifred wanted to move further north, and decided on Blackpool, in Lancashire. So that is where we went.

7

*"I will have it done, so I order it done.
Let my will replace reason and judgement."*
                              Decimus Juvenalis 60-130 AD

Winifred had a beautiful singing voice, a soprano with perfect pitch. Unfortunately, I had no voice at all, or so I was told, and I believed everything I was told of course. Once, quite early in our relationship, I was merrily singing *Twinkle, Twinkle Little Star* until I was told to cease forthwith as my voice hurt the ear. I tried whistling but was told that ladies did not whistle. In the end I took to humming, which I did in my head so nobody could hear, except me. I write this about our Blackpool sojourn which is a chunk of my life I don't particularly want to write about. The best thing about it is the little school I attended just a block away from our lodgings. I loved it there, and was a particularly ardent student who strived and won.

Our lodging was a corner house in Warley Road adjoining a fish and chip shop from whom our house was rented. There was little to commend it, but Winifred was a very good housekeeper, and really could make a silk purse out of a sow's ear. Downstairs was a large hallway, living room, a separate kitchen, a large backyard; upstairs had three quite spacious bedrooms and a bathroom with a separate toilet. In the far wall of the bathroom was a small hatch door, which the owner should perhaps have locked for Antony and I discovered a huge room on the other side. This was over the fish and chip shop and was filled with all sorts of old furniture, and bric-a-brac. When no one was about we would crawl in there and spend many moments of sheer make-believe. As far as I am aware, nobody discovered our secret so we must have become very adept at sneakiness. Regrettably, he was growing older and losing his imagination, and probably fed up with always having his sister along for the ride.

As we possessed a spare bedroom it was listed as available for the armed forces. This was the 'done thing' in those troubled times and those with available accommodation could, would or should have a person billeted with them. Whether with us it was by design or arrangement, whether Winifred applied, whether she was paid or not for the privilege, I have not the slightest idea, but a Polish Air Force pilot who had been shot down, and recently released from hospital was billeted with us.

Major Stanislaw Osianek deserves a very special place in my memories. His wife, together with his only daughter, had gone missing, and presumed dead in the terrible siege of Warsaw and the indiscriminate bombing during it when 18,000 civilians perished. He entered our lives, and became a very large part of our family. Antony and I, and probably Winifred, loved him. Antony was then 10 or 11 years old and a student at Blackpool Boys Grammar, a well-recognised school. Major, as we were told to address him, tried very hard to encourage Antony, who was not a very good student, and needed a discipline different from that delivered by Winifred. He bought books for the boy, and one for me called *Swallows and Amazons* by Arthur Ransome. I not only loved, but lived my books, and still do – perhaps that is strange. Major came and went. Sometimes he would be away a few days, sometimes as long as a month. Where he went and what he did, I never knew. Twice he took me along when it was a local call. This would occur in a room in a large palatial house, and I would sit patiently listening in a corner while several men around a table would discuss heaven knows what in a very complicated language, No chance of my hearing any secrets. It would be Polish of course. Then he would take me for tea. He had a very calming influence on Winifred, or maybe she was just being good in front of him, but we were happier when he was around. He didn't do anything in particular to keep the peace, he just did. I never even thought of whether they slept together or not. Only in later years have I wondered. The answer today would be pretty obvious. Families are, after all, held together by love.

That she was unfaithful to my father is, or was, a debatable point. Not far from where we lived was a rather nice public hotel with a good dining room and cocktail bar. Quite often she would go out in the evening to this hotel, but only when she knew, or thought she knew, we were asleep. One night during one of Major's absences, I heard her and a man's voice as they climbed the stairs. I screamed, although I'm not sure why, except I knew in all my uncertainty that something was not quite right. I could see from the banister rail at the top of the stairs, a man now descending them, saying he was sorry. Winifred saw me back to bed and said I was having a bad dream. Maybe I was. She was very, very strict, and could wither me with a look, and yet she would take me sometimes to tea in a restaurant beneath the Blackpool Tower where I sat, still as a mouse, mesmerised by the ladies in beautiful hats who surrounded us. I could sit for hours fascinated by them, sometimes concocting stories in my head about one or another in particular. It was a very special treat, and I always forgave her for all the bad times. The trouble was that you never knew when these bad times would occur.

You could never question Winifred, even about ordinary things that all children want to know. Sometimes, if she did reply, it was always "I'm not arguing with you, I'm telling you" and so we learned never to question or inquire. Signs of affection were there, but seldom surfaced. What she lacked in affection she made up for with temper. You could see it coming, building up slowly like a winter storm, and when it struck it was fierce and swift. Antony was old enough to beat a hasty retreat when he saw it coming. I was usually on the receiving end of the virulent explosion, and learned to remain very still and very quiet, and not look up until the rhetoric was over. It is one of the most difficult tasks for me to perform: remain silent. Punishment enough! Like Cervantes said: 'in me the need to talk is a primary impulse', and I can't help saying right off what comes to my tongue. Winifred did her best to knock this out of me, but never succeeded except in her own home. Years and years later, when an accepted boyfriend was invited to dinner, unafraid of his hostess, he remarked how strange it was that at the dinner table I never opened my mouth, but once I had left the house I never shut up.

Finally came the day when it was time for the three of us to visit Winifred's family in the city of Leeds. It was Christmas and we had been invited for the holidays. They lived in Adel, a suburb of Leeds, in Yorkshire. Her father was still alive but not well and spent most of the time in bed with occasional visits downstairs. Best of all, Nanna was there. We went by train and then walked to the family business which was a shoe shop and factory not very far from the station. We were met by Winifred's brother – Uncle Sydney as we were told to call him – who drove us to his home in Otley Road. There we met Lily, our new aunt, and Peter, our new cousin who was one year older than me. And there was Nanna of course, and her husband Grandpa, whom we didn't see much of confined as he was to bed most of the time. Winifred had two other sisters whom we met in due course, so all of a sudden we were blessed with a new family. Peter, Antony and I became the best of friends almost immediately it seemed. We rather filled the house with Winifred taking over Peter's bedroom and we three children sleeping in the attic which was a very large room occupying almost the entire space over the three bedrooms below. The boys shared a double bed and I had a single to myself. Thus began a period in my life that I had never experienced before: a happy family life. Winfred was as different from the rest of her family as beans would have been in a pea pod. She even failed to admonish us when we were in that home, as indeed she could not have done without admonishing Peter as well since we all three were inseparable.

It snowed that December and what fun the three of us had. Whatever the boys did I did too, from jumping off the cricket pavilion roof to sliding down a steep hill on a shared toboggan. We walked, the three of us, to Adel Church for a Carol Service, and Christmas morning awakened to pillow cases filled with all kinds of goodies. Dear Nanna and Lily made sure of that. I think Lily must have saved ration coupons for the whole year to ensure our holidays would be special. That first Christmas Nanna had taken me to Adel post office where I had seen a beautiful doll sitting in a box on the counter, and this little doll I found in my pillowcase, dressed in a pink woollen outfit. Angel. I have that little doll to this day, along with the teddy bear that Peter gave me as he was too old for it. Every Christmas was the same after that. Sometimes, if the weather was kind, we children would entertain the adults with circus acts devised by us. Peter would swing me around by one leg and one arm with my nose 5cm from the ground, and never once dropped me lower. We held bicycle events around strategically placed flags, with me balanced either on the handlebars, or tremblingly standing upright on the seat while Peter pedalled. I never fell off, much to the amazement of all. They were times to remember with joy.

I remember that our last Christmas there was different. Grandpa had died, the children's Christmas tree no longer stood in the corner of the lounge, and a huge wardrobe had been moved into the attic thus dividing me from the boys.

Returning to Blackpool was always sorrowful when life returned to normal. Major was never around at Christmas. On one occasion though, when I was about nine years old, Antony was farmed out to a neighbour, and Winifred and I went off to the Isle of Man to visit Major. We stayed in a little hotel just north of Douglas, and the next day off she went to visit him leaving me alone with strict instructions to remain where I was, and not leave the hotel. The owners must have felt sorry for me sitting alone, and one of the adult sons invited me to accompany him to the other side of the island to collect something. I was very happy to go along, and as we were back again long before Winifred I did not think it necessary to inform her of my disobedience. She found out though, as I should have known she would. She was absolutely furious with everybody, including me. I am not surprised when I think about it for she could have been in very serious trouble herself had anything happened to me. So why was I the one who had to suffer?

We had long since discovered that Daddy had been posted to Pretoria, in South Africa, and as I have written, some sort of official communication must have happened to ensure his children were cared for, so Winifred could not have been without money, as she frequently complained, otherwise how could she have afforded expensive trips here and there? She would correspond with my father from whom she received funny little photograph-type airmails which we collected from the post office. To these she would reply laboriously with the aid of a small, red, well-thumbed dictionary.

We actually received a food parcel from Daddy. Inside were two slabs of chocolate full of worms which Antony and I later commandeered from the bin, and a slab of dried snoek, a South

African fish, which was also sent to the bin, but this we did not bother to rescue! We licked around the worms and enjoyed the chocolate. Winifred would buy good chocolates now and again and gave us each just one having decided that our stomachs were not used to such delicacies. Even on Christmas Day she would allow us only one helping of Christmas pudding, until the aunts put her to shame. Nanna was a big Missions to Seamen supporter and she would arm us with tiny flags and collecting boxes, and send us out, rewarding our efforts with chocolate she had saved. Nanna introduced me to my first banana – she had acquired one from somewhere or someone. We each were given a third of it. An hour or so later I still had it in my mouth, now somewhat slimy, but a little taste of heaven nonetheless.

All too soon it was time for another of Winifred's trips. This time Major was in Edinburgh. The woman was either besotted or insatiable, and I the unwilling pawn. What the Major thought of all this I do not know, but then perhaps he was unwilling to look a gift horse in the mouth. We stayed in the same house with a nice family: the son was in medical school, and the daughter was a classical pianist and had been accepted into the Royal College of Music. Regrettably these two young people became innocent participants in the futures of Patricia and Antony. Winifred, from that moment on, decided that Antony would become a doctor and I would become a concert pianist!

There was no television in those days so my brother and I would play board games in the evenings, and make up our own table games too. Major had given Winifred a wire haired fox terrier which became her pride and joy, and at least kept her at home when he was away. He named the dog Basha, but he was not entirely successful for he was next posted up to Fleetwood, a tram drive away from Blackpool, so to Fleetwood we went. I'm sure she did not need me with her for a day trip, but this chess pawn was taken anyway. I was left to play on the promenade in a children's park, and became friendly with another little girl. We had a wonderful time rushing from swings to slides, and everywhere else. By the time Winifred returned I was flushed and exhausted with the sheer joy of the play. Unfortunately, I had lost the new yellow ribbons from my plaits, so was in trouble again.

Occasionally Winifred would go off to Leeds, sometimes briefly when we were left to fend for ourselves, at other times a woman would come to stay. I think Winifred was visiting her sick father who died while we were living in Blackpool, so there would have been much for her to do, sometimes however, I later discovered, to visit her husband. That little bombshell I might explain later.

Our day to day life in the school holidays was not unpleasant. We did not have such luxuries as sweets and chocolates but I seem to remember we had a shilling a week to spend (12 pennies each), and that we could get all the way by tram to the Amusement Park at the South Beach and inside there was, I think it was called, the Pleasure House. For the sixpence entry fee you could spend the whole day safely having fun. It was not a regular outing; sometimes we went on one of the piers, or into the Tower itself. If we had Basha with us, which we frequently did, we would go to the Boat Pool. This was an area on the North Beach protected from the sea by an enormous concrete wall which you could walk along the top of if you were brave enough. Inevitably, Basha fell off, on the seaward side. Never did two children move so quickly to retrieve a dog. Fortunately for us, not to mention Basha, the tide had gone out, and she had landed on soft wet sand, still filled with rippling shallow water. No one will ever know the relief we felt and I thank God that Basha could not talk.

We were often in trouble for some minor prank or other. Antony could lie with a straight face, and I can't tell you how many times I took the blame for him. Winifred would go on and on and on and I wanted to get the punishment over and done with. She would often punish us both even if one, or the other, or both was innocent. We had to stand in front of her, and she would say "elevate to the left" or "elevate to the right". Don't ask me where she got the 'elevate' from, possibly the little red dictionary. We would dutifully bend our heads (it should have meant raise our heads) either to the left or the right, as requested, and she would deliver the sharp slap. Mostly they were just childish wrongdoings, pinching the sugar or sticking our fingers into the jam jar. Once I suffered from earache and had to visit the RAF medical facility for ear drops. The doctor advised her not to slap me on the side of the face, but I swear she got worse when I reminded her of it. A second visit was required to the same facility after the cat incident. We had acquired a black cat and Basha, when the fancy took her, would chase the poor thing. One day, when we were in the middle of a meal, the cat leapt from under the table onto my knee. She actually climbed my leg by digging her claws into my knee cap. Naturally I yelped. I was told to stop being a baby, so that was that, until I rose from the table after the meal. My white sock was drenched with blood that was still dribbling down my leg. I have the scar still. It's my identification mark!

    Once I was locked in the toilet and told I couldn't come out until I had licked off a mark on the wall that someone had made with a finger. Antony swore that he didn't, and I know that I didn't. That 'someone' also dug a nail in my new shoes to make them more like brogues which I had wanted. Again it wasn't me, and Antony told me many years later that it was probably Winifred herself, and I think he might have been right. I got into terrible trouble once when I had wet the bed and was too afraid to tell her. But worst of all was a terrible thing that I really did do.

Here it comes:-

I was told to tidy out the little sewing cupboard and in it I found a box full of silver three-penny bits. I took a handful and then didn't know what to do with them. Brilliant plan: I cut out some sweet coupons from my ration book. No, that was no good, she would see the ones left behind. Better take the whole row. Still no good. She would see one ration book was a row short. Better take the rows out of the other two books, then she wouldn't know. I had to throw most of the coupons away as I didn't have enough money to use them all. Unfortunately I didn't think of the girl in the chocolate shop. Winifred was in the habit of buying all the rations in one go and would purchase good chocolates. Incidentally, and no excuse for my misdemeanor, she was not generous in dishing them out. That aside, I was with her when she bought them on the next occasion. I must have been the colour of a sheet, a particularly white sheet. When told by the chocolate girl that there were no coupons left, Winifred had only to look at me to know the truth, or some of it anyway. Oh God, I had to travel all the way home with her on the bus in stony silence while she debated my punishment silently. I was a nervous wreck and trembling like a leaf. I had not long to wait. She beat me with the dog lead until my bottom bled then sent me to bed. I was too afraid to cry, the most I could do was whimper, and I was still whimpering when Major arrived home to be told the whole sordid tale. I felt so ashamed. Certainly it had the desired effect as I never again stole a single thing in my entire life. Poor Major. He took one look at my poor bleeding bottom, gathered me up in his arms and took me to her bedroom which boasted a gas fire. He sent her for antiseptic cream, and told her to warm milk with sugar in it for me to drink. Then he nursed me and rocked me to sleep. For that I will honour him until the day I die. It is the only time in my entire childhood that I can remember having been truly loved. Almost worth the hiding.

The deed was never mentioned again and this is the very first time I have told the story for I was dreadfully ashamed. That was around the time that Winifred, because I had been wicked for some deed or another, told me she was not my mother and I was to call her Madam. It didn't last because I kept saying Madam Mummy by mistake.

Now and again she threatened to send us to Granny but stopped when Antony asked her when we could go. We both wanted to. Then there was the time when I caught German measles and she nursed me and bought me a bag of cherries. What could you do but love her?

There were other good times. Granny sent me a Royal Stuart Tartan skirt complete with pin. I loved it, and wanted to wear it all the time. Winifred told everybody she had made it, which I dare not dispute. Winifred made me a blue serge skirt with pleats at the front and back! Granny sent me a beautiful, ruby red, long-sleeved, high-collared velvet dress. I loved it. Wore it once, and then it was donated to the evacuee children. Winifred made me a silky straight dress out of parachute material Major had given her. I wore it to the school play in which I had a lead part. She didn't come to watch so my pride was wasted, then I hated the dress. Who would want to relive their childhood? Not me.

Then came the telegram, and at last my father was home, or nearly so. He had landed at Liverpool and would have some leave. Winifred went snow white as she read it, then burst into tears. I don't remember where Major was.

As I recall, Daddy must have arrived back at the end of a school year because I was very proud of myself and excited to tell him that I had passed my penultimate primary school year and been promoted to what was, in those days, the A stream of the final year. I was ten years old. Back at school, beginning our long division sums and decimal points and fractions – all very interesting – when wham bam, out came the suitcases and we were on our way again.

8

Education has produced a vast population of people
able to read, but unable to distinguish what is worth reading.
George Treveleyan 1876 – 1962

The journey was a long one this time: by train to London and from there to Devon. We were restless, the two of us, and were advised to look out of the window to see if we could detect the red soil of Devon. We couldn't. Eventually we came to Torquay, on the Devon coast hugging the English Channel. A beautiful town, rather as one would imagine a French Riviera town might be. One of the very large hotels on the seafront had been commandeered by the RAF and perhaps other Services. This was to be where Daddy would be working.

We lived in a large rented house, called Tor House, perched conspicuously on a triangular corner in what was known as Old Tor. It had one of those wide sweeping staircases flowing down to a large hall with a heavy wooden door that opened directly onto the street via a few wide steps. There was a second wooden staircase curling down to a spacious kitchen, and this was the one my brother and I were instructed to use. In those days I was not very interested in the layout of houses, but this house must have merited as one of the best, and a far cry from Blackpool. There was a grand piano which we discovered Winifred could play, quite well, by ear, and very loudly. Of course she could!

In due course I was entered into what could only be called the local village school where term had already started. I had no idea at all what they were talking about when it came to arithmetic. I must have missed something somewhere, but I was able to cope with everything else. Before I knew it the end of term came and it was school holidays again.

Major came down to visit us and to say goodbye it seems, for we never saw him again., but I have thought of him many times over the years. Basha was still with us, and produced puppies in the enormous cellars which were kitted out with small bedrooms, and one large room which contained an X-ray machine, so it was probably a doctor's house.

Antony and I explored the surrounding countryside by foot, and one of our favourite places was Cockington, a 12th century village four or five kilometres away, that boasted an old-fashioned, broken-down coach I loved to play lady in. In my bedroom at Tor House there was a copy of a painting of the Laughing Cavalier, said to be of one of the oldest owners of Cockington Manor which is believed to be haunted by him. It well might be true. Although I did not know that when I slept there, the picture frightened me.

Another ramble that took our fancy was Babbington Beach, a village as far away in the opposite direction. We walked many a kilometre in those days. All along the cliffs of Torquay were black holes, which were caves, but we never got that far. I think the beaches were somewhat restricted territory. After all, there was still a war on although chances of invasion were no longer likely.

A message came from Southsea. We were invited to attend the wedding of Aunt Renée, and joy of joys, I was to be her only bridesmaid. My father was delegated to walk up the aisle and give her away. New clothes were duly made by a dressmaker, that being the most convenient, and away we went. I loved every moment, even the now accustomed train journey. We arrived just the day before the wedding, so it was all a bit of a rush. There was a bit of a to-do because my dress was short and pale blue, but Renée wanted me in a long, muslin, tiered dress in palest pink. Of course, I much preferred that, especially because it was long. The shoes were a size too small but I told no one and just suffered a bit, in happy silence. I was given a gift of palest coral beads which I wore at the wedding, and still wear to this day. We were too late to have a practice run, but I was told very strictly to do nothing but follow the bride, take her flowers, and just stand there. Risky business this! The ceremony was held at Portsmouth Cathedral and conducted by the Bishop of Portsmouth. He eyed me suspiciously, I thought, and repeated the instructions to simply follow the bride. Oh for goodness sake, thought I, anyone can do this. They neglected to tell me how long the aisle was, and that when I finally stood still I was standing on the top of somebody's tomb. They also forgot to tell me that although I must follow the bride, I must certainly not go passed the Altar communion rail, which I proceeded to do until a very large hand came out before me in a definite Stop sign. Abruptly I did so, and promptly started to shake, flowers quivering in mute dissent, as were my toes, or what I could feel of them. After a very satisfactory reception at a lovely hotel, we waved Renée and her handsome Scottish Lieutenant Colonel, complete in glorious tartan which was the best thing ever for me, goodbye. Granny and Jean, the Scots terrier, returned with us to Torquay for a short break. Probably a bit sad for Granny, although she must by now be well-used to losing family one way or another, however temporary it might sometimes be. Difficult too, for she was the complete antithesis to Winifred.

A lot of talk was going on behind closed doors in our house. Antony had to sit a written examination to Bridlington Boys Grammar, which he failed miserably. Bridlington was to be our next destination, way up in East Yorkshire on the North Sea coast. It had been decided that a private hotel was to be purchased, thereby realising a dream of Winifred, and my father would retire from the RAF to help her run it. Antony was to remain behind in Torquay with father for extensive cramming and drilling by him for a second chance at getting into the school. The Headmaster had promised a place for him if the results were found to be acceptable. I was a different story.

We had to travel, just Winifred and I, by train in time for me to sit the Eleven Plus examination which I needed to pass in order to be accepted into the Bridlington Girls High School. Failure meant I would have to go to the Secondary Modern. Nothing wrong with that. I was beginning to have doubts. I had received little to no education since leaving Blackpool almost a year earlier, and I was very aware of having fallen behind. We travelled in reverse this time, from Torquay to London, London to Hull, Hull to Bridlington. Once there we booked into a local hotel, and the very next day I had to catch a bus to the government school where the examinations were being held and, alone and frightened, introduce myself, and ask to be admitted for the examination. The teachers must have been astonished, but they allowed me to sit for it. Oh what a horror it was. Everything was so terribly strange. There were two papers. One English and one Arithmetic. You had to pass both. I remember the IQ test in which I did extremely well, the English passably, but the Arithmetic, no, I was sure I had missed far too much. I made my way back to the hotel despondent and unhappy. The result would not be known for several weeks so there was little for it but to sit back and pray.

The purchase of the private hotel was duly accomplished and we moved in. Fully furnished there was little to do but clean it; there were no bookings, and as it was closed to visitors, there was plenty of time.

Meanwhile, I had to attend school. I was sent to the local junior school, by myself, and asked permission to start. Another astonished teacher. Thus began my final year of junior school which was already in full swing. Not unhappily, I settled in. The other children said I was posh because I didn't have a Yorkshire accent, so I had to try very hard to copy them. The schooling was alright but we had an arithmetic teacher who delighted in having the whole class stand upright while she shot times-tables questions at each pupil only allowing you to sit once you answered correctly. I was always the last one standing, and she took a dislike to me, which feeling was totally mutual. Came the day when I was requested to attend the Headmaster's office to be told I had failed the 11plus. I was not surprised, but nevertheless unhappy. All hope faded of ever taking up law, or being a journalist, and now I began to wonder if I would have to learn to play the piano.

At the end of the school year I was taken, lo and behold, to the Convent School where I was enrolled. I was happy to be there when the term started, and enjoyed it. However, we didn't learn very much. There were three classes in the entire school: one infants, one primary, and one senior class which was mine, where the girls' years ranged from 12 to school leaving at 16 or so. The youngest sat in the front row, and graduated row by row to 16, (or so!). We learnt music, how to sew a fine seam, how to conduct ourselves as young ladies and speak correctly (without a Yorkshire accent), a little arithmetic (not much), lots of literature and poetry, interesting bits of history and geography, and the Catechism. There was hardly a Roman Catholic amongst us, but we were happy little girls, at least at school. They also taught the piano. Part of the furniture in the hotel was an old German upright piano. This was removed to our private room in the lower living quarters, and I began my piano lessons at the Convent. It looked as if Winifred might realise her dream because Antony too had been accepted at the Grammar School.

I seemed to master the keys reasonably well. It was a few months later that I was transferred to a Miss Marjorie Taylor, (real name used here), who became my piano teacher. She was a spinster who lived with her aged mother within walking distance of our hotel. One of her pupils was at school with me at the Convent, and was an extremely talented pianist. She told me that Miss Taylor had asked her whether she thought I might be a student prepared to practise. Why Miss Taylor would ask another 12 year old is a bit of a mystery, but it worked. She, Miss Taylor, guided, encouraged and motivated me. For her I would have practised all day. Of course, I didn't, but for my first examination of Grade V, I received a distinction, and she was very proud. She always said that, although the meaning of examinations were obvious, she herself did not believe in taking lots of little ones that really meant nothing much, and which you were obliged to concentrate on for long hours, so she would skip them and go right to the heart. It worked. Between Miss Taylor and Sister Margaret I was a very happy little student. Miss Taylor also supervised my reading material, and managed to acquire an adult library ticket for me as the children's section was very limited in Bridlington. I leapt from Arthur Ransome to Hugh Walpole without effort. From him it was a very small step to Joseph Conrad. Thus began my love affair with the English language. I read anything I could get my hands on, and managed to acquire a torch – the better to read at night long after my light was switched off. My one problem was keeping up with the batteries which always expired much too soon.

The private hotel, I must pay note, was extremely hard work. If I learned nothing else I surely became an expert at household chores. My school grades at my happy little Convent didn't improve, simply because there were none. We had no homework but occasionally were instructed to learn poetry by heart, to be recited in the classroom. My dreams of a career within the world of words were put on hold. I thought perhaps I might be an actress instead. Life did not improve very much during those early years in Bridlington. Shortly after we had settled in there – I was 11 almost 12 – I contracted chicken pox from above, and bleeding from below, and was convinced that I was dying if not from one then certainly from the other of my diseases. However, I was assured that the pox was a childhood disease, and I was still a child, and the bleeding was just extra blood that my body did not need and would occur regularly, and with that I had to be satisfied. The one made me still a child and the other meant I had become a woman! Amazing what a child needs to accept as gospel. My brother finally set me straight in horribly school boyish enlightenment with both words actions. I was, quite literally, horrified.

I was very foolish. I courted trouble when trouble was not even within my hemisphere. I fell in love. I wrote, and received, beautiful little notes from a 12 year old boy in my brother's school, my brother being the postman. The notes were mostly about the string of donkeys his parents owned. I longed for a horse, and a donkey was the nearest I could get. I never actually spoke to the little boy and only knew his name was Mike, nor did he speak to me. Foolishly, I left one of the notes in my shirt pocket, probably declaring my undying love for the donkeys, or perhaps for him, who knows? Seized upon by Winifred, Antony was commanded to instruct the young boy to appear before my parents, together with me, the following day after school. I don't know whether he did or not, because I was so terrified I ran away. I had a little friend at school who lived some miles away in a tiny village, and lifted me home on her bicycle. I told her mother I was on my way to my aunt in Leeds. Of course, the father cycled back to Bridlington to tell my parents I was quite alright and they would send me to school the next day. It didn't work out that way though. Winifred and Daddy arrived by taxi and took me home again. Winifred told the poor parents that I had no aunt in Leeds, and that, I suppose, was true. It broke my heart because I was so sure that Aunt Lily was a real aunt and Peter was my real cousin, so firmly had I been brainwashed. Nanna, who by now was living in an apartment in Bridlington, collected me and I spent two nights with her. I don't know what the outcome for the little boy was. Antony never told me, and I was too afraid to ask. However, two people, a man and a woman, came to speak to me at the hotel in the presence of Winifred and Daddy. They asked me if I was happy at home and Winifred answered before I had chance to, but she was told to be quiet as I must answer. Taking my cue from Winifred I answered as I thought she would want me to, although it was not really what I wanted to say. Just as well because had I spoken out there might have been a dreadful outcome. Once again I was ashamed, not so much for running away, but because I was too afraid to speak. Everyone else seemed satisfied and things settled back to normal.

Winifred said my head was too full of love stories and I should read Shakespeare. I had never read a love story, and she had certainly never read Shakespeare, but I read the Bard avidly and I think that she might have later regretted her remark!

Nanna bought me a bicycle, an old secondhand one she had spotted at an auction house, and took me with her to bid for it. My first bike. It was fantastic, with low handle bars and very narrow tyres. I don't think I ever walked again in Bridlington. Meanwhile, shortly after my 'love affair', I was sent down, by myself, to visit Granny. I managed the train journey with some success, even crossing London with the aid of a taxi – I was a bit young to venture on the tube. The return journey was bit more difficult because Granny had loaded my suitcase with the *Children's Encyclopaedia Britannica* and they were mighty heavy.

Life settled down in Bridlington. We were no longer obliged to 'elevate' but that did not mean punishments were not carried out, just differently. We remained not respectful, but rather fearful, of our stepmother, for such she had become although we did not know until many years later. In fact it was only when I was researching the facts for this book that I discovered she had been married to one Alexander Smith from Bradford in Yorkshire from whom she did not divorce. I can recall something of this during our period in Blackpool when something was once mentioned about Alex being alcoholic, but not knowing who Alex was rang no bells for me, until now. He died at the end of 1943. Winifred and my father were married in Leeds in September 1944, which would have been just before we went to live in Torquay.

The only real difficulty with the hotel was that the season was such a short one during the summer months, and an even shorter one at Easter. There were constant debates about money, or rather the lack of it, yet there was sufficient to provide us with a living, if a stringent one. Everything was still on ration of course, and Antony was given the task of calculating and then cutting out the coupons required from the visitors' ration books in order to feed them. He had other tasks too, as I had mine, which had to be fitted in with my piano practice which had quickly developed into two hours a day: one for scales and exercises, and one for pieces. There wasn't a lot of time left for getting into trouble. My hours were not strictly adhered to during the season as there was a great deal of manual labour required in the twelve bedroomed hotel plus our own quarters. Daddy was, as the expression goes, chief cook-and-bottlewasher which meant he did all the food shopping and then confined himself to the kitchen where he concocted the most amazing meals out of very scarce products. He was the only cook I knew who could mix roast chicken with roast rabbit and no one could tell the difference. No one was allowed to assist in his kitchen. Once I wanted to watch him skin a fish in his kitchen sink, but after lifting up the cod and showing me the marks each side of its head which, he said, were where Jesus had held the fish, I too was banned. He had a very long wooden table, scrubbed white, upon which were laid all the vegetable tureens and meat dishes prior to serving. Only then was anyone allowed to assist. These were all then carried into the Stillroom in which had been installed a rope-pulled lift used to haul the dishes up to the dining room He was a wonderful cook which all seems a bit of a come down from being a Wing Commander, Retd.!

It was Winifred however, who worked the hardest. She cleaned, washed, scrubbed, painted and polished, and by the end of the first year had papered every bedroom wall. I was roped in to help with the latter, and quickly learned to duck when the paper fell before she had quite managed to attach it to the wall, and she was left with two little bits stuck to the end of each forefinger. I also learnt to swear, under my breath. There were only two bathrooms, not unusual for the times, so each bedroom had a small closet for chamber pots where guests relieved themselves during the night, and occasionally became more venturesome. It was my job to empty these, help make the beds, clean each hand basin and polish the mirrors. We were all expected to help with the washing up, except Daddy who did his own. This was all seasonal during the summer months when the schools were on holiday. Unfortunately, we were not. We had a woman who came in daily to wait on tables, but that was all. We had no wage, but I had pocket money of two shillings a week.

(about 20c)

I had long learned to keep my mouth shut and my tongue still within it, and although the work was hard you just had to get on with it. I read somewhere that a German monk had said it was better to obey rather than to rule, and that was very true. The war had ended in 1945, shortly after our arrival in Bridlington, with little affect upon any of us, except that Daddy had retired from the RAF. We had actually stayed in one place for over two years without packing a single suitcase, except at Christmas. I had reached my teen years without further incident. I was happy at school, had a few friends, lots of library books, and Miss Taylor. What more could one ask?

Do not tempt the gods for the lightning was once more to flash across the sky. We were to move to South Africa where father hoped to start a new life. So the plans were made. We were to go for a trial period, Daddy to go first to find a job, and accommodation. The hotel was to be retained and run by Edith, Winifred's elder sister, with Nanna to help. Antony was to remain with them so as not to interrupt his schooling. Basha too was to await results. I, of course, was different. I was not to remain behind, but would accompany Winifred later once Daddy had settled.

I had to leave my books, my piano, Miss Taylor, my friends, my happy school, and travel to some distant land about which I knew absolutely nothing.

And Winifred was seven months pregnant.

9

*Parents can learn a lot from their children
about coping with life.*
Muriel Sparks 1918 -?

On Christmas morning 1947 at 6am Winifred and I flew out from the old London Airport on a Skymaster aeroplane taking two days and one night of flying, to Johannesburg, South Africa. She was sick for the entire flight and at seven months pregnant it was a bit of a worry, especially being her first child, but every time we touched down she quickly recovered.

The first stop was Tripoli and we were all herded into a pub on the airport where everyone was celebrating Christmas Day. Next was Khartoum which we reached at midnight, then Kisumu on Lake Victoria. The poor woman filled bag after bag, and kept the hostess busy. I, sitting next to the window, only filled one and that was from all the chocolates the air hostess kept delivering into my lap – it was Christmas Day after all. I made friends with the man behind me, and when we were over the Nile I thought it was a great crack in the earth and told him so. I had managed to tie the porthole curtain behind my head to shut out the night light which needed to be on for Winifred to find the next bag, and I left enough space at the side to talk to my new friend. I remember him saying my education had been "sadly neglected" – his words. He explained about Khartoum, and why the streets ran out like a Union Jack; the death of Gordon, and the revenge of it by

Kitchener. The man would not have known it, but I have never forgotten his story, and my love of history was born that night so far above the bloodied land below.

Kisumu was the next stop. Winifred overheard my chattering with a stranger, and I was told to stop. So that was that, and unfortunately I learned nothing at all about Lake Victoria! We were taken in a rattling bus to a hotel on the banks of the Lake where we were given a room in which to rest. Later we were given breakfast in the dining room, and I had my first taste of a grapefruit crossed with an orange, and my first taste of the Africa I came to love in later years. Africa, north, middle or south, has a taste peculiar to itself, and there is no other taste or smell in the world quite like it: a dry, hot smell, the smell of woodsmoke, of parched veldt, of the rain before it arrives, of animals, of Africa.

It was eight o'clock in the evening of Boxing Day when we landed in Johannesburg to be met by Daddy. It also happened to be his birthday. He had found us a rented house just north of the city, a pleasant little home with a stoep – the South African word for patio – overlooking a small front garden facing a road that led to a bus stop two houses away around the corner. There was little behind the house, just a garage at the top of the driveway, with a kia attached. A kia is a small room where the African servant, if you employed one, lived. Everyone had a servant – it was work for them; they were lodged clothed and fed all for free, and from their wages managed to send much needed money home. In South Africa the servant was usually female, or could be a male, but further up on the continent the house servant was always a male. My father had employed a male. He was huge and very black; came from Nyasaland, or Malawi as it is now called. When my parents were out in the evenings the light in his room never went out until they returned home for he was baby-sitting me, he said. I think he was a little shocked that I was left alone at night, which was probably alright in northern climes but was a bit of a no-no in Africa. He was one of the old school servants who were worth their weight in gold.

My father had found a good job in the city, selling cars. Quite a lot of ex-servicemen seemed to do this. He was fortunate enough to be allocated a car in which we would explore the countryside around the city, or tried to. Winifred complained that there were no trees on the surrounding veldt and when my father pointed out a whole forest she replied there were no bloody leaves on them! A difficult lady to please. The Union buildings in Pretoria, a very pretty sight to see, and on a very pretty site, but "they must have been built with English money" said she. Not very happy. Even I could see which way the wind was blowing.

I made friends with a girl of my age, Tania Reid, who lived on the corner of our road, and spent as much time as I could with her. She was from an Afrikaans family descended from those people who had been in the land long before the English arrived to take possession. Her family had a peanut farm outside what was then a village, called Brits, just a little further north of Pretoria, and would sometimes go there for a Friday and Saturday night, occasionally taking me along with them. Slowly, very slowly, I was beginning to learn a little Afrikaans, a bastardised version of Dutch. Just as well my brain was exercised with something. I had my music but no piano, no school and little or no books. I did find Forever Amber, and Lawrence's Lady Chatterley's Lover behind the curtain in their bedroom hidden from my tender eyes, and managed to read them both in the evenings when my parents were out before they themselves had finished them. My knowledge of life was expanding. I met the boy next-door. He was epileptic, and like me, did not attend school but was privately tutored. We would spend many an evening chatting over the fence. He explained the red in the skies over Pretoria where the refineries were and explained too about his illness and how you lived with it. He taught me quite a lot about the country. I wonder what happened to him. My father had made a few friends at work and both he and Winifred were invited out occasionally. Sometimes I went too. But it was tedious because I had to sit quietly for long periods doing nothing much, and entering the conversation only when invited to.

The arguments continued, the usual subject finances. I still cannot understand why we always seemed to be poor. I remember taking my much loved coral necklace, my only jewellery, into their bedroom and saying they could sell it for it might be worth a bit. But of course, it wasn't. I must say those arguments were very one-sided as all you could really hear was a female voice going on and on with only low mumblings from my father. She hated it when he hid behind a newspaper or had his head in a book. He thought a soft tongue turneth away wrath, yet when I tried a soft tongue in defense I was told I was insolent, and wrath descended in heavy showers around me. It really was best to remain silent.

One day, late in February, Winifred and I were out shopping and had returned to the little car Daddy had obtained for our use, when she stopped at the open door, and holding onto it, made a huge puddle of water on the ground.

"Phone your father," she told me. No mobiles in those days. I flew to the nearest shop.

"My God," the woman exclaimed, "her water must have broken."

I hadn't the slightest idea what she was talking about. If I was kept anywhere, it was in the dark, which trait continues to follow me to this day! I am still always the last one to find out about anything, even my own pregnancy when it occurred. Anyway, the phone call was made; father arrived with a driver who took me home, while he drove Winifred, in her car, to the nursing home. Robert Samuel Part was born that night.

It was not very long after his birth that we moved to the Berea, a hill to the north of the city, and lodged in a Toc H establishment. This was a boarding house dedicated to assisting ex-servicemen and their families in times of need. (That's a much shortened version.) I shared a room with a young working woman, while my parents, with baby Robert, shared a bed-sitting type room.

It was shortly after we moved into the Toc H that visits to the Children's Hospital began. I thought perhaps all babies visited the hospital shortly after being born, but nothing was explained to me. I became more and more concerned with sick feelings developing in my stomach. Eventually, I was invited to spend another weekend with my friend Tania on the peanut farm. I even wondered then if that was contrived, but I will never understand why no one was prepared to tell me what was wrong. One day while we were having lunch a phone call came for Mr. Reid who, on taking it, looked directly at me. I knew immediately that the phone call concerned me and something was very wrong. But even he did not explain. What could he have said? Well, perhaps the truth, but it was not really his place to do so. He simply said your parents want you back at once, and promptly took me, with Tania holding my hand, until I was deposited at the boarding house. I really cannot remember anything more about those dreadful days. They have been completely obliterated.

Winifred was an RH Negative blood group. Very rare indeed. Robert was one of the last blue blood babies. The medical profession had not yet developed the blood transfusions at birth that would have saved his life. I think the hospital they visited was the Experimental Hospital where all sorts of tests were seemingly tried, but all to no avail. It must have been a terrifying, heartbreaking experience for my parents. It's still hard for me, even as I write this in my old age.

The Dominican Sisters of Bridlington Convent had instilled in me a certain degree of Christian belief which brought me some solace to which I clung after Robert's death. Today, as a reasonably intelligent adult, I firmly believe in a Supreme Being whom we call God for want of a better name. We are able, with the same minds we are all born with, to believe in Him, no matter under what name or in what manner. We stray, we falter, and sometimes we are lost, but with faith we have the strength to find our way again. I have sought for the record of little Robert's birth, and I'm sure by law he would have been registered, but I have not been able to find any record of either birth, or of death. I know he was not christened, unless that was kept from me too. His little box of ash was retained and eventually interred in the Wall of Remembrance in Lawnswood, Leeds. On it were inscribed my words from a poem I had written 'a little Robin who flew away'. These were removed when our father's name was added by my brother in 1960. I can only assume that Winifred's name was added by her surviving relatives. I do not know where her ashes are. I was not told.

It was a difficult time indeed. She was not a religious woman, yet she seemed to recover quickly from this great sadness. Her character was one of a strong, self-controlled woman whose temper always got the better of her. She continued to visit the hospital to give her blood, but now I was allowed to accompany her – not to enter the place, but to wait outside, which is where I discovered the cowshed full of cows. To this day I don't know why they should be there, and no one answered my question.

It was perhaps May or June of that year that I ventured to suggest that I should go to school. Two blocks away from Toc H, I had spotted a girls school called Barnato Park which housed the Johannesburg Girls High. Yes, I could go there if I liked, and I liked so very much indeed. By now I was adept at introducing myself, was accepted, and started immediately. I still had my Convent gymslip, the black uniform universally worn, and all I needed was a white shirt or two. I also needed the school girdle about an inch and a half wide in the school pink, and white, which tied around the waist and fell down one side. I didn't receive pocket money but was given enough to purchase, from the school, one white and one pink ball of wool. I borrowed a pair of knitting needles and knitted myself one – necessity is the mother of invention. It was only for the winter months. In summer we wore white dresses which the school called utility dresses, and were at a much reduced price.

I couldn't have chosen a better school and the remainder of the year that I spent there was the happiest school year of my life. The terms in South Africa began in January and finished in December, unlike England where they began in September and finished in July. I had only missed the first term, and as the standard of education at that time was at least a year behind that of England I managed to fit in quite well. I was also rather lucky because Algebra and Geometry were only to begin the following year. Barney Barnato, the mining magnate, had bequeathed his beautiful home and grounds to the school and the lovely house itself was used as the boarding section. Barnato himself had apparently never lived in it. Even when I was not in school I was quite happy to work very hard, and spent many hours in my bedroom, out of the way, studying.

Hardly had I begun my schooling than we were on the move once more, this time to a rented flat on the 5th floor of a block above shops in the centre of Johannesburg, but there was a trolley bus that dropped me off almost at the school gates. Winifred appeared to be happier there than anywhere else. The lovely city shops were literally right on the doorstop. For a born shopper that was an enormous temptation!

I was learning to swim at school, and beginning to speak a little Afrikaans. All the English girls were obliged to take lessons while the rest of the class sewed. I was given a special ribbon for gymnastics and, wonder of wonders, I was chosen at the end of the year to be in the choir for the following year, albeit as a contralto. A poem and an essay of mine were chosen for the school magazine, and adding to my pleasure, I came Second in the end of year examinations.

Christmas was not celebrated, except for a very nice roast chicken dinner Winifred cooked, and Daddy's Boxing Day birthday went off unremarked. They also totally forgot my birthday in January which I was a bit miffed about.

Other things were taking precedence: they had booked tickets to return to England in February. It should have been obvious to me that the experiment to settle in South Africa had failed. There was no happiness to be found there for Winifred. I asked if as a special favour they would take me to say goodbye to my little Afrikaans friend, Tania. The family had moved to the East Rand and we were invited for lunch on one of the last Sundays remaining. Tania and I went off on bicycles as was suggested by her parents and we spent the last few hours together sitting under a tree a few kilometres away, just chatting as little girls can, and swearing eternal friendship. I never saw her again.

We travelled down to Capetown by train in a small sleeping compartment. It was a very long way and a very sad journey. Halfway along we stopped at a station in the middle of the Karoo called De Aar. It was so hot you couldn't put your foot on the platform. It did not matter to me. My whole body felt numb and I thought that I would never laugh again.

10

*I began to believe nothing of what I heard
and only half of what I saw.*

Myself.

We finally arrived in Capetown, travelling over the vast Karoo and through the land of sleeping giants, as I liked to call the mountains, which looked as if they had all fallen sideways as we slipped along in the valley between. I felt like falling sideways myself: perhaps the world from that view would look better. But who could not be moved by the extraordinary beauty of this fairest cape in all the world. Slowly but surely I emerged from self-imposed misery.

We boarded the *S.S. Arawa,* an Australian one-class passenger vessel of the Shaw Saville Line sailing from Sydney to Liverpool. It's difficult to recall the voyage. We were all three sharing a cabin which fortunately had a porthole well above sea level that needed to be opened whenever possible as Winifred was extremely seasick. I spent most of my time on deck, or in the music room where there was a piano. Not that I wanted to play but because one of the passengers was a music teacher and had won an Australian prize of two tickets to London. He and his very pretty wife made friends with me, and he would often play for everyone's amusement. Just a couple of times I played too. I had sheet music and one or two little things in my small school suitcase which, to save returning to the cabin, I stashed under the couch in the music room. Bad idea. They disappeared and were never recovered.

Leaving Africa at the height of summer we arrived in Liverpool in the middle of winter, on a cold, wet and blustery day. Going through Customs was unpleasant, but the officials made it as comfortable as possible. One man approached my parents saying he understood there was a small box they wished to declare. I was asked to step aside, which I did willingly enough. Little Robert had arrived in England.

Leaving Liverpool behind we entrained to Leeds where we made a short stop-over in order to inter Robert in the Lawnswood Cemetery. We arrived in Bridlington on the following day, feeling very much worse than when we had left. Antony met us at the station and I thought him horribly formal and distant. One of the first things he said was "'I may as well tell you all that I've got a girlfriend". Gone was the big brother whose footsteps I had dogged. Instead I had an aloof, superior young man for a brother.

We settled down once again. It was out of season so there were no guests. I returned to Miss Taylor, resumed my lessons and thought about school. Barnato Park had given me a letter for the Headmistress of Bridlington Girls High, in which was stated "Patricia made a very promising start and we were sorry to lose her." along with my final report. The letter was an official document giving me a transfer from one high school to another. The irony here was that this was the very high school to which I had failed the entrance examination in the 11+. This school was at least eighteen months ahead of the school in South Africa. What was I in for? I soon found out.

Once again I presented myself to the Headmistress armed with my letters and very little else to commend me. I even lacked the normal obligatory parents required to meet the Head. However, Miss Smith as I will call her, – not the real name as she was not too happy to meet but was obliged to accept me. Her very manner shouted displeasure. She placed me in the right class for my age, so she said, although I met another girl from the previous little junior school who had passed the examination, and she was in the year behind me.

It was fortunate that I was with a great bunch of girls – all the naughty ones, all boarders, all bright – who took a fancy to this knowledgeable but dim girl from Africa. The mathematics which they had been doing for three years was beyond me. The maths teacher stood me up in front of the class, and asked me to answer a geometry question on the blackboard. Someone whispered the answer. "And how did you reach that conclusion?" barked the crow. Another time the crow actually taught something new, and we were given several of the sums for homework. All correct, the book was returned to me with, written in red ink, "Who did this work for you?" Upset, I raised my hand. The crow expected me to remain by my desk, but I went to the front of the class holding my book open and very politely asked why she had written these words, and I quoted them, at the same time saying she had taught and I had learnt. She gave me an A, with a face as red as the pen she had used. It's the only A. I ever received in my history of mathematics.

All the other subjects were manageable, except French in which I battled. We had to sit the Junior Certificate in the mid-year, after which you could, by law, leave school. This hardly ever happened in a high school most students continuing until matriculation. The maths paper was an abomination from start to finish. I read the entire paper, but could complete none of it. When the results went up I started looking from the bottom, and there was I as large as life, right at the end with 2%. They must have liked the way I had written my name! All the other subjects were passed, except French. When the English results were displayed I started at the top, and there I was, right there, with 98%. I figured 98 +2 gave me a pass of 100! I've often wondered whether teachers discuss their pupils in the Common Room?

Strangely, 1949 which began so dismally began to shape up. The school year had ended at about the same time as the hotel season had begun, and I was needed! With what I considered perfect timing I asked if I could leave school. To my surprise, the idea was accepted with alacrity. There was however, a proviso: when not attending to my hotel duties – a polite way of saying cleaning and polishing – I had to increase my piano practice to six hours per day, to which I agreed somewhat reluctantly. It did not last long since I spent two hours each day on scales, and drove everyone demented so it lasted about a week. I had not even bothered to inform Miss Taylor. Not that I would ever make the pianist Winifred had hoped for. I practised because I had to. I loved Chopin and other classics, and had no time for modern music, but I was no pianist. It was hard slog all the way for me. Miss Taylor knew it and I knew it, but we both pressed on. It was often difficult even to practice for Winifred would call out "wrong" if she thought she heard a bad chord. I would laboriously point out each complicated note and slam all five down, but she would not be impressed. At least Miss Taylor decided to postpone further exams as I had been without a piano for over a year anyway.

So ended my formal, if haphazard, education. Quite tragic really, and a downright disgrace too. But as Winston Churchill once said "it's a good thing for an uneducated man to read a book of quotations" so I did!

Of course, one must bear in mind that being ill-educated in the modern sense does not make you unintelligent. For those lucky ladies better schooled than I but far less bright or knowledgeable, I suggest read, provided, of course, that one can.

Then again, it's no good reading if one has no idea what to read.

It was decided I should have my teeth straightened. Once again without parental help except for the initial consultation of how it should be done, after two extractions and other various indignities inflicted in my mouth over a short period of time, I presented a smile showing a gold bar with a silver wire across each tooth attached to it. All this with no one around to hold my hand. It was sore, it was painful, I needed a hug, so I went to Nanna. Oh well, at least I would have straight teeth.

It was around this time that Shirley, Edith's daughter and therefore Winifred's niece, a very pretty woman, was married. I mention it here because I was to present the silver horseshoe at the church door. Winifred dressed me in a crepe de chine dress with baggy puffed short sleeves, and smocking across my chest which already had little boobs sprouting. The indignity was a big bow that tied at the back. I have a photograph to prove it. I was 15 years old for Pete's sake! My hair would have been in pigtails too had it not been for Nanna who put it in rags the night before so that I could wear it loose. It would be another year before I was allowed to wear a bra, and that was given to me by one of our daily maids.

That Christmas, Antony and I were allowed to throw a party. He invited his school friends, and I invited the friends I had rediscovered from Convent days – a typical teenage party for the age. No drugs, no alcohol, and no smoking but loads of food. Winifred had gone all out with what baking skills she had. We played the usual party games we had enjoyed at other parties. The teenagers of today would have been horrified. Postman's Knock, and I received my first kiss from another boy called Michael who told me not to be tense but to relax and enjoy it, so I did. Far too brief I thought. He later told my brother I would be quite lovely once I put my hair up! Oh dear, those pigtails!

Before Easter of 1950, I was sent down to Granny again, which I always enjoyed. She had sold the tall house in Helena Road and lived with a lady companion in an apartment facing the Ladies Mile in Southsea. It was close to where I had lived as a baby although Granny would not elaborate due to the ill feeling amongst the family. It was to be the last time I saw her.

Once again the busy Easter was the prelude to the summer season. The money rows began again. Actually, I don't think they ever stopped. Basha, the dog, became ill with a phantom pregnancy and it was decided to purchase a wire haired terrier puppy for her to nurse. He was to be under my care so I called him Chippy. One day, in ball play, he slid across the floor, banged into the far wall, and broke one hind leg. There being no veterinarian in Bridlington at that time, Antony and I took him to the nearest one by bus, and the poor little chap's leg was encased in plaster for some weeks, but he managed. No walkies though. I was holding him one day some time afterwards, when the entire cast slipped off leaving one very straight and very pink skinny leg. I was the one who telephoned the Vet. who assured me all would be well.

Winifred had two sisters, one Edith, who had helped with the hotel while we were away, and Marjorie, the prettiest of them all. She and her husband Jim lived in Rotherham and Jim had two sisters, one living in Leeds and one in Scotland. The Leeds sister owned a holiday home in Bridlington and that summer the entire brood descended for a month. These included a boy, John Prior, a first year veterinary student, and Frances Templeton a blonde, petite and lovely girl. My brother had long since forgotten his first girlfriend and soon took up with Frances, so I teamed up with John. Just a summer friendship for him – don't forget I was still in pigtails – but I was a bit more serious. I would be, of course, since he was the first boy, or rather young man, who had ever expressed an interest in me. I begged to be allowed to put my hair up, was refused so I cut it off! What a mess. Daddy cried, Winifred scowled, and Antony laughed. But they couldn't stick it back on again.

Miss Taylor had decided it was time to start in earnest on my next examinations. As the season drew to a close I began to work at the local jewellers retail shop. The wage was very little, but would help to get through the winter months which was always a battle with no guests, and I could keep some back for pocket money. Antony left to complete his National Service having passed his matriculation with an exemption. That Christmas Winifred's entire family joined us at the hotel. I was still at the jewellers when, in the New Year of 1951, the hotel was put on the market for sale, and was sold by Easter. WHY?

This time my father, as well as Antony, would leave for South Africa as soon as Antony had finished his National Service. Winifred and I were to follow later, again. I have no idea why we couldn't have all gone together.

The week before we left I sat my Grade VII Theory in the very classroom I had used during my last years at Primary School! The practical I took in the music room of Bridlington Girls High! Déjà vu.

Then I gave my little Chippy away.

11

A child becomes an adult when he realizes that he has the right, not only to be right, but also the right to be wrong.

Thomas Szasz
1920-2012

Our last few days in Bridlington were spent as guests of the woman who worked with us. I had given my Chippy to her daughter and, as they hit it off together pretty well, my sense of loss was eased. We went by train to London, and booked into a hotel between Piccadilly Circus and Leicester Square. We walked from one square to the next, had tea in Swan and Edgars, and taxied the next day to Tilbury Docks where we embarked on the Union Castle ship *Llangibby Castle*. I tried keeping a diary to make a note of all the changes in my day to day existence. Winifred read it without my knowledge and then made derogatory comments. I stopped writing.

This would be my second trip on an ocean-going passenger ship. It was all one class and a pretty old vessel but offered the opportunity to have a holiday break, and be waited on hand and foot. Unfortunately for Winifred this was not to be the case. We had no sooner eased our way out of the Thames, before we had even reached the Channel, than she became violently sick, and that was the state in which she remained for the next several days. It was a tub of a ship, and rolled happily from side to side so that even I thought I would succumb. The weather was absolutely foul, but the thought of the stifling cabin prompted me to remain on deck wrapped in a warm blanket on a damp deck chair. An officer found me there, fed me a hard green apple and brought me a hot drink of Bovril, or some such beverage, all of which stayed down. It wasn't snack time, and there was no steward in sight so I was fortunate. Only about six passengers made it to the dining room and on that occasion we all sat at the same table so it was not necessary for me to eat alone. On about the third day I made the decision to visit the ship's doctor for advice for Winifred was indeed very ill. He decided that as the weather would be calming a little we should wait another day to see if she might recover, but I knew from past history that this would not happen. Sure enough, push came to shove and the doctor explained to her in one of her more lucid moments that he would give her an injection that would knock her out for at least 48 hours, and she would never again throughout her entire life suffer from travel sickness. In years to come I was to regret that I had ever interfered!

As we pulled into the dock at Las Palmas she had recovered sufficiently to come on deck. We did not go sightseeing but stayed aboard and watched the other passengers bantering with the local women who lined the dock displaying their exquisite embroidered linen. For a couple of cartons of cigarettes, or something similar, you could purchase a truly lovely tablecloth. Quite shocking to imagine these days, so little given for so much work.

The voyage continued and I became friendly with another teenage girl. We vied with each other for the attention of a young man, perhaps in his twenties, travelling out to join the Basuto Mounted Police, making absolute pests of ourselves. I don't think we spoiled his trip. I think he enjoyed enthralling us with tales of his various exploits as much as we enjoyed listening to him and asking questions. We two silly starry-eyed girls agreed that he was indeed film star good-looking. Winifred meanwhile had hitched up with some man who was the life and soul of the party but had broken his ankle while playing deck tennis, and spent the rest of the trip with it in plaster.

We docked in the roads off St Helena and passengers who wished were taken by jolly boat to shore where we had to leap from the boat to the jetty, making a change. It was an interesting island because of course this was the island where Napolean Bonaparte was imprisoned and then died. Not in gaol though. His incarceration was a lovely house in very beautiful grounds, where he probably died of boredom. The next port of call was Ascension Island, a lump of volcanic rock of some use to the British Military and also these days as a useful base for tracking orbital debris. Finally we awoke to the magnificent view of Table Mountain and once again entrained for Johannesburg. This time we hit De Aar in mid-winter and it was so cold we didn't even open a window never mind put foot to platform.

My father and Antony had settled themselves into a truly lovely rented house in Parktown North in the northern suburbs of Johannesburg. It was old and unpretentious, but it exuded charm and had an orchard of fruit trees at the rear. There was a semi-circular drive at the front of the house with two gates, and two magnificent jacaranda trees – a picture to be painted from the road, as it frequently was, especially when the trees were in full bloom. In fact we met, and befriended one of the artists whose name I have long forgotten. Surely Winifred would be happy here at last.

It was here that Nanna and Marjorie, one of the sisters, visited us, and stayed couple of weeks on holiday. It was only after they had gone home that I think the rot set in. The shouting began again, in fact I don't think it ever really stopped. Antony always retired to his room with the excuse that he had to study. I once plucked up the courage to ask her why she had bothered to make this second trip, or why she did not return to England. She showed me the back garden ablaze with blooms from the fruit trees, and said that was why she stayed! Daddy bought her a Pomeranian dog, and we acquired a stray white bull terrier we named Bogey. The two of them hit it off and became strange allies. I loved Bogey: he knew he was not allowed to sit on laps so he would put his head, followed by first one leg, then the next leg and finally the third leg, leaving one leg on the floor, and that was his idea of being on the floor and not my lap.

Antony had a room with its own entrance and attended Witwatersrand Medical School as a second year student. Once again the 18 month difference in education in the UK triumphing in his case, whereas with me it had been the other way around. I was to be enrolled as a student of the mad man who taught piano on the opposite side of the road. He also had a studio in the City. I had to play before he would accept me, beginning in his house, before being promoted to his studio, where he boasted a Bechstein Grand.

A friend of Daddy's from work had found a job for me at a very exclusive jewellers' shop in the very centre of Johannesburg. I began in the small goods section on the top floor. I had not been there long when I sold a customer a canteen of cutlery, and the gentleman asked my name and where my father worked. He asked too whether I might like to work with a lot of other girls, how long I had been in South Africa, and where I had been to school. Innocently I answered all questions. When I arrived at Daddy's place of business to collect my lift home, Daddy told me I had an appointment with the Personnel Manager of the Standard Bank Head Office for the following morning. After a school reference, and a short test, there I was, a Bank Clerk. I never looked back. Fortunately they never saw my final math examination.

Working with a team of girls was a great pleasure and I made my first seemingly adult girlfriends. This was before the days when large company canteens provided meals. Instead we shared a lounge in the basement where we munched our sandwiches at lunchtime and discussed our boyfriends, if we had any. My special friend, Meg, taught me to smoke. Some friend! It was, of course, the done thing. Not such a bad thing by today's standards; sex was simply not discussed, booze oo'd and ah'd about, and drugs unheard of.

Daddy had a friend at the car company who suggested I might like to meet his daughter Betty. We hit it off immediately, and although she never came to stay with us because she simply didn't want to, I was often at her house for a weekend. They lived on the West Rand in the suburb of Florida, a small town, which was really an extension of Johannesburg, and it was through her circle of acquaintances that I met my first proper boyfriend, Nicholas.

Meanwhile my piano studies continued with the mad man. I call him that because he actually was, a little. An ex-prisoner from one of the Nazi Concentration Camps I think he was a bit wounded upstairs given the seemingly crazy things I had to do. For example, he made me stand on the corner of a busy street while watching the second hand of his pocket watch, for concentration; practice the piano with the lid down; sit on the floor and reach up to play the keyboard, and endless, endless, endless Czerny Studies. The metronome was always ticking when sometimes I wanted to put my own interpretation into a piece, when I had a piece that is. And oh that counting: I had to say aloud "ba de riddle ba de riddle ba de riddle" instead of 1.2.3.4. for instance. I was joining the group known as the-sandwiches-with-no-filling! I began to loathe it and bunked off on several occasions until I was discovered. An enormous earsplitting argument ensued which I lost, and that was the end of that – no more piano, not even Chopin. My one regret.

Antony, at the same time as my music finale, had simply left his second year medical studies without a backward glance; walked out of his separate entrance and disappeared into the night. Two days later he telephoned to say he was working for a chemical and explosive company in Durban.

Thus did Winifred's dreams of a doctor and pianist in the family dissolve into nothingness.

Unfortunately her wasted dreams brought down further vitriol upon my head. You cannot drive children, certainly not adolescents, to your way, for in the end you will drive them from you. Not only from you, but from that which the child might really have wanted, but was now too afraid to attempt in case of failure. This was so for both of us, but Antony escaped.

I did not. I lived in constant fear of reprimand. Her continual shouting and the constant bickering went on month after month. It made me nervous, and when you are nervous you lose confidence, and when you are aware that you are losing confidence, you become afraid and insecure. In future years I was to regain confidence and overcome fear, and in that strength was my salvation. For all that, I never ceased to be afraid of Winifred, but in the end it didn't really matter. Today I wonder if it ever did.

My friendship with Nicholas continued. He had a small motorbike and worked on the airbase on the East Rand and would ride over on the back roads to visit me in Parktown North. His family owned a fruit farm in the rolling hills of Natal. I think he was considered a very suitable companion for me. Even Winifred liked him. However, I overheard a conversation when it was decided I was much too young for a steady relationship. In any case, there was never any thought of actual love: we were more like very close friends. He was a Roman Catholic which did not concern me in the least and I sometimes attended Mass with him. No one having had any interest in my religious education I was half way there myself.

I remember a special time when Winifred and Daddy wanted to visit Durban for a holiday. It coincided with Nicholas returning to his parents and it was arranged that I would meet his parents and stay with them for a few days. I loved it, and remember sitting absolutely still watching a tiny buck not three metres away munching on the soft grass. We were so still you could almost hear the beads of sweat drop from my brow. For two glorious days I enjoyed the hospitality of kind gentle people in beautiful surroundings. Then they took me halfway to Durban where Daddy met us, and I was transferred back to the realities of life. With the right encouragement, and better guidance something might have come of it, but due to my stupidity, it did not.

I met a much older boy, a man really, for he was 26, an ice hockey player who worked for a stock broking firm. My head was totally swayed, probably because he taught me to skate. His elder sister gave me her dancing skates, and I was in seventh heaven. He wasn't particularly welcome in my home, and I think I might have been trying to be defiant in bringing him home at all. I came off worse than when I began, which I should have known I would. He wanted to marry and had a diamond he wanted to make into a ring. A ring? A ring for me? A ring for the idiot child? I was about to be an even bigger idiot. Established and older, he caught me in a net. Then one evening when we were alone, he introduced me to sex. I didn't like it. Not one bit, although he assured me it would be better next time. But there wasn't going to be a next time. I actually felt molested and unclean. Too late, I wanted Nicholas back, but I was too ashamed and afraid to tell a soul, least of all Nicholas. The damage was done and I could do no more than get on with living. The last I heard of Nicholas was of his departure to join the R.A.F. as a student pilot.

At the bank I was sent for Ledger Training on the Bookkeeping Machines. They did the math for you! At the end, I came out Top, but when I reached home to tell of my accomplishment Winifred did not believe me. I went back to the tutor and, much to her astonishment, asked for a letter of proof.

Arriving home from work one day I could not find Bogey. I was told he had been taken to the Vet. to have the warts on his mouth examined. The Vet. had said nothing could be done, and he had been put to sleep. I looked at her aghast.

I should have known. We were leaving for Durban. This time I was happy to go. We packed again, but there was a small difference as I was to be left behind in the rented house, living camp-like as caretaker until the new lease holders arrived. This had been pre-arranged with the house owners. Very odd indeed, but I did as I was told and left by train for Durban during the month following.

Perhaps having to do things by myself was supposed to make me independent, but it had the reverse effect. I was afraid to do anything without prior approval. If approval was not given, I did it anyway, nine times out of ten, but then the result had to be hidden, and was usually a disaster. In the end I struggled to make any decisions. Why should I when they were all made for me?

12

What we have to learn, we learn by doing.
Aristotle. 384 – 322 BC

Durban has outstretched arms to the north through long, low hills of green sugar cane, beside the blue of the sea. You can hear the thrashing of the surf on the golden sands long before you see, approaching by car from the west, tall white buildings glistening in the distance. Mecca of the surfers and haven to the sailor. Below the Bluff are the calm waters of a natural harbour open to those who seek shelter if stormy seas cry havoc. To the south the arms reach delightful small towns nestling in coves by the sea. Inland she has sanctioned the establishment of beautiful suburbs before finally reaching the lush rolling hills of Natal. I have always loved Durban and always will. In that I am constant.

At first we lived in a rented house in Durban North, split-level and very pretty. Antony, who by now had established himself in rented rooms near his work, visited. All was forgiven, and perhaps now we could settle down. As a matter of interest, Antony had won a scholarship through his company for a three year course in Science at a University. I was pleased for him as he had always wanted to go into the permanent army, and at last he seemed to be happy, even if it was a far throw from the army.

Shortly after we arrived I was introduced to a man by my brother – also an Antony but known as Tony. He, bless him, had two horses, and stabled them in a small horse stables with an enclosed horse ring, in the swampy area along the beach just below where we lived. This was in the years before the Hypermarket which stands there now was even dreamt of. I dearly loved Tony, or rather the horses, Elusive and Cost Price, the latter being an ex-racehorse, nice and gentle. Elusive was just that, with a wicked temper. There was also a little quiet pony upon whose back I learned to ride without the benefit of a saddle or stirrups. Around and around the ring we walked, then cantered, but for trotting we introduced the saddle for my backside, and the pony's relief. I was invited by Tony to visit some friends of his in Kloof, a country suburb, and ride their mare that had not been ridden for months due to the absence of their son. She was very, very frisky, and Tony put me on a lead rein until the mare and I got used to each other. I was never happier than when I was either at the ice rink or in the horse ring. Of course, you might guess it couldn't last: we moved.

Nanna visited us, once only, when we were in our second house. It was slightly further to the north but still in Durban North. Tony moved to Johannesburg so that was the end of my horse riding for the time being. I worked in the head office of the Standard Bank to which I had been transferred from Johannesburg. It was lovely to have Nanna around even if only for a short time. Winifred behaved herself too. Nanna introduced them to some friends of hers from Peterborough in England, a race horse training family who had settled in Durban. False names here: Tim and Shirley and their horse training group became frequent visitors and Shirley, her antitheses, became what can only be called Winifred's best friend. Perhaps that's why they got on so well. Shirley was very pretty, with a simple outlook on a life in which everyone was kind and happy. Her husband, Tim, had been a pilot during the war. She and Tim introduced Winifred and my father to the Durban racing fraternity within which

Winifred settled comfortably. Tim was followed everywhere by his little dog, Winkie, a Maltese terrier, and because they had moved into a luxury flat, they were looking for a home for Winkie. She was given to me, and what a little love she was. She fretted badly for the first few days, and I would let her sit on my lap while I fed her bits of food, otherwise she would not eat. It was a week before she seemingly forgot them and became my pet.

You would think that with enough money to attend the Saturday 'meet' and throw lavish parties, with change left over for dinner out at some noted restaurant, their squabbling over finances would be over, but they were not. In fact they had only just begun!

As for me, amidst these sudden flows of prosperity, I carried on regardless. I was allowed out and had a pretty constant flow of boyfriends, but I had to be home by 10.30pm otherwise there would be consequences. Completely unnecessary as I couldn't lose what I had already lost, but they were not to know that! Not many of the boys had transport, but usually we would go out in groups where at least one had a car. They were fun evenings, not always dancing and partying, but quite often at a local hotel where, if it was fine, they had outdoor dancing. Sometimes we would play cards at one or another's house, never mine, or perhaps Monopoly or some such. I joined up with a group to play squash and saved up to buy a racket. More than anything I enjoyed my skating and managed to get to the rink at least once a week and met friends there. In those days a boy would ask you to 'go steady' and if you agreed you would never date anyone else. We were all the same. Sometimes this sort of relationship became serious and might end in marriage. Never me. A boy had to be introduced to my parents before I was allowed to go out with him alone. Groups were accepted, but not single dates. This somewhat restricted my chances of 'going steady'. However, I had my share of boyfriends but they came and went quite quickly. I was in love with none of them although I admit to having a heart flutter now and again, and a little weep if I lost one. All healthy enough I suppose.

We were living on the Berea, the ridge of hills overlooking the City when I joined the Shakespeare Club and attended their readings once a week. There I met Julie with whom I became very friendly. She was of Portugese extraction with very strict parents so we had something in common. The sixth of seven children, all of whom had a University education, Julie herself spoke seven languages.

I was very happy at the Bank, working on the Bookkeeping machines we had in those days. My wages were not high, but as usual I gave it all to Winifred. She gave me back what she considered to be an appropriate figure which was never quite enough but had to do. She figured she fed, clothed, watered and gave me shelter, so what did I need with money? I had one dress on, and one in the wash, and that was all that was required. Thank goodness we had compulsory dresses at the Bank, and I only had two of those. I was not permitted to wear trousers, but I managed to save for a pair of khaki slacks which I changed into when I went out and changed back into when I went in. (Excuse the grammar, it is my own!) I once saved for a grey top with bright red stripes that Winifred decided was downright ugly and I thought beautiful. I gave it to a friend, Lucy, and she kept it for me temporarily.

There did not seem to be any chance of further promotion at the Bank and some of my friends were leaving for greener pastures, so I thought that I too would make that move. Before I did so, Winifred packed up and went to England to see Nanna. She wanted me to go too, but I pointed out that I only had a certain number of days due so it was decided that they would pay my fare from Durban to Capetown and back, while she carried on to England. I wasn't going to refuse. It was the sort of holiday many of my friends had taken and was quite popular. Even Julie had been. So away I went on the *Edinburgh Castle*, First Class of course – when would Winifred ever travel otherwise. Her seasick days were long gone and she loved the attention. In Capetown I hopped aboard the Castle ship of the same name, *Capetown Castle*, for my trip back to Durban. After all my experience I should have known better than to attend a First Class dance alone. When I danced with the Purser and thanked him afterwards he replied that it was his job to dance with single lady passengers. I went to bed early that night.

Back home, I applied for a job with the United Building Society and was accepted. The work was different from the bank. For a start we were strictly controlled in both our dress form and social behaviour. We were not, for instance, permitted to hold private conversations in the Banking Hall, and permission had to be sought before leaving the Banking Hall for the bathroom. The result was that many girls would not like to work in such circumstance so those that did were highly sought and of good calibre. We were looked after, and happy. All the rules made sense. Pity they have fallen away over the years. It was during these convivial lunchtimes that I learned from my peers the facts and the pitfalls of married life. A much renowned book by Marie Stopes, covered in nondescript brown paper, was handed around and borrowed by those who wished to be enlightened. I was one of the them. I even mentioned it to my father in passing, who made the remark "Good, good. Very popular with women in Victorian times. Won't do you any harm. Good, good," or something similar.

In due course I became a cashier on the counter. We had huge

National Cash Registers so it was pretty hard to make an error, unless you pressed the wrong button. If you didn't balance, no one could go anywhere or do anything until the error was found – very much 'all hands on deck'. My good friend there was Lucy whom you will hear more of later.

Daddy taught me to drive. He took me to a steep hill, stopped halfway up, and told me if I could reach the top without sliding down, I could drive anywhere and anything! That's how the lessons began, and three Saturday mornings later I reached the top of the hill. From then on it was straight, fast driving, changing gear from top to lower at high speed without grinding, followed by driving in heavy traffic. I passed my Test! We got on very well together, the two of us. Many times I wondered why he stuck it all out. The trouble, I thought, was that he spoilt her. And let her have her own way. Not because he wanted to, but because it was the easiest thing to do. At home I was similar in that I had learned to turn the other cheek, and to hold my tongue. On our trips home from work we would take little bets on who would be on the firing line that night. Once I sneaked out in the middle of one of her verbal attacks on Daddy. When I returned he was busy collecting his clothes from the pavement where she had thrown them from the upstairs flat where we were living at that time. He also had a black eye the next morning.

I should mention here that during our time in Durban, on this occasion, we lived in seven different houses or flats, two purchased, the rest rented.

Once again, through my brother. I met a boy who was working toward his Masters Degree in English at Pietermaritzburg University. He had a big bearing on my life. False name here: Paul. He read a thesis I had written on William Shakespeare and was astonished that I was not at University. I still have that thesis, in faded blue ink, in one of my scribble books. We remained friends for many years, even after we were both married to other people. Mostly our friendship was conducted by letter – remember we had not yet heard of computers or mobile phones – and we both moved around so much that landlines were difficult to find, and public telephones a godsend. Anyway, it was good practice for our letter writing skills at which he was particularly good. I discovered Winifred was reading his letters when she put one back incorrectly in the envelope, but I didn't say anything. The last time he took me dancing we arrived home at midnight to have Winifred pull me from the car by my hair calling me all kinds of descriptive names for being late. Exit Paul, although we remained friends. I still have some of his poetry and a list of authors he wanted me to read. Exit many similar boyfriends in very similar circumstances. I had another lovely friend, a science student who finished up as a scientific zoologist in London somewhere. Gleefully, Winifred showed me a photograph of his marriage in London and was surprised when I showed a lack of interest. I had moved on, as had many. I once had a doctor friend who told me sadly that I would marry eventually, but first they would have to marry my mother.

We moved to Kloof, and behold it was the house next door to the frisky mare I had ridden a couple of years earlier. The people were only too happy to have me ride her again, and I swear that horse remembered me. I would rise at four in the morning so that I could ride before setting off for work. The ice rink was too far away so I could ride at weekends as well if I wished. I started to teach Cherry to jump, not that I knew how to, but she seemed to be teaching me. Once I hadn't put her curb chain on and she sprinted with me down the freeway which was in the dirt stage of construction. I knew that we were nearing where it rejoined the highway, and was getting frightened because I couldn't stop her. Eventually I turned her off the dirt and uphill where she slowed slightly and I managed to slip off. All those years of practicing circus acts with my cousin paid off! By the time I caught up with her she was standing in the middle of a bowling green at the local bowling green club. Thank heaven it was midweek and only the Africans were around, laughing and clapping. I climbed aboard and rode sedately home where the Africans there already knew of my ignominy. Such is the bush telegraph of Africa! It didn't last though. I had to kiss Cherry goodbye as we moved again.

Granny died when we were in a flat on the Berea. I was not told of this but remarked on my father's black tie at breakfast which had replaced the R.A.F. one. It was the same year I reached my 21st birthday. I can't recall anything special occurring, no dancing so we probably dined out. I was given a rolled gold watch, my very first watch, which has long since disappeared. A neighbour who was leaving gave me a young budgie, cage and all, and I spent hours in my room teaching him to fly around free. He began to talk quite well too although that required a lot of patience.

We moved from house to house like wandering gypsies and each house had to be packed for, and unpacked at, so to speak. I became an expert at both! The Personnel Department at the Building Society refused to bother with my constant notification of address changes. They simply wanted to know if my income tax was updated. I told them that my father saw to that side of things. Giving over all my wages and retaining but a small portion I supposed he did. I was too poor to be concerned about taxes.

Father, poor Father. This kind gentle man, so well read, beautifully educated and highly intelligent, was quite unable to cope. He had gone through one divorce that had lifted him out of the frying pan and his second choice had landed him slap in the middle of the fire. It was disaster. What else could it be? When

I asked him why he did not retaliate he always, as I have repeatedly said, replied that 'a soft tongue turneth away wrath'. When I asked him why he didn't leave her, he said, "For the same reason you don't, I am afraid". knew what he meant, but could not explain it, or wish it away. All this was long before she committed the first of her two Cardinal Sins.

We bought a house in Westville, the nearest suburb in Durban after travelling inland. While there, Winifred departed for England again. I am not at all sure, but I think it must have been about then that Nanna died. I took some leave and Daddy and I started painting the inside of the house while she was gone. Much laughter when, while he was at work, I painted a black wooden door white without putting a base on first. Took two whole days to get it right, and white. She would have freaked out, but father just laughed and told me to get it done. We would go to the local café-restaurant for supper and eat fish and chips on their verandah, on one occasion with a screwdriver poking out of my back pocket. Or I would cook way-out meals for the evening: soft boiled egg in the middle of a mound of fluffy potatoes was one. I thought it original, but apparently it was not. Then we would sit on the verandah of the house and sing raucously, without a care whether we were flat or not. Just pure natural fun.

Once she returned from England it became my habit to ask Winifred if I could borrow her dilapidated Ford Prefect to reach the ice rink. She always said yes as long as I filled it with petrol. I would put five shillings worth (50c) in. It generally registered around the zero line. My top up would probably last until the next time I borrowed it. She kept going on about this marvelous pianist who played the grand piano in the beautiful Edward Hotel, as it was then, and I should go there to hear him. I kept crying off because I had been approached at the rink to perform in the stage show they were about to take to South America. I had to ask permission, even though I was 21. Naturally it was not granted. Dancing on the stage, even on ice, in a European country was a definite no-no, but dancing on stage in a Latin American country was not even to be considered, and I was an idiot even to think it, never mind raise a voice to it, and so on ad infinitum. I agreed to go to dinner at the Edward after my session at the rink. I did not need to ask for the car as I would go after work to the rink and would be getting a lift home with them. After skating I walked to the Edward, pony tail swinging and ice skates slung over my shoulder, not exactly dressed for the Edward. Geoff was playing as I entered the room. I found my parents and as I sat down he began playing Some Enchanted Evening, You Will See A Stranger Across a Crowded Room. I swear it was pre-arranged. Winifred was delighted. This then was to be the pianist in the family!

Geoff was a tall, handsome man who hailed from Harrow in England. His parents and mine would sit together listening to him play, and drinking whatever tipple it was they drank, and of course he would join them as often as not. He was a Freemason, which interested me a lot as I had been probing into various religions and although Masonry is certainly not a religion, it is extremely interesting. Geoff was amazed at my knowledge as it is supposed to be a huge secret, which it is actually not. There are such places as libraries around which I had been finding myself for many years, and after all, the truth would still be a secret even if shouted from the highest treetop!

He was a tremendous pianist and played in concert with the Durban Orchestra, and other orchestras. He made more money playing at the Edward Hotel. I was mesmerised when he played. We went out together on and off, and off and on. He took me as his partner when he was invited to the Governor's Garden Party – for which I had a new pretty blue and yellow dress – and took someone else to the Durban July Horse Race! He suggested we should get married, but not in Durban because half the racing community would come to the wedding. I had already tried the suggestion of marriage before, in Johannesburg, and somehow I was still not ready. I hadn't fallen in love, at least I didn't think I had.

Before I knew it another year had passed. We moved to yet another flat on the Berea. This time it was fully furnished as we were to rent it for just six months. The house at Westville was sold, along with the contents, but I doubt if there was much left because there was an enormous mortgage. The little black Pomeranian dog had died while we were in the new Berea furnished flat, and I smelled the next move without being told of it.

Some sort of plan was afoot which did not seem to me to be entirely kosher, as they say when something seems not altogether right. I was to go with Winifred to England and my father was to follow when we had decided where we wanted to live.

It was to be that terrible time again. I had to give away my little budgie, who was now very talkative, to a very close friend recently married, and he was immediately loved. Then one day, with my dog Winkie in my arms, Winifred and I met Tim, and I, crying, handed Winkie back to him.

The arrangements were made. This time we were to travel by Holland Africa Line instead of Union Castle Line. Today I have cause to wonder whether Winifred had been banned from Union Castle, or perhaps she had just grown tired of them. She had certainly sailed often enough with them, almost once a year and always first class, despite all the talk of penury. The fact that I did not have the least desire to go was not given any consideration, and for some reason, which I cannot possibly fathom, it did not enter my head to complain – wouldn't have done the slightest bit of good anyway.

A Going-Away party was held in the cabin that Winifred had to herself. Geoff arrived with a record he had cut especially for me where he played my favourite: Chopin's Fantasia. I couldn't show anyone my cabin as I was sharing with an elderly lady just a little further down in the same alley. I was happy about that as I preferred not to be with Winifred, but it does beg an intriguing question? Finally a bell rang, everyone departed, we went on deck and waved goodbye. I just stood against the rail, and cried as the ship passed out of the harbour then turned southward under the Bluff, knowing I would never see it again.

13

In the fell clutch of circumstance,
I have not winced nor cried aloud,
Under the bludgeonings of chance,
My head is bloody but unbowed.
     Invictus.
     W.H. Henry, 1849 – 1903

I stood at the rail of the *Oranjefontein* as we crossed the bar and turned south to pass the Bluff which the Zulu's call "Bubulonga" – meaning big and long, loosely translated – and the rest of us call The Bluff because it hides the natural sheltered harbour. I wondered what the hell I was doing there. I had tears in my eyes, a lump in my throat and an ache inside wondering if I would ever see it again. It was too late now to do anything, like leaving home, so I simply had to accept the inevitable and soldier on. There is no doubt about it: I was a coward. Oh well, best foot forward, and as I did so bumped into a young man, who bumped into me. Let us call him Robert.

"Hello, are you alright?" he enquired. "Are you leaving someone behind?"

I stupidly replied, "Only bloody Africa."

He laughed, took my elbow and guided me to the aft lounge, and sat me down. I protested that I ought to go below and assist my mother in unpacking, and he asked quite seriously if she was handicapped, which made me laugh. I don't think that had been his intention though. We chatted for a while and he told me he was a doctor en route to Scotland for take a further degree in Edinburgh. I think it was Edinburgh, or it might well have been Glasgow. So began a shipboard acquaintance that bordered on romance and luckily for me lasted for the entire voyage.

It was a two class ship and I must confess I didn't visit 2nd class. Why would I? I understood it was really little better than steerage. This was later confirmed because a day or so after we had left Durban, Robert had met a young man, Brian, who asked if he could upgrade himself, and share the two bed cabin Robert was occupying on his own. I don't know how the arrangement was made, but the appeal was successful and Brian joined our little group. Winifred, as often as not, joined us too, although from Capetown onward she found friends more to her liking and was often in the company of a professor from Oxford.

I shared a cabin with a pleasant, elderly woman. We were hardly ever in it at the same time, except to sleep. She always had an afternoon nap, I did not; she went to first sitting, I went to second sitting. She was always in bed before me; I was up early, she was up late, so everything worked out like a cuckoo clock. I borrowed one of her long white nighties for the fancy dress ball, and her hot water bottle. She was shocked when she saw me dressed, on Winifred's inspiration which I thought quite canny, as 'The Morning After the Night Before'. The barber refused point blank to put my hair in steel curlers. He said I was totally mad, and should have gone as a fairy princess. I blacked out two front teeth as well! When I saw myself I thought the barber had a point.

Robert, Brian and two other young men went as the quartet from Swan Lake. They emptied the shop of crinkly pink paper and then went back and emptied it of the white paper too. Some ladies, in semi-secret, made ballet tutus for them, and gave them ballet lessons too. They won a very popular First Prize.

Meanwhile after the judging, I made the biggest transformation ever in the animal kingdom!

We had to dress for dinner every night which was a bit tricky as neither of us had much to choose from. The food, by the way, was superb. The Captain was a lovely elderly Hollander who said he wished I was his daughter! He allowed us to play the grand piano in the main lounge which was usually kept locked – not that I played for those days were long gone. Anyway, nobody wanted classics.

We went ashore at Las Palmas, Winifred and her friend the professor, a Spanish Diplomat and his very pretty blonde girlfriend, Robert, Brian, another girl and I. The Spaniard took us to a local dancing establishment where there was much music and much more dancing. None of us danced. We were only guests and just watched. I sat enthralled by the Spanish girls who wore the most beautiful dresses, all frothy and sparkling. When they returned from dancing to their seats, they lifted their skirts high to their waists before they sat down, and then dropped the skirts over the back of the chair to avoid crushing them. It was all so pretty and charming. Robert put a finger under my chin and pushed in order to close my mouth.

When the journey came to its end and we docked, Winifred made me stand beside her until we had disembarked. I wondered why a few people were staring at her until I discovered that the Professor's wife and daughter were in full view waving at him. I, being ever the innocent, gaily waved back.

Almost everyone on the ship travelled up to London by train. I said goodbye to Robert and Brian and the other people who had befriended me, and away we went. We were to stay with Carla, a family friend from South Africa, one of the racing fraternity. She was wont to spend six months in South Africa and six months in England and it was presently the turn of England.

She owned a tall house in Orme Square, just off Bayswater Road, opposite the Park. This house had recently been renovated into apartments. Carla was, at the time we arrived, living in one on the first floor. There we deposited ourselves for the time being. I don't think it was much longer than two or three nights. I would leave the two ladies and go off by myself. One day I went to the cinema. I've forgotten what was showing but the short was about Durban which did me no good at all. I did not know London in those days and was a very solitary tourist with little more than bus fare in my pocket. I looked at all the touristy places like the Regent St, Lambeth Palace, Piccadilly, and Buckingham Palace and finished with a walk through Hyde Park on the way home, all places within walking distance of Orme Square, if a little far for the feet.

It was decided that we would visit Brighton as a possible place to live. I felt as though I was just along for the ride as my opinion would not have accounted for much. We stayed in a very pleasant B&B near the seafront on the way to Hove, and used this as a base to explore Brighton. I was used to the golden sands of Durban, and the green hills of Natal, and my first impression of Brighton was not a good one. Everything was concrete, everywhere you looked, even the beach! We went to see the pre London film showing of *The King and I*. Winifred bought me a wonderful adult coat so that I could at last dispose of the one I had worn for the last eight years. That more or less heralded the end of our Brighton tour, and it was time to try somewhere else. We were no help at all to each other. Where to go?

Back at Brighton station we boarded a London train and started inspecting a map we had purchased. A man facing us across the train table asked if he could be of assistance. He suggested, after we had explained what we were about, that Richmond might be a likely place. After promising him that we would meet him at the end of the day if we did not like Richmond, we deposited our cases at the station and set forth. It now dawned on me that it was I, in my nice new coat, that had attracted him, not Winifred, and I did not think a further meeting with him would be a good plan. I resolved to cross that bridge at the end of the day knowing that we had to collect our suitcases, and it could be a tricky decision that needed to go my way. It was pouring with rain when we arrived at Richmond so we asked a taxi driver to take us to a suitable B&B – taxi drivers always know the right places.

There, in a tall terraced house not far from the station, we were given a room at the back of the house and at the top of the stairs, clean and pleasant enough. We carried no suitcases so I wondered what the landlady thought of us.

Off we set in the pouring rain, not torrential, but wet and unpleasant. This was not the Richmond I came to know many years later, but a wet and dirty facsimile. No town can be shown off to advantage around a railway station, especially in the rain, and Richmond was no exception. We returned to the boarding house, couldn't find the owner – she was probably out getting stuff in for our breakfast – so we left the key on the hall table and walked out again. I wondered again what the poor woman thought. Back on the train to London I suggested that it was a good seven hours before we could meet 'that man' so perhaps we could collect the luggage, phone Carla, and pitch up there again. Thank goodness, this is what we did.

Poor old Carla, she really was a brick. She had a partner called Harry, but I think it was she who had the money. I never discovered her history although she was a good friend to me too. Winifred now needed some moral support and in some confusion we set off into the City for a meandering walk. On passing a shipping agent she had a wonderful idea. "Shall we go back to South Africa?" she asked me, one foot already in the door. You must know my reply. And so it was decided, a temporary booking made, and that was the end of it. But the chickens should not yet have been counted. On arrival at Carla's she waved a yellow envelope at us. It was from father and it read "arriving in London on such and such a date" which happened to be the very next day. I wanted to send a reply immediately saying "Don't come!" but it was far too late. Winifred was in a state of shock, poor woman. I had no idea what the hell was going on. Why had we come? Was nothing decided before we left? I thought it had been arranged to give us time to settle. Was Daddy wanting to be rid of both of us? If so, why was he coming? He was not really expected for another month or so.

Then there he was, looking worn and weary, another lost soul on Carla's doorstep.

Back to Brighton we went. Another couple of days in the same boarding house, except this time I had my own room. Within another day we had found accommodation in a very nice furnished flat in Hove.

Hove is a lovely affluent suburb of Brighton a little to the west along the coast. I know I had a streaming cold, but nevertheless I was sent out in dreadful weather to 'clear my head' while they discussed battle plans. I remember sitting in an enclosed promenade shelter looking at the channel and wondering what to do next. The 'next' came soon enough for on the following day I applied in person for a job at Barclays Bank in Brighton and started a day later. I, at least, would have some money coming in so we would not starve. I expect there was money coming in from the Westville house, but again, I was not told.

The Bank was easy although I was back in Clearance, and not in the actual Banking Hall. I was not popular with the Personnel Section as they had to register me from scratch with all the necessary Government Departments. I caught the bus from just outside the flat, which actually was the first floor of a normal house, the ground floor being another flat. The two together looked like a pretty private house from the outside. It was only a one-bedroom apartment, but had a wide passage in which someone had once placed a bed. That was mine. I thought I could be quite happy living there especially after my first week at Barclays when a young chap in the bank, who travelled to and from on the same bus, invited me to join the local amateur dramatic group. I went home full of the joys of spring.

Forget it, I was told. We're moving to Eastbourne. The only person who might have been more horrified than me at this turn of events was the Personnel Manager at Barclays Bank who had just finished all the paperwork!

It transpires that while I was at work they were at home, plotting. A solicitor had been engaged and the three of them had sought a suitable business which had now been not only found, but apparently purchased with, I understood, the very last of their funds. This business was not in Hove, not even in Brighton, but in Eastbourne, eastward along the coast towards Hastings. The business, as it turned out, was a fish and chip shop! How the hell did they pick that one out of the pot? Ye gods! Was I to be included in a dreadful urn, shaken about, and then tossed out sooner or later, into Charon's boat and even have to pay a penny for the crossing? My apologies to Horace, Roman Poet around 70 BC.

At last I gave vent to my anger, but it was of no use. I could have saved my strength and stilled my heart for I could do nothing. It was easy for Winifred, who had always wanted a fish and chip shop after hearing the ringing tills of the shop we were attached to in Blackpool. Much easier for her, the unpaid nursemaid as she had become in the habit of calling herself, to hide behind the truth than it was for my father to confess it. He gave in to her, spoiled her, and in doing so made life more bearable. The truth was that between them they had made an ungodly mess of everything, and landed me right in the middle; the truth was that she was a spendthrift and impossible to please; the truth was he coddled her every whim, getting himself into deep financial dirt, for want of a more appropriate word.

My father, this kind and gentle soul, weak, but willing to sacrifice anything for Winifred, whom I am sure he could not emotionally love, had left South Africa through the back door, so to speak, using the company car and, with the help of my brother, had driven up to Lourenco Marques. From there he had flown to London while Antony had driven the car back to Durban with a letter of explanation of sorts.

My father had not paid his Income Tax. Nor had he paid mine. None of us could return to South Africa. We were now poorer than the poorest church mouse. But it's okay, we had a fish and chip shop! I thought perhaps I should kiss a frog!

The solicitor they had used to purchase the business very kindly transported us to Eastbourne. I thought that rather odd, but by now I was kind of numb, and prepared to accept anything. My first impression of the shop was not too disheartening. It was situated a block from the seafront and ran parallel with the promenade. The door opened to a long shop with a staircase along the right hand wall. The cooking facility ran straight across the back wall. Between the counter and the front window was a café area with seating for about a dozen people. It was behind this room the horror began, for here were two rooms next to each other with cold brick floors and stone walls. This was where the fish were to be gutted and cleaned by my father. In those days there was no such thing as prepared fish – they were collected or delivered fresh and whole. The room next to this held a large white bathtub into which were finally poured the chips which were then kept in cold water. Of course, there was no such thing as a prepared chip either: Winifred and I between us washed and peeled potatoes, and then put them through the chipper.

The staircase led to our living quarters above. There were three tiny rooms which would depress even the hardiest. The largest was the front room which overlooked the street. In one corner there was a frosted glass partition behind which was the bath. That was fortunate – it could have been downstairs where the lavatory was, or even, worse, outside!

This then was to be our lifestyle for the indeterminate future. Meanwhile, before we had opened the door for business I had gone to Lloyds Bank thinking it wise to give Barclays a miss, and had been employed to start the following week. It had been impressed upon me that we were not only very poor, but would have to live a hand to mouth existence, literally, until the shop started making money. I actually thought that my small income would at least be reliable. However, I was told I was needed in the shop, and had to return to Lloyds with that decision as my apology.

It was towards the end of summer, and therefore the end of the season, when we took over. Eastbourne had little to commend it, but then I never went out, so how could I judge. The most I ever did was visit the local cinema on a Sunday afternoon. I wondered, when nobody sat on either side of me, that perhaps I smelt of fish and chips! It was indescribably terrible, but no doubt there were people in the world much worse off than us. It was many years later before I would cook or eat fish and chips.

The year continued in like fashion until father, that remarkably impossible man, came up with the idea that I, me, this poorly educated, unobtrusive, silent, mouse-like creature with an as yet untapped high IQ, might be coming into some money. Me! Wow! What was money? From nowhere came the idea. My real Mama came, after all, from a wealthy family. Perhaps, I, me, should go up to London and visit the family lawyers to find out!

Another of Winston Churchill's comments is "When you are going through hell, keep going". I kept going. Indeed, I would have walked through the hubs of hell if I had even an outside chance of getting back to Africa in one piece. An appointment was made, and up to London I went, just like Dick Whittington but without the mythical cat. Of course, father had remembered the names of the family lawyers, and clutching their address I deposited myself once more with Carla who had extended her stay in London.

It took quite a bit of nerve to walk into that distinguished ancient company of lawyers and present myself to one of them in particular. His opening words were "It's easy to see who you are" but whether he was referring to Mama whom I do not resemble, or to her mother, I have no way of knowing, but the new black coat carefully cared for above the fish and shop, was proving its worth. Mama, now widowed, was certainly alive, and delighted to know that both her children were. I must have given the lawyer a brief outline of my circumstances which he related to Mama in front of me by telephone, and asked if I would like to meet her. I'm afraid I had to decline as I did not know how Winifred would react to the proposal. I'm sure a certain amount of fear must have been obvious in my demeanour as the lawyer did not pursue it. Mama was living off the income from the Trust Fund that had been drawn up for her by the family executors years earlier. Apart from the interest generated, the Trust itself was untouchable until after her death. She now named my brother and I as her beneficiaries and with this information I returned to Eastbourne.

What happened next I should perhaps have foreseen. Nothing short of battle plans were put in place, once again behind closed doors, and the next thing I knew I was sent again to London, this time with Winifred, in order to visit a Money Lender. We asked if we could borrow money against the eventual interest in the Fund. He gave a very definite no, but was prepared to actually purchase the Trust. This was a long term interest for him since Mama was still very much alive and reasonably young. In any case he would have to approach the Executors, and with that we had to be satisfied.

By now I was feeling a little upset about the whole thing. What would the Executors, and Mama, think of me? I'd only just been made a beneficiary to a substantial sum of money, and here was I trying to get my hands on it long before due date. Granted Mama had dumped us which had resulted in a sad and disconsolate childhood from which I had yet to recover, but that was no excuse. I was older and should be mature enough not to participate in such a nefarious scheme. In retrospect I can only submit that I was totally under Winifred's domination, and for some psychotic reason was unable to oppose her. I was also sorry for my father, but he was no help at all. Back to Eastbourrne went the unpaid nursemaid and myself to await the result of what I now thought was to be a very explosive situation. It was not a long wait.

A letter arrived from the London lawyers addressed to my father with the request that I, and I alone, should return to their offices in order to meet an executive of the Trust Fund. I never saw the letter and don't know what the contents were, only that I should present myself. Thus did the plot of my life swirl around and thicken. Winifred came along too, why I do not know since she could not come to the offices with me. Perhaps she had visions of Mama being on the scene. We both agreed to meet at

3pm in the tea lounge of Swan and Edgars, not too far from where I would be. In the office I was introduced to a tall distinguished man, probably in his mid-sixties. I will call him Mr. Exec who after some small talk and a question and answer session, asked me if I would like lunch. I accepted and a taxi was ordered which took us to *Simpson's on the Strand*, or was it *Piccadilly*? I played safe and ordered roast beef, as he did. It's difficult to hold conversation while eating so nothing much was said during the meal. We had already spoken at length and I had answered questions honestly and carefully. We got on very well indeed, and I felt I had known him for much longer than an hour or two. He told me that my grandmother had been very kind to him when he was very young. I wondered if he was the adopted son of my grandmother, but did not like to ask. When the meal was finished I laughed when he looked at my plate and remarked that I must have been hungry. I had been! He was almost at the end of his questioning. Then he said that he would consider what he could do to help me, but it would be only a temporary help as he was no longer a young man, and he had his own family to consider. I asked him if he would like to meet Winifred who was waiting for me, and he accepted. I was dreadfully conscious of the fact that I, in my snobbishness, did not think he would actually approve of her, and I wondered what he would think of her five strands of false pearls! However, all was well, and she was sedately charming. He declined to sit after I had made the introduction, gave me a perfunctory hug, and departed saying he would be in touch.

Strangely enough I felt no after-affects from this obvious interrogation, instead I felt a sense of happiness in that I had tried my best and done well.

About two weeks passed and then one Sunday morning the doorbell rang. I ran down to answer and there was Mr. Exec. He had come, he told me, with good news. Of course I invited him in and took him upstairs where I introduced my father. It seems that they had met years before, and at that time had been in Mama's court, so to speak. Winifred arrived a few moments later having been given enough time to look reasonably presentable, minus my father's dressing gown, and no sign of the pearls. I made tea and after some desultory small talk Mr. Exec got down to business.

Firstly he made it plain that he could now allow Eileen's (Mama's name) child to live in such circumstances. I crossed my fingers and prayed Winifred would not explode. He said he would pay my father's back taxes out of his own pocket, and Winifred would repay him once probate was granted on Nanna's Will; and my father was to be escorted to a South African bound ship by a lawyer. He turned to me and said that he was sure that I would return there too, as was my wish, either with my father or at a later convenient date. Then he sternly admonished me never again to try borrowing money from a money lender, or anybody else come to that. None of this could take place until my father had ensured that he had been offered his job back, and proof of this could be produced. And that, as they say, was that. He left very shortly afterwards. I wondered how he had travelled down from his home near Guildford, but presumed it must have been by car. After I had seen him down the stairs to the front door and thanked him, in tears, for what he was doing, I returned to our living room weak at the knees, wondering what to expect, but there was total silence. I should have basked in the stillness of Winifred's tongue, instead I said I would go to the movies, and asked for ticket money. I understand that the very same evening Father wrote to Durban to inquire about a job!

I can only assume the paperwork that was undertaken to finalise all this. The shop could not be sold, or any further steps taken until father heard back from Durban. For my part, the whole thing from beginning to end was nothing more than a sordid tale. Except for another whim of Winifred's we would all still have been in Durban and the tax could have been paid off monthly against my father's wages. Her constant desire to trail back and forth as a first class passenger year after year had taken its toll. The money should have been better spent. As it was, she was still the unpaid nursemaid for monies from the Trust Fund would not be forthcoming, and she would have to pay the taxes from her own legacy from Nanna.

I waited only days and then began to look for the postman whose delivery arrived very early each morning. One day I could see a blue airmail envelope from the top of the stairs, but it was a letter from Geoff, the only one I received, and which I could barely read because the writing was so poor. Then there it was, a letter for my father. This was it: with baited breath I watched my father's face as he opened the envelope and I knew before he spoke that it would be alright.

So began the ordeal of selling the shop. I could almost guarantee it went for a song, just to be rid of it, but I kept such a low profile in all the affairs and just quietly got on with the job. We had a man in the shop helping us by then, a nice fellow of about 40 years, who was on the dole and willing to work for a fish and chip dinner every night which was all we ever ate, except for the odd sausage. Thank goodness he was there because after we had sold the shop, and father had left, duly escorted, we needed Alfie to help us, and besides he gave us a room in his Council house when we needed accommodation prior to our departure.

The same lawyer in Hove who had helped us buy the shop, this same lawyer delegated to accompany my father and see him aboard the ship for South Africa in case he did a bunk, now for some reason beyond my ken took us from Eastbourne to Hove where he and his wife put us up for the night. Winifred gave me a sleeping capsule to take, to calm me she said. But I slipped the capsule apart and dropped the contents down the lavatory before putting the two sides together again. Why she wanted to give me a sleeping pill I do not know. Later I took the now empty capsule in front of her. The next day we departed Hove for Southampton, and the lawyer saw us off on the train. We had the window of the compartment down, and he and Winifred gave each other what I would call a clinch of a kiss. Surely that wasn't in the contract too! I didn't care. We spent one night in Southampton grateful for the knowledge of a taxi driver who found us reasonable accommodation, and the next day we were on our way to Durban, and home.

14

The wisdom of age is a poor substitute
For the optimism of youth.
Unknown

The Holland Africa passenger ship *Jagersfontein*, sister ship of the *Oranjefontein* on which we had arrived in England, lay at anchor in the Southhampton Waters, the tidal estuary north of the Solent. We were transferred to her by lighter from the docks and boarded up a very short gangplank. It was a little embarrassing when all the other passengers, obviously hailing from the Netherlands, were lining the ship's rail watching us – we were foreigners boarding a Dutch ship! I learned a little about these same passengers later, some still bearing a bit of a grudge towards the English for the debacle at Arnhem (which actually applied both ways) but 98% were a marvelously friendly bunch.

This time Winifred and I shared a cabin, indeed, money was so tight but I would gladly have travelled steerage. The cabin was a short way down a little off-shoot of the main passageway. It boasted a fairly substantial porthole beneath which was a small bed, mine. Opposite, against the inner bulkhead was a bunk. No shower or toilet, but these were conveniently situated nearby.

It was not long before we left the cabin and made our way to the decks where everybody else had the same idea, to watch take-off, or up-anchor, or full steam ahead, whatever the term. It was a mild day, an English Spring day, a good day to wave goodbye.

We remained on the starboard side where we could see the edge of the New Forest as we glided almost silently by, a mass of dark green foliage, with here and there a boat ramp visible leading from it to the water. Eventually, as Southampton Waters gave way to the deeper waters of The Solent, we passed Calshot Castle, build by Henry VIII to repel any invading French or Spanish. Extensively modernised to keep pace with the centuries, it was still used during the two World Wars of the 20th century as a successful deterrent to any German invasion. Finally we came to Hurst Castle, another of Henry's defensive forts. The white chalk needles of the Isle of Wight were on our left so near you could almost touch them, and then the English Channel claimed us. I felt quite sad as I realised I had left behind my birthplace in the very Forest we had just passed, my birthright, this green island no longer mine.

Winifred by now had become bored with my recitation, both the history lesson, and with the receding coastline. We moved on for a turn around the deck.

Walking through the forward lounge we passed three young men sitting in a row on a settee and Winifred made some remark about them being likely lads! I hadn't noticed, but the next time we went by I made a point of looking. Two very green eyes met mine. It was like an electric shock.

Going down to dinner that evening we scanned the board outside the dining salon and discovered we were seated at the Captain's table. This must surely be wrong, but the Head Steward approached us and confirmed the seating. We had only reached this exalted position because the captain was the same dear old man who had once said he wished I was his daughter: the captain from the *Oranjefontein*. It was a decided honour but carried with it certain etiquette that must be observed: in the evenings one could enter the dining salon but never begin ordering, and therefore eating, before the Captain arrived. nor leave the table first, so timing was of the essence. Fortunately the captain generally entered the aft pub just prior to dinner so we had plenty of warning! In any event, we had time to get used to the idea as the captain does not usually leave the bridge on the day of departure.

The following day during my perambulations, while Winifred was elsewhere, I was approached by a young man who introduced himself as Henk. Speaking perfect English with that very attractive Dutch accent, he said he had come at the request of his friend who wanted to escort me to the dance that evening. I replied that the friend should ask me himself, but was sorry because I had to know who the friend was. Henk said "Come with me, we're all playing cards in the lounge, and I'll introduce you." Away we went, I gullible as ever, with heart beating, and there they were, about five of them. The only one that rose to meet us was Jan, the boy with the green eyes.

There were about six of these young men, in their early twenties, all straight out of Officer Training Courses in Vlissingham, all qualified Fourth Officers travelling as civilian passengers. They were en route to Durban where they would join their ships of the Royal Interocean Line plying between South America and the Far East. They would spend about twelve months at sea before returning home for further training after which their journeys would begin again. As time went by these turnabouts were much quicker as the airways became more available but that was in the future.

And so we met. The boy with the green eyes and me. The mutual attraction was immediate. There wasn't a thing either of us could do about it. From that very first moment we were inseparable. The only thing we didn't do together was eat and sleep. Sometimes in a crowd, sometimes just the two of us, but always together. Winifred said it was nothing but a shipboard romance; I was being foolish; I had a wider choice, but for once I wasn't listening. It was kismet: I had met my Jan. When we were together everybody else simply disappeared, although they were there before us.

Was this love? I had been too closely guarded, boyfriends too closely inspected, or dangled inappropriately before me to even remotely fall in love. Yet here was I, totally and inexplicably suddenly made aware of emotions I had never felt before. Could I be in love? Was this it? I couldn't possibly know. And yet it must be so. Everything I did was suddenly pleasant, even talking to Winifred was pleasant. Even if he wasn't with me it was pleasant because he was there, within my mind.

After four or five days we reached Las Palmas and we all three went shore together, poor Jan having to endure sitting in an expensive hotel while his mates were all enjoying the attentions of the bevy of lovelies I have already written about – those glorious dancers with their beautiful dresses uplifted over the backs of the chairs. Fortunately he didn't know what he was missing!

Thus the voyage continued. A square canvas bag was erected on the aft deck, much too deep for this non swimmer, but Jan and Henk were always there to keep me afloat. I didn't neglect Winifred, she was frequently in our company, or in the company of all the younger people aboard. Mostly when not playing on deck we congregated in the forward lounge while the older set met in the aft pub. Jan and I always joined her, if she wasn't with us, and she and I would go below to shower and change before dinner. Jan and The Boys occupied a table about as far away as you could get from ours, but Jan swopped his seat so that we could at least see each other. Afterwards the whole bunch of us met in the pub, unless there was a function in the lounge. Always together, he and I, and anybody else who cared to join us. We didn't mind, we never really noticed them. In a group, the boys became known as the Banana Boat Boys after the Harry Belafonte hit tune then popular whose record one of them owned. Jan had a small portable record player on which the tune was played when the occasion demanded. I mention this only because travelling with us was a journalist who was elected to write the ship's newspaper, and in which he wrote an article commending the Banana Boat Boys whose second favourite record was "And Mother Came Too". Winifred was not amused!

The dances were held in the main lounge to the tune of a gramophone playing the old 78 records. Jan had a particularly lovely record which began with a quickstep, followed by a fox trot, then without missing a beat became rock and roll. While dancing one evening, totally engrossed, unaware that Jan had contributed his record to the Purser for playing, Jan whispered in my ear that I should open my eyes and look. I did so and discovered that everyone else had formed a circle around us and had stopped dancing. We were on display. Even the Captain, and the passengers from the pub, had been called to watch. When the music ended everyone applauded, but looking and finding Winifred's face was not so pleasing. The one time in my life when she had ever actually come to watch me do anything, only merited a scowl.

The main part of the voyage was almost at an end. The Captain's Cocktail Party and Dinner heralded the end of the trip for we were fast approaching Capetown. Many of the passengers would disembark to be replaced by South Africans doing the little coastal trip from Capetown to Durban, or perhaps the other way around, as I had done a couple of years earlier by Union Castle. This would signify the end of the silver cruet sets! They were replaced with glass ones for apparently cruet sets and ashtrays made excellent souvenirs.

I had particularly wanted to be on deck when Table Mountain was spotted, that magnificent sight of majestic majesty guarding the southern tip of Africa, the flat-topped looming giant of a mountain, rocky bastion of the mother city. In days of yore the first mariner to sight Table Mountain was rewarded with a tot of rum or brandy, or even a silver piece, by the captain. However, I overslept and by the time I awoke we were about to be tied to the dock. The three of us decided to catch a bus to the base of the mountain, and from there take the cable-ride to the top. This was not to be because Winifred and I could not afford the tickets and we couldn't expect Jan to pay for all three of us. He'd already paid for the bus fare and didn't even get the chance to sit next to me! In the end Jan went up on his own and came down again on the next car. But the view was almost as good from where we were. Back we went to the ship and spent the remainder of the day hanging over the rail watching the newcomers board.

Unknowingly we were hurtling toward the first of Winifred's Cardinal Sins.

15

The stupid neither forget, nor forgive,
The naïve forget, and forgive,
The wise forgive, but do not forget.
Thomas Szasz, Psychiatrist.
1920 -2012

I am not sure whether it was the evening we sailed from Capetown, or the following evening, a dance party was given on deck to welcome the new passengers aboard for their coastal trip. It was to be great fun with balloons and streamers and party fare. At one stage I was watching Winifred who was sitting alone. She had not yet made friends with the new lot and most of her old mates had disembarked. I remarked to Jan we should sit with her for a bit, which we did. After a while she said we should return to the dancing and reminded me to be in the cabin by 11.30. My Cinderella time. The time was soon upon us and we looked around for Winifred but she was nowhere to be found, not even in the pub on her favourite stool. I was starting to worry but Jan pointed out that she had probably gone below earlier. I thought this odd because normally she would prop up the pub until closing time. We departed the dance floor and went below.

As I wrote earlier, our cabin was at the end of a small passage leading from the main corridor, and it was there that we usually kissed. We stayed hugging and kissing for few moments then reluctantly parted and Jan turned to go just as I opened the door.

I did a double-take and rebounded, closing the door and turning to Jan. There had been two people on the bunk. Was it a mutual thing? No, it couldn't have been. There had been nobody special around, and she knew none of the new passengers. Had someone attacked her? Were they waiting for me behind the door? What to do?

Jan said he would go in first. My rescuer, my big brave Jan. And so he did, with me close behind. There were still two people on the bunk. They had not even heard or noticed either of us. Then Jan and I began to whisper as we realised there had been no attack. We both went to my little bed and kneeling upon it looked through the porthole with our backs to the lovemakers. There was nothing out there but the blackness of the ocean. Jan said he knew who it was. I didn't. I begged him to stay because I didn't know what to do. Jan suggested we ought to leave them to it. However, we didn't need to decide anything further as Winifred said, quite normally, "You can turn around now. He's gone." So Jan went too. It was fairly dark inside the cabin so I simply removed my dress and got under the covers. Winifred said nothing, and neither did I. Thus she successfully passed the first Cardinal Sin, and I wasn't counting the little ones!

The next morning she tried to explain herself. Probably she had been awake most of the night wondering what to say. She was lonely because I had left her by herself; I had been enjoying myself running around the ship with Jan and disappearing into ironing rooms; she knew what went on in ironing rooms! (I thought they were for ironing). A long tirade of what I had been up to, followed by tears of regret, which always got me; many apologies, and please don't tell your father.

It was only much later that Jan told me it had been one of his student officer friends! I really didn't know whether to laugh or cry. I felt shamed.

The following day nothing was said about this episode. I went to breakfast on my own to find two new passengers at our table, whose names I have long forgotten. Later I accompanied Winifred on deck and sat with her in polite silence. Jan walked silently passed and acknowledged my unspoken request to leave us alone. Slowly but surely the atmosphere went back to normal, while I never left her side. We even went down to dinner together, but of course, the Captain didn't put in an appearance as during the coastal trip he seldom did, or at least this was the reason I was given for his non-appearance. The following day we docked at Port Elizabeth, and Olaf, the offender, was transferred from the ship to hospital with a suspected appendicitis which certainly eased the atmosphere. I wondered whether it really was an appendicitis, and hoped so because a reprimand would have been much, much worse.

The remainder of the voyage was something of a damp squid. Jan returned to my side and we managed to put on brave faces all round.

We had no idea where we would be living in Durban but Daddy had found a two bedroom flat somewhere on the Berea, the low hill that overshadows the City to the West. Jan had no idea where he would be living either, or even if he would be posted to his ship. We hatched a plan that the day after we landed I would visit the Royal Interocean Line offices and they would head me in the right direction. On our last morning the Head Steward asked me if I would kindly visit the Captain after breakfast before disembarking. This I did and the kind elderly gentleman wanted merely to bid me adieu with the promise that I would visit on their next visit which would probably be his last as he was due to retire.

The Custom and Immigration formalities had, of course, been completed in Capetown so my father was able to meet us as we disembarked without any problems, and we were off to our next 'home'.

Here I must mention Harry. He was the husband of Carla, our London hostess, and it was he who had organised the rental of our flat. It was actually quite a pleasant place, near a bus route. Arriving there we were greeted by a number of boxes, all of which had to be unpacked and the contents duly distributed throughout the three rooms plus kitchen and bathroom. This we, but mostly I, accomplished within the day of our arrival. I knew I had to be out of there fairly early the next day: one to get my old job back, and two to track down Jan, not necessarily in that order. However, early the next morning, there was a loud bang on the front door. It was Geoff, and with a Haloo and Whoop he lifted me, in my dressing gown and, whirling me around, announced that he was taking me flying! I could do without this, but was persuaded and by seven o'clock we were airborne out of Stamford Hill Airport, just down the road. Being afraid of heights, and particularly tiny aeroplanes flown by newly fledged pilots, I couldn't wait to be grounded. It was a nice welcome home to Durban and I was happier than I had ever been although poor Geoff. had to be told I couldn't see him again because I was in love. Geoffrey had a habit of cropping up now and again throughout the rest of my life, though nothing ever came of it.

The same day I found Jan and took him home to meet my father. I also managed to be re-employed at the Building Society and was to begin at the start of the following month. Jan and I had a full two weeks together and at the end of that time he was to be posted to his first ship. These young men did not always stay on the same ship but were posted to others during their tour, and one never quite knew when.

We played on the beach; went for long walks; ate junk food in bad cafes. Sometimes we ate with my parents and then played chess at home. Jan had taught me the moves on the ship but I never managed to beat him. On those evenings I would borrow Daddy's company car and drive him back to his hotel in town, dropping him off at the door. We went to movies; and if we could work the car in, we danced. Oh how we danced.

One evening at the Edward Hotel Causerie while we were dancing Jan whispered in my ear, "Look, they're doing it again," and they were: standing in a circle around us. It wasn't even rock and roll.

The R.I.L. ships came and went. The Banana Boys disappeared one by one until only Jan was left. All too soon it was his turn. I did not go down to see him off. During our entire relationship I never once did, but I was always there when he arrived. Once I could see his ship anchored in the Roads off Durban for three days while they waited for a harbour berth. Jan asked his captain if they could launch the Jolly Boat to come ashore but was not surprisingly ignored.

I was very happy at the building society but was not quite so joyful at home. One day my father asked me if it was true that Winifred had slept with one of Jan's colleagues. I looked at him in sheer horror. He said he didn't want the details, just a Yes or No. He would not tell me how he knew. I wondered if she had taunted him with her accomplishment, but then I thought maybe someone had written to him. I never found out, indeed. I did not wish to pursue it. Shortly afterwards during one of our one-sided exchanges, she accused me of telling Daddy what had happened, but this was hardly true because he already knew. I would never have told him because of the hurt it might cause.

We moved flats, and went to live a block away. I had no bedroom and slept on a pull-out bed on the open balcony. I liked it because I had a good view of the Indian Ocean. Jan said next time he arrived he would send a ship to shore signal! That didn't occur because we moved again, further up the hill but with no view at all. At least I had my own bedroom.

It was about this time Antony informed us he had met a divorced woman four years older than himself, with a three-year-old child. They were living in Pietermaritzburg, an hour's drive inland from Durban. Antony had won a bursary from his company some three or four years earlier, and had been sent there on a science course. The relationship was frowned upon by my parents and I remember Daddy sitting down and writing to him at Winifred's dictation. The words that I heard being written were not at all pleasant. A private detective was hired – no doubt at great expense – to discover if any bit of dirt was to be found clinging to the poor woman. She emerged unscathed. I wondered how Antony would react. He didn't. Quite simply he packed up his ready-made family and moved to the furthest reaches of Zambia, then Northern Rhodesia where he joined a government national park, dealing with conservation and Tsetse fly control. He carved for himself a very happy lifestyle adding a little girl to his family.

Thus was a wedge driven between Antony and myself, not to mention his father who was still unable, like me, to stand up to Winifred. Antony was made of tougher mettle than my father and I put together.

Our new flat was a semi-detached home in a very old building. This time I had my own bedroom in which I spent many hours trying to learn Dutch. My father gave Winifred a tiny miniature Pomeranian dog they called Susie in the hope that it might give her some added interest. I don't know what they did during the day, but in the evenings it was always my job to take her for a walk. I became very fond of the little sausage. She would wait for me to arrive home in the afternoons and then, after the walk, we would have a session of 'Hide and Seek' together. I even taught her how to put her paw up for 'How do you do'.

Meanwhile, the Probate on Nanna's Will was granted and Mr. Exec was repaid his Loan, so now father heard from Winifred the repetitive "I've been nothing but an unpaid nursemaid to your children" and I heard a new one: "I brought you back to South Africa. I paid your father's Income Tax for him". Would it never end?

One day, when Jan was in port, he asked me to marry him and was then brave enough to enter the lion's den and request permission from my parents. Permission is surely not required when the participants are over twenty-one, but it was the 'done' thing. They must have been expecting it. As Jan pointed out, we only hoped to become engaged since we could not marry until he was further ahead with his career. He returned to me in the kitchen grinning from ear to ear. It was decided that the engagement would be announced on his next return when we would then throw a party and he would have time to let his parents know. That was seven weeks away and I could hardly contain myself. I told Lucy at work, and nearer the date I invited several girls to the expected party so that Jan's friends would have someone to dance with. Winifred even bought me a new dress.

Jan docked on a Friday. They would be sailing on the Sunday so it was to be a very quick turn-around. Arriving home with him we were again in the kitchen when Winifred called him through into the lounge as they wanted to speak to him. When he returned to the kitchen he was unable to speak and white as a sheet. He looked at me, then cuddled me and said they had changed their minds: he was too young; we must wait and see how things turned out. It was too much for me, and for him. We left the house and took two buses back to the ship, arranging to meet in the morning which was my Saturday off, and our Engagement Day. I was heartbroken. I went home. My father said nothing, Winifred said exactly what she had said to Jan. I was numb.

The next morning I had to go into the building society and let my friends know there was to be no party. Private conversations could not be held in the banking hall so all they could do was look at me in blank dismay. We did not have mobile phones in those days, so contact was limited.

It was a damp and windy day. I met Jan, and he and I visited a jeweller's shop where he bought me an aquamarine stone mounted in white gold, very pretty, in place of an engagement ring. He told me that, in the Netherlands, Roman Catholics wear their wedding rings on the right hand so we could pretend we were Roman Catholic. We sat on the beach, even on that damp dark day, and I could not stop weeping. He said he would rather sail away and never see me again than have me cry like this. That stopped me. Nothing had really changed. We still had each other.

The following day – Sunday, the day Jan sailed – I took my parents their early morning tea and showed them the ring on my right hand. Winifred asked to see it. I took it off and she held it up the light, looked at it, handed it back and said "Humph. He got that one out of a Christmas cracker". My father grunted, which was quite something coming from him.

What makes a person so cruel?

I just wished I could pluck up the courage to leave home and live on my own somewhere, somehow, but was fearful of the consequences. Whatever happened could not be good for me. Jan had sailed and I was desolate. My period arrived that same day and I bled for a month instead of the normal week. I felt incomplete and I found it hard to function, but I did. The world didn't stop. But Winifred capitalised on my weakness, and whatever confidence I might have found, I lost.

Lucy, my good friend at work, was a great help. She seemed to know when to speak and when to be quiet. We would spend hours together at her house just reading and hardly talking. She and her fiancé John arrived one Saturday when they knew my parents were at the races, packed a suitcase for me, and took me home to her folks. I left a note for my parents telling them not to worry, I had left with Lucy. Big mistake. That evening we were just sitting down to supper when Winifred arrived at the front door, leaving my father in the car. The scene that was played out was Oscar material. I was pulled out by the hair and one arm, and bundled into the car.

Slowly but surely I regained a small amount of self-control and buckled down once again. Jan and I wrote regularly, me a little in Dutch, posting and receiving from and to, each port of call. I discovered my letters were being read by the manner in which they were returned to the envelopes so, out of the meager funds returned to me from the salary I handed over monthly, I purchased a handbag with a small lock attached. I was asked, laughingly, where I kept the key.

I replied, "Around my neck on a piece of string."

Nothing further was said. What pleasure could she possibly get from reading Jan's letters? A lot of them were partially in Dutch for me to translate.

Next to my bed was an empty wicker laundry basket which doubled as my bedside table. On this I had propped Jan's photograph. Every day when I arrived home from work I found the photograph turned face down. I asked what reason she had for doing so and she said she dusted it! A wicker laundry basket? I gave up.

For the first time ever when Jan docked I went aboard. I saw his cabin, went on the Bridge, met his Captain and a couple of his friends. If I could I would have slept there. The Captain would probably have allowed it, given the circumstances. But Jan said that was something for our future together. Perhaps it was as well that I didn't.

We moved yet again. This time to a dreadful building one block from the beach. I was without a bedroom again and slept off the main bedroom once more, but this time it was enclosed and afforded no privacy at all since their bedroom windows opened above my bed. Little Susie, Winifred's Pomeranian dog, became my great comfort. Very intelligent little thing, who seemed to sense my loneliness. One day I arrived home to find her gone. She had been given away.

Winifred added to her vocabulary of the "unpaid nursemaid" and "I paid the tax", the added salt of "he's too young, you need someone older and established". It went on and on unabated.

Jan arrived once more. I was a nervous wreck, so worried she would say something to turn him away, frightened to cry in case Jan should leave me. He very likely would at this rate. It was another quick turn-around for the ship, this time to South America again.

Then the bombshell fell. Lucy and I had started the habit of going for coffee every day after work to prevent my arriving home before my father. Even a grunt was better than not having him there. We lived now within walking distance of town as well as Winifred's favourite seafront hotels! On this occasion Daddy and I arrived home together. The atmosphere was bleak, something was afoot. I was soon enlightened. She had received a visit from Jan's Uncle who was visiting on another ship. He had come on behalf of Jan's parents who were concerned that Jan was too young to be thinking of marriage, and the relationship had come at the very beginning of his promising career. The visit was strictly confidential. Jan was not to be told of it, in case it caused conflict between him and his parents, and further distress. It was suggested that the relationship be terminated.

What was I to do? The ball had been thrown very squarely but most unfairly into my court. I could not tell Jan, for he would be furious with his parents, and that could cause no end of problems. I was left to ponder my decision.

In a way I left it to fate. I wondered if Jan had been instructed in similar manner, as I had not heard from him. I decided that if no letter was forthcoming from the next port, I would write to say I could not cope with the distance and the time apart. I do not know how I put it down into words.

I told no one, not even Lucy. Jan's ship arrived. I heard nothing. On the second day I went down to the docks, boarded the ship, and went to his cabin. He was about to depart for town so after a few embarrassing moments on both sides, neither knowing quite what to say to the other, we walked together to town. On the corner of West and Gardiner Streets, outside a chemist shop, I kissed him on the cheek as he did me, and said goodbye.

I walked home with breaking heart and unshed tears. I faced Winifred and said very clearly, without emotion which was boiling inside me, "You will be pleased to know that I have just given up Jan so you can stop turning his photograph down. I shall now marry the first man brave enough to ask me."

For once, she did not reply.

I had reached a crossroads in my life but all the roads had 'No Entry, Under Construction' signs up. Shakespeare no longer appealed, I wept over poetry and could find no solace in reading. The same page was constantly re-read. I asked Winifred if she would please increase my allowance so that I could extend my purchases to deodorants and the like. She suggested soap was good, and handed me half a packet of king-size pads. Poor Lucy: I spent longer hours over coffee, and usually arrived home just in time for dinner.

Slowly but surely I resurfaced, almost at the same time as the 'roads' completed their construction. Finally, with Lucy's help, I took one of them. I was twenty-four years old, for God's sake. It was time to take possession of my life.

INTERLUDE

Oh God, I pray that I may not be shamed
Ever in my heart,
Or hear a voice whispering against me
That I knew not love.
Clemence Dane 1886 – 1965

Before I close this particular period of my life I must write that some thirty-five years later I met Jan again. He told me that he did indeed have an uncle, but that the uncle had never sailed except around the Zuider Zee and certainly never visited South Africa. His parents, at the time, were surprised to learn from Jan himself about our broken relationship. Thus did the Greek handmaiden of Ate strike again!

There are many kinds of love, but between a man and a woman, I believe, there are only two:

My own love, a smile across a room, a glance my way, was like a floating bubble which even the mere touch of a hand would ignite into something beyond description, a warm whirlwind of delight. The kiss that created a fountain of falling stars; a waterfall of molten silver splashing into an infinite pool, followed by the stillness, the closeness of him. Ours was an age when sexual gratification was all but forbidden outside marriage, to my everlasting regret. Oh, to have that wild passion of absolute joy, a madness if you will, when a scalding hot desire tempered with sexual intimacy, is perfection indeed. I was blessed, and it was indeed a blessing, with the experience of that all-consuming love, but it never came to full fruition between Jan and I, because it was never consummated. Even so, I am the better for having known of it, even though I burst the bubble.

Then there is the other love, rich and rewarding , when two people love as a comfortable partnership. They know each other's feelings, often their thoughts, certainly their wishes. Theirs is a satisfactory teamwork. Oh yes, there is sex, exploratory and good, and I think safe, even secure, but without that floating bubble of ecstasy which can burst, as mine did. These are the favoured, the fortunate. I am one of those, and I count my blessings doubly.

But my goodness, if you have never known the mad kind, even unconsummated then, my friend, you have not lived.

16

If a man points to the moon,
only a fool will look at his fingers.
                Confucious.

It was Lucy, my friend from the building society, who came to my rescue. She invited me to be her only bridesmaid at her forthcoming wedding which was to take place in about six months. Initially this caused me some concern but Lucy immediately realised the reason for my dismay and put my mind at rest by insisting she would be responsible for my dress. She involved me in everything and as a result I seldom had time to feel sorry for myself. I tried not to look out to sea, and lost count of vessel movements.

One evening Lucy's parents invited me to supper and on arrival I was introduced to a young man who had arrived from the Copperbelt of Northern Rhodesia, now Zambia, and was hoping to purchase a business in Durban with the assistance of Lucy's father who was an estate agent. A Yorkshireman by birth, you could still hear the slight accent. He seemed quite a pleasant man of about thirty, but I felt no butterflies, and thought no more of him. However, the day following, he telephoned me at the building society and invited me out, but I refused. So began a courtship of telephone calls. I began to run out of reasons for refusing until one day Lucy's parents invited me to the theatre, and arrived to collect me in a car full of people, including the would-be-businessman. He manoeuvred himself into a seat next to me in the theatre, tried, unsuccessfully, to hold my hand, and that I thought, would be that. But it was not, and that was how I became aware of John Frestel.

After the theatre episode John trod carefully. We met frequently at Lucy's house for the wedding was imminent. John was to be the photographer. I found him to be a gentle person, kind beyond comparison. Lucy had told him of my situation and he was considerate enough not to question me. The big day arrived. My parents had declined the invitation but nevertheless, just as we were about to begin our meal, Winifred sallied across the empty dance floor to congratulate the couple, to my deep embarrassment. Father, to his credit, remained lurking behind the door. The fact that the reception was held in a room within the complex where they had attended the Saturday Meet was no excuse. I think it was partly in defiance of her that I had accepted John's invitation and joined a group of others who planned to visit a nightclub after the wedding. This meeting of two people possibly about to merge had its comic side. Had I not accepted the invitation, John had decided not to pursue the issue. At midnight I was having misgivings about getting home for I still fell under the rule of being home before the witching hour struck. However, I thought permission at my age ridiculous and as I hadn't dated for some six or seven months I would do as I pleased for once. John, bless him, took me home without even being asked, and then returned to the nightclub to rejoin our friends, all of whom knew me.

So began a love affair that was solid in its foundation. If Jan had been my prince, John was to be my rock.

What was he like, this John, for few are left alive who knew him? He was one of the good people of this world, strong, quietly spoken, not roused easily to anger. A kinder, more generous man you could not wish to meet. Well-liked by men, he was adored by women, but never seemed to notice, except for the odd blonde. As he said, men could look at me as much as they wanted, as long as they didn't touch, and it worked both ways. Not terribly handsome, he nevertheless, with his clear direct grey eyes, one cheek dimpled, and very strong jaw line, possessed a natural charismatic attraction. He was a typical Yorkshireman, not given to outward shows of emotion, and solid as the land from which he came. Incidentally, he also had gigantic shoulders which were hell to knit for!

His mother, Annie, a hard working woman, had been widowed when John was only four. His father had been a bricklayer's mate, offspring of the Irish navies who had fled the Irish Potato Blight from 1845 well into the 20th century. My offspring, like it or not, have very mixed genes: one side from the high echelons of the English upper classes, and the other side from the solid stock of English working class.

John had, according to his mother and I had no reason to doubt her, passed with honours the examination to a prestigious high school but had refused to go, electing instead to join the army, for which he unofficially upped his age by one year. Thus he spent the latter half of the war years in the British Army Royal Tank Regiment as a tank driver. This regiment is the oldest tank regiment in the world. I retained the army beret badge which I passed on to our son, and I hope that Peter has it still. John served in both the North African and Italian Campaigns. I had to drag information from him for he seldom spoke of it. Once I teased him of his possible wartime descendants, to which he replied that there might be the odd little Frestel running around Italy, but definitely none in North Africa. On the minus side, for historical reference sake, he told me that he was not enamoured of Montgomery, nor of the civilian canteen van whose individual name I cannot state here, who would empty their tea tanks into the desert sand rather than give away a free cuppa.

I took John home to meet my parents and quite frankly could not have cared a tinker's curse whether or not they liked him. John had by then purchased a petrol station and Winifred said how nice it was to have someone who was not only established, but a Yorkshireman to boot. My father said nothing. I wondered how long the peace would last and how long it would be before she found some fault.

Durban Bay is actually a natural harbour which in those days had, along with fifty eight berths for commercial vessels, a naval base for the South African Navy. The Bay also protected a very reputable yacht club, in which was once a very disreputable small boat with an equally small inboard motor owned by one John Frestel. About six of us would squash aboard on a Sunday and chug around Durban Bay admiring the ocean-going yachts and getting as near as we could to the greater ships of the sea. Then somewhere in the middle, we would drop anchor and play cards. Sometimes we would sing raucously, or John would tell jokes of which he had a bountiful supply. Much laughter always. On one occasion the engine failed and we all had to find something to paddle with. The potty I found was too small and my arms were too short so I became Cox. We, or rather they, paddled to the nearest ship and asked them to throw a rope down, up which John climbed, laboriously, then pulled us around to the dockside. We had no drugs, a few beers and plenty of cigarettes, and we ladies made numerous cups of tea. Whenever I thought of Jan, which of course I did while chugging round the Bay, I would push the thought to the bottom of my being and leave it there. John never told me he loved me, nor had I said so to him. We were just comfortable together.

One Sunday, as I was about to leave the flat to meet John elsewhere, Winifred turned on me furiously, pinned me against the wall by my throat and began to throttle me, shouting she wouldn't allow me out. I was about to pass out when quite suddenly she dropped at my feet. My father, who had been reading in the bedroom, arrived at that moment, took one look then sent me to empty the fridge of ice. After I had done so he looked up and told me to go quickly, just as she was surfacing, so I bolted, and left him to it. The odd thing about these acts of hers was that they were never remarked upon again. But this time I do recall hearing her say "God struck me down". This I found to be sacrilegious coming from a woman who was quite the most irreligious woman I know.

Once again it was time to move. I was functioning a bit like a robot, just going, and doing, and accepting, and marking time, in order to sail along without too much trouble – probably getting a bit like my father. It was only a matter of time before I would break out of this self-imposed shell that I was temporarily quite comfortable in.

We were in the worst flat of all being almost on the beach front itself, above a row of shops and behind the main hotels. It had absolutely nothing to commend it except its proximity to all the hotel bright lights just around the corner. The glass front door opened upon a very long passage. The first door on the left led to the main bedroom, the next door to a bathroom and finally a kitchen, all in a row. On the right of the passage stood a wardrobe which contained all my possessions, and the end of the passage opened to the lounge in which was my divan bed. At least I had a bed and it was inside!

We had no sooner settled in this flat than Winifred was off again to England. I never discovered the why's and wherefor's of this latest venture. At least I was not commanded to accompany her this time and that was an achievement in itself. Furthermore, she actually handed my passport to me for seemingly no particular reason. She left in the company of a man who, I was told, was to set her up in the hotel trade, and that was about all the information I could glean. I didn't even know which ship she travelled on and anyway I was at work so could not go to the bon voyage party. The entire undertaking was a bit of a mystery. However, something must have gone awry aboard the ship because a letter arrived for my father.

As he perused it I leaned over his shoulder to read what I could. All I could see was a bit of a sentence similar to: 'I have never witnessed such disgraceful behaviour…' Then my father, who knew what I was doing and seemed quite content, suddenly folded the letter and said he would read it later. We got along so well together, he and I, without Winifred around, and I was a little hurt when he said the contents were not for my eyes, and that was the end of it.

John and I developed a routine. He moved into a boarding house on the Berea and became friendly with a couple newly arrived from England, Bob and Lillian Rowlands who became great friends of ours. John was a little too generous in his petrol station. He seemed to have a plethora of out-of-work mechanics in the garage section and on top of that he never pushed his customers to pay their monthly petrol bills. Bulk petrol had to be paid for and he didn't have the capital to pay for his customer's petrol, regulars though they might be. It happened that at about the same time as Winifred left for England, trouble loomed at the garage and John decided to put the business up for sale.

His few furnishings arrived from Rhodesia and were scattered around our flat. His bed went into my parent's room, the only occupant now being my father, and the small table fridge slipped into the kitchen. A nest of tables joined my divan in the lounge, and his 100 or so miniature liquor bottles arranged along the old fashioned plate ledge around the room. This all has a bearing on what followed a couple of weeks later.

One day John collected me from work, and tipped into my lap a pile of money saying, "Count it, it's all we have." It so happened that the Lebanese Jew who was buying the business came in a week before the end of the month, when the customers were supposed to pay their bills, and said they were taking over immediately or not at all. All John could do was empty the tills, the contents now being in my lap.

Where to now? Immediate necessity for him was a cash income and he found employment as a tallyman on the Durban Docks. It was a temporary, honest work for the immediate future. He worked a twelve hour shift. I would rush home from the building society – no coffee with Lucy these days – and cook for Daddy and myself then keep a plate of food for John each evening, because the boarding house dinner finished before he did.

We heard nothing from Winifred for about a week and I remarked to Daddy that maybe she was on her way home.

"God forbid," he said. "If she is I'm on the next boat out."

My rely was "No, it's my turn," or words to that effect.

Believe me, the laughter that followed was very quickly stifled by a noise at the front door at the end of the long passage, and there she was, the handmaiden of Ate once again!

"How did you get here?" was my immediate reaction.

"I bloody well flew. How do you think?" was followed swiftly when she spied John's bed, which he didn't sleep in, by: "What's this? Is John Frestel sleeping here? You can tell him to get his bloody bed out."

I was still standing, aghast and shaking, by the front door, through which I bolted out of the block of flats to the corner of West and Gillespie which I knew John would pass in order to reach his supper. I knew it was too early so back I went to the flat and peered between the curtains on the glass front door. I could see her at the end of the long passage, with forefinger extended and admonishment in the muffled angry voice. My poor father. What had he done, or not done to deserve this?

Back I went to my street corner just in time to see John. I almost met my Maker leaping into the passenger seat babbling almost incoherently, "Mummy's back".

John started to laugh and I started to cry.

Bob and Lillian had moved into a flat in Morningside on the northern brow of the Berea, and that was where John took me, bursting in unannounced and unscheduled, so to speak, with John still chuckling saying: "The Dragons Back."

It was a well-earned nickname that stuck. Lillian fed John, and John placated me. In a way he made it almost worse because he said: "Be here tomorrow night with your toothbrush, or you won't see me again."

He took me home, leaving me to try sneaking in. Fat chance. The bedroom door was open and they were both sitting up in bed. Nothing much was said to me so I turned to plod passed my wardrobe. Winifred called out "You'd better tell John Frestel to move his stuff out, but he can store the fridge here, and the bottles."

Just like my father, I said nothing. Instead I went to tidy my possessions in my wardrobe which served as a vanity table, with drawers always open for inspection, neat and tidy. It struck me that I would need a very small suitcase.

In the end it wasn't a suitcase at all but a large blue trunk! The day following was a Friday which I spent at work in a perfectly normal manner although my stomach was growling angrily, not from hunger but from anticipation. I had made a decision, and a plan. After work I phoned home and explained that Lillian was collecting me and taking me home for dinner. She wasn't collecting me but I caught a bus and arrived there as planned albeit without my toothbrush. I had a battle plan in mind for Saturday and needed Lillian's help to polish it up before John arrived. Invariable my parents went to the races on a Saturday and my stepmother would want to see, or be seen by, her friends. It would be a good time to collect John's possessions, and include mine, not forgetting my toothbrush which was now in my wardrobe. John arrived and the battle plan began in earnest. We polished it up and I returned home to sleep for the very last time in that flat.

The first necessary hurdle to be faced was accommodation for me from Saturday night onwards. Taking past experience into account I knew what I must not do, and I had to hide. It had been decided that Lillian and I would go room hunting while John with two friends raided the flat armed with my key. Bob, not wanting to face the foe, was to be the van driver, and we would all meet at Lillian's in the evening.

Of the two ventures, mine was the most difficult. John's boarding house, or any house wherein my friends lived, were all out unless I wanted a third hair-pulling experience. Licensed hotels were not considered and the YWCA was full. In the end I chose a private house which had a spacious room available, with a bathroom next to it. It was owned by an elderly Polish couple, and at the opposite end of the road where John lived. No food was provided but there was always the coffee shop on the way home, and there was always John, but never at the boarding house, just in case. I worried a little about Lillian's flat because I had a feeling that it was known where Bob and Lillian lived, but not exactly which block, and certainly not which apartment. I hoped that even Winifred baulked about knocking on doors.

What had begun as a battle for the boys turned out to be a bit of a damp squid, for nobody was home. Bed, bottles and fridge slid nicely along the lengthy passage and out of the front door, followed by the entire contents of the wardrobe, including my toothbrush – the whole lot filled only about one third of the large blue trunk. All this was deposited at John's boarding house with the exception of the large blue trunk which somehow made its way to my room.

That evening from Bob and Lillian's, I telephoned my parents to let them know I was alright and spoke briefly to Daddy. I could sense my stepmother hovering at his elbow and sure enough in seconds I heard her voice. I was about to speak when she made a caustic comment and promptly hung up. Needless to say I was not offended although I was somewhat shaken. However, this time I was surrounded by friends, all of whom were laughing and chatting, enfolding me with warmth. In due course I was deposited at my new home feeling numb and exhausted, together with a kettle, a mug and the large blue trunk at the bottom of which was my toothbrush!

In the middle of my first night there I was awakened by a strange sound like the rustling of small dry leaves. I rose from the bed, padded across the floor to the light switch by the door and flicked it down. Then I screamed, for my hand alighted upon a cockroach, and everyone who has ever lived in Durban knows that here they are bred to enormous proportions. What was worse, when I looked, all four walls had a small army of them, now scattering madly to wherever cockroaches scatter as soon as a light is turned on. I pulled my bed away from the wall, sat in the middle of it and remained there until dawn, now and again shaking a newspaper extracted from the bottom of the big blue trunk, the noise of it keeping my enemies at bay. Fortunately one of our friends worked in the laboratory of a chemical production company and at a special request arrived the next day, Sunday, armed with an enormous spray-gun filled with some deadly stuff and soused the room with mist. Some days later the man renting the room below approached me asking if I was troubled by cockroaches!

It was not very long after my move that John took me to supper at one of our favourite café/restaurants on the seafront. We ordered curry and rice and no sooner was the plate placed before me than he said it was his intention to return to the Copperbelt. My heart sank to my boots. Now what was I to do? I began to eat the curry, swallowing painfully. It was like swallowing lumps of rock. From a great distance, just as I was about to shovel in the next batch of rocks, I heard him say:

"So you'd better make sure your passport's in order because I think we should get married before we leave."

That was typical of my John: no going down on one knee – no bunch of roses – no champagne. Just the honest Yorkshireman stating an obvious fact. I didn't even reply, had no need to, but couldn't for the life of me eat any more rocks.

We saw a great deal of Bob and Lillian. They had acquired a miniature Schnauzer puppy, and John would present himself at their flat at about 6am almost every morning to take the puppy for a run on the beach. We would frequently join them for supper but normally John and I would eat together somewhere. Only once did I join him at the boarding house when one of the other lady guests pounced upon me and berated me for giving my mother such heartache. I never visited again. Often we descended on John and Lucy and played cards until late in the evening. Then came the night when we met Bob and Lillian at a beach front hotel, and Lillian's first words were that we had better get married quickly because The Dragon was on the warpath. Apparently Winifred had induced my father to park close to the block of flats where Bob and Lillian lived and then apparently sat in the car and waited like two third-rate detectives, watching everyone return from work. Lillian was the one they copped. She had told them she had no idea where I was and suggested that Winifred approach the building society. My place of work was no secret. Poor Lillian. She had been quite shaken by the episode and did not want to be caught again. Shortly thereafter I received a phone call just as I was leaving work. It was Winifred.

"Do you know who this is?" she asked.

"Yes." I replied. "It's Mummy."

"Exactly," said she, and hung up.

Our marriage plans and departure for northern climes progressed. I bought a pretty air-force blue dress, a booking was made at the Durban Law Courts, my passport was changed to the name of Frestel to be handed to me on our wedding day, and all the other preparations concluded, of which there were more than I could possibly have envisaged.

One lunchtime I walked down to my father's place of work and invited them to my wedding. I don't think he was very surprised. I remember he asked if I loved John which was as good a question as any I suppose, in the circumstances. I returned the following day and he was apologetic saying they could not attend. When I asked why he said it was because Winifred didn't like Saturday weddings. I wanted to ask whether he was a man or a mouse, but refrained, and simply said that the invitation was an open one. There are few people alive who would believe this sorry tale, but it remains the truth and I cannot sugar-coat it. I have made many mistakes when typing this for even today, after all these many years, I find myself tearful with the pain of that memory.

The big blue trunk was packed once more and disappeared, along with John's few possessions, into the furniture van for points North. The parents' of one of my friends very kindly offered to act as my own, and arrived to collect me in a car bedecked with lace. After an emotional goodbye to the Polish couple who had been so kind to me, we departed. John, along with our dozen guests, was waiting on the Courthouse steps. As I greeted him I looked hopefully to see if my parents were there, and I could see them at the bottom of the little lane that led to the main road. I went down the lane and taking them both by the hand led them back to John and our guests. I thanked heaven for my foresight in previously warning my friends not to speak about our wedding breakfast just in case they arrived unexpectedly. By this time my nerves were somewhat frayed as although I was pleased to see them, I was anxious as to what Winifred might say, true or false, that might throw a spanner in the works for she was quite capable of saying anything. A magistrate conducted the ceremony using the exact same vows as those made in a formal church. He congratulated us both then promptly departed back to his Court where a case was in session, leaving his clerk to complete the paperwork and hand me my passport. After posing for a few photographs, we said our goodbyes and finally reached John's car. The last photograph taken was one of us inside the car where we both looked not only happy, but relieved. It was only much later it struck me that Winifred was wearing white while I was in blue!

The full English breakfast, followed by champagne and wedding cake, was a great success. Everyone had driven around several blocks, as had we, before arriving at the lovely old Majestic Hotel. Afterwards, John and I went off to the movies because we both wanted to see Doctor in the House. When we returned to the car it had been broken open and John's small overnight bag removed from the back seat. My own was still in situ in the boot. We had to crash in on Bob and Lillian for replacements and arrived at our lovely honeymoon hotel with John carrying a shoebox filled with odds and ends needed for an overnight stay, that being all we decided we could afford. As we left the next morning, John carrying his shoebox, was asked if he required a company receipt. Initially the reference was lost on me, but I later hoped that I had looked more like a bride than a mistress.

Back in Durban we collected our suitcases from Bob and Lillian and also picked up Mike, a young bachelor friend who was attached to our group and wanted to make a fresh start. Typical of John to offer succour to a lost soul who joined us on our honeymoon!

We piled into our little Morris Minor ND 10216, which number I have never forgotten, and away we went. I had John beside me, intelligent, kind, liked by all who met him, positive in his attitude to life, and too generous. His second name was Edward and he had warned me never to call him Teddy, but to me he was just like a great teddy bear with his massive shoulders but gentle soul. I was beside him, but rather he was beside me, and behind me too. He was everything I could wish for and I loved him dearly. My John. How lucky I was.

We travelled north, far beyond the borders I knew. I was leaving all my friends behind once more, but I didn't care. I would never lose them, and I would make new ones. I was safe and I was loved. You would think that would be the end of my story. Alas not. It was simply the end of the beginning.

17

Woe to the man who has not learned, when young,
To hope, to love and to put his trust in life.
Joseph Conrad.

It was a long, weary trip from the Natal coast of South Africa to the Copperbelt of Northern Rhodesia, as it was then called, but now of course, is Zambia. In those days the roads were not the freeways of today. Even the road between Durban and Johannesburg was a winding one of two-way traffic. Once over the great, grey, green, greasy Limpopo River* which serves as the border between South Africa and Zimbabwe, the roads were, for the most part, quite torturous with six feet wide tarmac known as six-footers, which often developed into strip roads. These were two strips of tarmac strategically placed to take one set of tyres, one front and rear tyre on each strip. One never quite knew which bend on a six-footer, once manoevred, would suddenly present itself with these two strips, but it always seemed to be just when it was my turn to take the wheel! Once during the trip I asked if we could stop for water but John said, "No. Look, there are elephants," but look as I might I could see nothing but the impenetrable bush that lined each side of our narrow roadway, about two metres of brown dirt gravel stretching along on each side both left and right of the road. Then I saw a large mound of manure. Elephant droppings, and still steaming! Our Morris Minor, being black, might well look like a rival, at least to an elephant anyway.

However, we sang happily, munched apples, and somehow the miles went by. We were liberally sprayed with obnoxious insecticide at the Tsetse Fly Control Stop, and dropped down and into the wild Zambesi Valley. Then over the river and up the hills on the other side, and we were in what is now Zambia. Of course it wasn't all driving non-stop. It was more like a honeymoon for three, except for the nights! We stopped en route at several small towns and odd motels with comfortable accommodation. Since then I have driven that long journey many times. The roads over the years gradually became wide enough for two-way traffic, with luxurious stops. The Tsetse Control disappeared but I suspect the fly remains, along with the Kolokolo bird.

My introduction to the Copperbelt town of Nkana was a little weird. We were all very tired so John took us to his Aunt in the mine township. She, poor woman, had recently undergone a lobotomy operation. This totally destroys, or renders a section of the brain either immobile or incomplete, leaving the patient half barmy. The operation has long since been banned. The first person I met in Nkana was therefore Nellie, a lovely lady, but half daft. It did not make her welcome any less warm for both she and her husband made it a very happy occasion. We did not stay long and continued our long journey through the attached town of Kitwe and a further twelve or so kilometers, reaching the suburban district of Itimpi just before midnight.

Here lived John's mother – Mum – and Cliff, his stepfather, although Mum was away in England, and Cliff was fast asleep! John warned us that there were three dogs and one was rather an unpredictable bull terrier mix. It was very dark when we arrived at this ten acre plot but John managed to park near the front door, and promptly disappeared leaving Mike and I almost on the doorstep. We stood a little foolishly wondering how long John would be when I felt something against my leg. I lowered my hand and discovered a silky ear. It was the bull terrier who had decided to investigate. So much for the vicious dog!

Eventually John reappeared with Cliff holding a lit paraffin lamp which gave a shadowy light so at least we could see the front door. One by one we followed Cliff while the lamp bobbed uncertainly through the house to the kitchen where further lamps were lit. Cliff had married John's mother some years after the death of John's father who had died when John was only four year old.

Cliff? What can I say of him? He was a short stocky man not quite one and a half metres tall. He had, honestly, two left legs – well, that's what he called them and, although I never examined them, I think he was absolutely right! By trade he was a Master Builder and had built the house we were in, and others in the area. At first sight I was a bit taken aback. I came to know and love him very quickly. His sense of humour and gentleness warmed everyone within striking distance, especially children. Cliff: he was what kindness is.

Within the hour, which by now was an early one, he had fed, watered, and bedded us down. Somehow or other he had accommodated the three of us who had appeared without warning and descended upon him. I remember he woke John and I, who were squashed into a single bed, with a cup of tea at nine the following morning.

So began the first day of the next ten years which were the happiest years of my entire life. I was enveloped in a cloud of peace and tenderness. This was new to me, and I basked in the atmosphere of friendship and love. I look back on them with joy and tenderness. How fortunate I have been to have lived them.

The ten acres of land, and the house, are worth a story on their own. There was no electricity so light was obtained from a number of paraffin lamps which gave off quite enough brightness to play cards beneath them. The light emanated from a very delicate mantle which disintegrated if even very lightly touched, as I quickly discovered. Cliff had a very tall African servant, who insisted on wearing a very tall chef's hat, beautifully starched. This made him twice as tall as Cliff. He very kindly set up the ironing board for me that very first day and offered to iron my very creased skirt, but I refused, and said I preferred to iron it myself. As I lifted the iron up the bottom dropped off. It was a coal iron. Those irons had a space along their base into which hot coals were inserted and clipped in. The clips had not been clipped. Fortunately no damage was done, except slightly to the concrete floor. The African's response to my dismay was "Ow Khosisaan, meenahaas"´or words to that effect, which freely translated means "Oh Princess, I didn't know." It was a phrase I heard frequently in that part of Africa. It also means, "me sorry" or "wasn't me" whichever phrase best suited and thereby covered a multitude of errors!

Hot water would have been non-existent without the aid of the good old Rhodesian Boiler, as it was called in that lovely country. By its very name you can imagine the bountiful supply of hot water. But from whence came the water? There were no municipal water pipes. After I had ironed my skirt we all, including the three dogs went off to explore the plot with Cliff as our guide. For the first time I could see the Rhodesian anthills close-up. They are enormous mounds of tightly packed soil of varying size, some as high as the house, some higher, the result of furious ant excavation. On the top of the one nearest the house stood a large galvanized iron tub, suitably lined and filled with water that was continually pumped from a nearby well. Cliff had three such wells on the property, all in use. The water was pumped up the well, across the ground, then up the anthill and then down into the boiler. Plentiful until the rains stopped and the wells ran dry. After that it was a case of all-hands-on-deck for Cliff would load his enormous truck with empty 45 gallon drums and half a dozen labourers and drive off to the Kafue River, already pretty low, where once again the eternal pipes were put to good use. On return, the water was pumped directly into the holding tank on the top of the anthill and there would be water again. This labourious exercise would be repeated several times over the weeks, until the dry season was over and the rains came.

Meanwhile, with Mum being away in England where she had gone for some female operation, and to see her family, I had to learn the intricacies of the great black wood-fired stove. It was just that. The sort you see in cowboy movies and great for cooking stews or fries or boiling. The oven, however, was a kind of hell for me. The only side that got hot was that nearest the wood. I had countless disasters, all eaten manfully, by my three hungry male mouths. I longed for Mum to return.

My life was abundant with excitement. I met John's friends, Marie and John Hopton, who became over the years like a brother and sister to me. At the time they had two small boys, Alwyn and Shaun, and a newborn little girl, Julie, to whom I became godmother. Cliff threw a welcome braaivleis, (barbeque) for us, with my new friends, the Hoptons, invited and some neighbours in the area who had befriended Cliff. It was at this time that something occurred worthy of mention. We were sitting around the fire outside when John asked me to fetch his cigarettes from the house. I jumped up immediately and hurried in to fetch them. When I returned John took my hand and said it was no longer necessary to fetch and carry every time I was asked, and he hoped to knock that out of me, or words conveying the meaning! It was a lesson I was happy to learn.

We had one small problem in those early months of marriage. We had no work and therefore no income. John had previously been employed at the Uranium Plant which had since closed and there was nothing available. He was put on the waiting list. Mike, who still lived with us, found work with a tyre company, so there was a tiny income, but John and I were definite 'guests'. John applied for a job diamond mining which was quite funny because the man who interviewed John, collected him and insisted I went along too. He was a very rich American who drove a very expensive American car at some 230 kilometres an hour some 50 kilometres distant to show us the accommodation. That was when I realised why I had been invited along. It was not a caravan as we had hoped, but a tent, albeit a sturdy looking one. Outside a woman was busily cooking, and inside was a sickly-looking child. The husband was presumably off drilling or digging or generally looking for diamonds. We were driven back to Kitwe at even greater speed and the man was never seen or heard of again. I wonder if he made it home?

Kitwe, on the outskirts of which we lived at that time, was the town that had grown up beside the mine of Rhokana Corporation Copper Mine whose massive residential area was known as Nkana. All the people who lived thereabouts call the area Nkana-Kitwe. Nkana was the mine where the money was, and Kitwe the town of commerce where the miners spent their money. The people of Nkana had their own hospital and medical service, which is where my son was eventually born, and Kitwe had recently built the Kitwe Central Hospital. Kitwe was a lovely little town – in my opinion quite the nicest of all the Northern Rhodesian (Zambia) towns including the capital Lusaka.

John accepted a job as the swimming pool superintendent of Nkana Mine Recreational Swimming Pool which was really not much of a job but certainly better than nothing. Mum returned from England to my most welcoming arms. I had met her when she had passed through Durban and liked her enormously although I never quite forgave her for being the first person to tag me with the name of Pat.

Out of the blue disaster almost struck because of our minimal income, but like a tornado that rolls and roars upon you, it missed, and instead became the most significant, splendid and awe-inspiring event of my life: I was to have a baby. Marie Hopton laughed at me, for I had earlier announced smugly, while cradling her newborn, that John and I would wait a couple of years.

"Like that was going to happen," she had thought!

I had found the local Mobile Library and ordered Grantley Dick Reid's book *Childbirth without Fear** and determined mine would be without either pain or fear. I carefully followed every word. Marie held her tongue!

October and November came and went. Finally when even the Kafue River was running dry, the rains arrived. The drums were filled and the wells replenished for the last time. Mum had returned and I was relieved of my post at the black stove and instead became the cashier at the swimming pool taking the silver sixpences from the children. Every now and again up went the 'Please Wait' sign John had made while I disappeared to heave up insides that came to nothing. In the evening arriving home, Mum would often present us all with an enormous meat and potato pie topped with thick luscious crust oozing with gravy. My stomach would revolt and I'd settle for a boiled egg and a cup of tea. The happy heaving continued!

Bob and Lillian sent little Chippy, their dog, up to us by air knowing we would give him a good home. They had received warning that dogs were not permitted in their flat. We were still with Mum and Cliff, but somehow Chippendale of Farnhill, the only miniature Schnauzer on the Copperbelt, settled in happily despite the other three dogs, although we were diligently aware that fights might ensue while it was decided amongst themselves who was the leader of the pack.

Marie and John asked if we would look after their house and dog over the Christmas period while they went on holiday down south, as we called anything south of Lusaka, and we were thrilled with the invitation. It meant John and I would, for the first time, be alone together. Mike remained with Mum and Cliff – I couldn't understand why he didn't look for other accommodation. One just didn't like to ask him, and really he was no trouble.

John, still on the waiting list for a mine job, took a transfer to the Rhokana Cinema as manager and projectionist. It was a great little theatre and always well attended. It meant that John had to travel to Ndola, 65 kilometres away and the nearest air link, there to exchange and collect movie reels for the following week. It also meant that I had my very own seat on the back row. No television in those days.

At last, two days before the Hoptons returned, we were allocated a mine house. They were more or less fully furnished and we had little to buy except for two new mattresses. There were no curtains or carpets but the floors were polished red concrete. These were kept shiny and red by applying thick red polish. Oval brushes with elasticised bands sideways across the top were given to the African servant who slid one on each foot and danced happily across the polish, keeping his feet on the floor. My servant was David, who stayed with us the entire period we were in that wonderful country. I wished we could have realised his dream and taken him with us when we finally left the Copperbelt.

The happy heaving continued and finally we were fully fledged members of the Rhokana Corporation Medical Scheme and I was able, at six months pregnant, to register with Nkana Hospital.

The doctor to whom I was assigned was a little taken aback to find I had not yet sought medical attention, but being poor we couldn't afford private consultation without borrowing money and that I refused to do. There was nothing wrong with me except the morning sickness. The doctor vehemently refused to control it. I had not heard that babies were often born limbless, to a degree, if medication was given to relieve morning sickness. I was therefore grateful, and suffered for the entire pregnancy. The poor mad died in his sleep before I came to term, the latter a cause for debate. I actually knew the date of conception, and however or whichever the date was reckoned, it always came out as 6th June. (D. Day for WW2 buffs.)

I look back with pleasurable feelings for that little house. Mike came with us and I rented him the little front room which had its own entrance. It came with basic furniture, and this was a tremendous bonus, although it had no cooking stove or refrigerator. Fortunately we had John's bar-fridge and small Belling stove.

One good thing about mine work is all the perks that go with it. Accommodation at a minimal rate, even David, our servant, was accommodated in the Mine Compound in a house with his entire family. We enjoyed a good pension scheme, six weeks paid holidays annually, all-inclusive medical, etc., and of course my free cinema seat! John bought a secondhand Kombi to go with the Morris. We visited Mum and Cliff on Sundays and they visited us on Fridays which became known as Mum's Day. Almost every evening while John was at work, I would have visitors, usually old friends of John from his previous years in Nkana, and we would play Canasta or Twenty-ones. I had made a couple of new friends. One was Gertie Fleming, a Scott, pretty as could be and a great dog lover. She had a habit of picking up dogs in the street and taking them home as strays only to find they lived just down the way or around the corner! Marie, horrified to find I could hardly knit, bought me a bootee pattern and a ball of white wool, handed me some needles and instructed me to get on with it. I still have those bootees, grey with knitting rather than age, but I never looked back and became a knitting freak, making both Johns' fairisle jerseys in multiple colours. Once, years later, when the Hoptons were robbed in Johannesburg, Marie told me all John Hopton worried about was his jersey, knowing I was unlikely to ever knit a third.

June 6th came and went, as did the 7th and the 8th. By now I had a new doctor who was quite high in the hospital. He said there was nothing wrong with me and my date must be wrong. I could not believe this because I knew the date of conception. I was overdue.

One Sunday, on the 19th June, on our way back from Itimpi, John turned onto a dirt bush road and told me to hang on. I grabbed Chippy and held him while we bounced along the pot holes. That night, midnight, I knew my time was ready and John awoke to find me in the bath, finding relief, and getting ready for hospital. I thought it too early but John was not hanging about and took me there immediately. Twenty strenuous hours later my son was born. Having read the Reid book I had refused any type of pain control but was cursing the book. John was with me but eventually I told him to go away because I was much too busy. The doctor arrived after he had finished his dinner and told the hovering sister to prepare for forceps. I heard him through a haze. The most ridiculous command to give a woman trying unsuccessfully to give birth is to instruct her to stop pushing. I was still doing so when they tried to shove a tube down my throat and I heard someone say to shove it up her nostril. Someone else asked if they should break the water. I gave up. The child was caught between a rock and a hard place in the birth canal. Too far gone for a Caesar, or anything but a good grip on the forceps and a good tear of everything else. By then I was out for the count. Apparently there was some difficulty in bringing me around from the anaesthetic but I remember being awakened by John telling me I had a lovely son, and with that I went to sleep again. When I awoke in the morning I was told to lie flat and it was late afternoon before I saw my baby. Difficult to inspect a newborn when you're lying in a prone position without so much as a pillow as an aid, but I managed and was pretty pleased with what I had achieved!

My dear friend Lucy and her husband John had arrived by car that same day thinking my baby long since born, so on my first evening as a mother I was surrounded by friends both old and new. They had all seen him earlier in the day, before I did and that upset me a little, but I was so proud of him.

There were to be no more children. John adamantly refused to allow me, never mind himself who had been worried silly, to undergo those rigours again. In a way I'm sorry I never had more children, especially a girl because they remain close. But as things turned out it's just as well I didn't.

We spent over a year in our little mine house. Peter was christened and passed his first birthday there. I grew carnations by the kitchen door and when Marie nipped them all in the bud I was hurt but discovered it necessary to produce beautiful blooms. I entertained and cooked on my little Baby Belling electric stove, a relic of John's single quarter days. It had a tiny oven and one square hotplate and I wonder today how I ever coped. Yet I did, with the aid of a marvelous pressure cooker I had picked up at an auction. I also found a cot at an auction and painted it a glossy white. Our circle of friends grew and grew. We would all meet at the swimming pool, or the Mine Dam where some had boats. There was a Club too, but we hardly ever went there for some unknown reason.

We had a close circle of very real friends and I list them for my future generations: Marie and John. Pat and Ken, Joan and Brian plus a few children. We taught each other to ski on the little farm dam someone found. Permission always had to be sought first from the farmer who was agreeable provided we kept the numbers down. We camped there overnight when possible and I was the butt of many jokes because I couldn't swim, yet I was the first to learn to ski wearing the contraption John had made to keep me afloat when I fell off.

One day I sat on the edge of the bath and watched a few ants making their way through a crack in the concrete floor. Within ten minutes a pile of excavated soil had risen about 4cm. No wonder they erected such enormous ant hills. Regretably, that and they had to be disposed of.

One night, long after the last film had finished and just as I had begun to worry, John arrived home with a shocking story. The Belgium Congo, a few kilometers to our north, was in revolt. This was a time when a mobile phone, or any phone come to that, would have been a blessing. John stayed for a few moments and was off again. The Congo Border was not all that distance away and the people were in full flight with whatever possessions they could squash into their cars, dogs, cats and other pets included. John did not return until six in the morning, had a little breakfast, a quick bath, (we had no shower) and was off again armed with all I could give: a dozen hard boiled eggs with a paper twist of salt and some bread. All day people were ferried from the border, some to local accommodation and some on their way south of the Zambesi. The Cinema and the Recreation Club were closed and used for congregating points, until day by day the people, bereft of everything, were assisted on their journey to an uncertain future. Many of the animals found willing homes in

Kitwe, and often in later years you would hear "oh he's a Congo dog", now grown fat and happy. I wondered whether he remembered his past owners who had loved and left him.

With half an eye on the future, would we be the next on the list and have to move too? Thank goodness we stayed or I would have missed the following years of happiness. Ask anyone who worked on the small Copper Mines of Northern Rhodesia (now Zambia) and they will say the same thing:

"They were the best years of our lives."

18

Oh the days gone by, the days gone by,
The childish faith in fairies and Aladdin's magic ring,
The simple soul reposing glad belief in everything.
When life was like a story holding neither sob nor sigh,
And my happy heart brimmed over in the days gone by.
                                            John Whitcomb Riley.

It would perhaps be wise to condense the following several years which were, indeed, the happiest of my entire life. John had, by this time, been re-employed and had left the Club Cinema to become once again a miner in the true sense of the word, although not underground I was pleased to learn. He worked in the Power Plant above ground as a shift worker which took a little adapting on my part but once you became used to shifts they were really quite enjoyable. What was lost on one shift was gained on another. Nights were not as bad as I thought they would be beginning at 11pm and lasting until 7am. He had every afternoon and evening free. The afternoon shifts meant he was in bed every night with an entire morning free. That left the day shift which was pretty dull because we never had an entirely free day! All in all it worked pretty well and we missed it when he eventually reverted to a normal day's work. He had also undertaken a correspondence course in electrical engineering which augured well for the future.

One day John arrived home excited to tell me we had been offered a Bancroft type house at the new end of the residential area. They were so called because the first prototype had been built in the town of Bancroft nearby. They were lovely little houses of three bedrooms, a breezeway-cum-dining room and separate lounge, plus the usual mod-cons, a large garden, garage and outbuildings. I was thrilled. It faced semi-cleared bush, devoid of houses, which stretched down to a tributary of the Kafue River. Immediately to our left was no house as the plot had the remains of an anthill which was like concrete and not worth excavating, by humans anyway. This meant that we had access to even more garden but our side was already quite big enough so we left it barren, as did our neighbours on the further side. Here we settled for the following seven or so years. No one could have been happier than we three. Needless to say, Mike, who had tagged along with us from Durban, came along too, so that made four.

The house was about four kilometres from the actual Mine. The area was reached along a straight road that ran alongside the Rhodesian Congo Border Power Plant just prior to our area. From this Plant huge pylons stretched electrical wires above the road. I was quite frightened travelling beneath them by car during powerful electrical storms, and would hold my breath and shut my eyes for the seconds it took to do so. Today I wonder which was the most dangerous.

One night, shortly after we had moved there, I had another frightening experience, if you could call it that. I awoke from a dream that Winifred had arrived for a visit. John laughed and said that was no dream – it was a bloody nightmare!

When Peter was about sixteen months old we took our first holiday. By now we had disposed of the Morris Minor and purchased a secondhand Volkswagen 'Buggy' and in this we set off for points south. We hit Salisbury, now Harare, at about midnight, none too sure where to sleep. We passed Meikles Hotel and John decided to investigate but quickly returned. It was hardly worth the huge tariff for the brief period we would be sleeping there, so on we pushed into the darkness. Exhausted, we pulled into a lay-by at the side of the road and bedded down, John curled around the steering wheel, Peter and I curled in the back. We were awoken from sleep, if that's what it was, by the mooing of cows milling around us.

Not too much further down the road, had only we known it, was the village of Hartley and there in the hotel we were allowed to use a bathroom, and bedroom in which to change, for the price of a marvelous full English breakfast. Kind people, Rhodesians. We had hoped to make it all the way to Capetown but the weather turned drearily cold when we reached De Aar and we side-tracked to the coast. After a short stay in East London we pushed up to Margate and finally headed for Durban.

We took several holidays over the next years. All of them hold memories, some happy some sad. Once Ken and Pat, part of our crowd of close friends in Kitwe, joined us quite by accident. We had not pre-booked, a bad mistake, but we managed to find accommodation in a holiday flat in Point Road. Not as bad as it sounded as it was actually quite acceptable once you got inside. I am not quite sure how Pat and Ken found us there, but we had been logging each other all the way down from the Copperbelt. In any event, they joined us, also having arrived without pre-booking, and it was arranged that they could sleep in the lounge on a pull-out bed while Peter, John and I shared the bedroom. We were woken in the early hours of the morning by a tremendous crash coming from the living room. Pat and Ken had collapsed the pull-out bed!

That was one of the best holidays we ever had even though it was cold and wet almost every day, so cold the milk – in those days still delivered in a glass bottle, cream at the top showing yellow through the glass crowned with a silver lid – bursting through and the overflow freezing down the side. Too cold to even venture on the beach, but we had the greatest fun. John and Ken were chosen by the competing African dancers to do the judging at a local company's annual competition. This was hilarious because they each had to bang the head of the winning dance leader with a knobkerrie, (a wooden stick crowned with a wooden knob) and then they were, themselves, in competition! We were rolling around with laughter. Those Africans could really dance. Then we spent hours watching balloonists landing at another competition, Pat and I bored to tears while John took a million and one photographs. At the end of the holiday we followed each other's cars and the fun continued all the way back to Kitwe.

You may think that Winifred had departed the scene. Alas, not so. I received regular letters from her mostly on the pet subject of being the unpaid nursemaid and having repaid the Trust Fund with the small inheritance she had received from Nanna, and she had therefore paid my father's back-taxes herself. My own back taxes had by now been paid by myself, or more correctly, by my husband. Now the new note: she had also paid to bring me back to South Africa. She would continually bemoan the fact that there was no Trust Fund to fall back on, and I should pay out, and pay up. I talked to John about it and wondered if I should sign it over to her. After all she could not sell it. My own mother was very much alive and the Trust tied up until after her death, and she was considerably younger than Winifred. The most Winifred could do would be borrow against it, and after the last debacle, that was highly unlikely. John said to let her have it as it was really only paper and in any case he was well able to look after his own family without touching what seemed to be blood money. I wrote and told her to send me the papers and I would let her have it.

Sure enough, the solicitor in Brighton whom I had last seen kissing her goodbye through the open window of the train, was the man who sent me the papers. I signed and returned them. Shortly afterwards I received a bill from him for completing the job. This was too much to stomach. I replied that I might well have been an idiot to hand the trust over, but was not sufficiently certifiable to pay for the privilege of doing so, and sent a copy to Winifred. I never heard again from the solicitor. Winifred did not even bother to say thank you but at least the Trust would never be mentioned again. Or so I thought!

Chippy, our dog, had a coat that needed to be regularly trimmed from time to time, he being a miniature Schnauzer. This was done by the woman who owned not only the local Pet Shop but also the only Boarding Kennels. A true animal lover we became quite friendly, and she convinced us to show Chippy at the annual Rhodesian Agricultural Show. An enormous event with contestants from both the Rhodesias, Nyasaland and South Africa. It was easy for Chippy to win Best of Breed because there was only one other Schnauzer, and she from South Africa. The woman who owned her told me she had imported the dog from England and paid three figures for her. It was not so easy for my Chippy to come second in the entire Show but he did, much to our joy.

One day I was walking along our only shopping street pushing Peter in a pram when who should I bump into but Julie, my old friend from Durban, with three tousled haired boys in tow. So Julie and her husband Tony Hearty, joined our group of best friends. When they left for South Africa a couple of years later they gave us their little black mongrel, Blackie, who became a much loved companion to me in later years, after Chippy had gone to the place beloved dogs go when they die.

The Rhodesians, like the Kenyans, had acquired the name of

a hard drinking lot, but this was totally unfounded. Parties would be held in private homes from time to time. John and I, for instance, would throw one annually, ask our nearest friends, and they in turn would do the same. Alcohol was purchased for this event and it was still around when it was time to order for the following year. Of course, we would visit the homes of our very closest friends on a regular basis, but never consumed alcohol. Sometimes we would splurge and throw a dinner party but mostly we would meet weekly here or there and play cards or board games. No television until much later when we bought a black and white set, all that was available, and sat glued to it for hours at a time. My favourite evening was visiting John and Marie Hopton, especially in winter for John Hopton would make piles of pancakes on a little primus stove in front of the fire, and we would all eat as many as we could loaded with cinnamon sugar or dripping with golden syrup. Once he came in from the kitchen with a plate laden with fruit cake beautifully cut. Marie had a fit, for it was the cake she had baked ready for Christmas. After that she always hid future Christmas fare. When it was our turn I usually did fried chicken served in individual oval straw baskets, all the rage in those days because the most popular song of the time was Eve Boswell singing *'Picking a Chicken with You.'**

We all had braai's, or barbeques as they are known elsewhere. Sitting outside on gloriously warm nights, a 45 gallon drum sliced lengthwise filled with ice, held beers and cold drinks, and sometimes our feet, to keep cool. Flying ants gamboled overhead in their hundreds wherever there was a light to be found, dropping their wings from an inky black sky so studded with stars you wanted to reach up and touch them.

The parties were held annually as I have said and the best one of all was at our house: a shipwreck party. It took three days to prepare just the room. All the furniture was removed from our lounge and John carefully lined all the walls with chicken wire then covered the lot with white paper, the end rolls of the printing presses of the local newspaper and painted it a splotchy greenish/blue. This was the Cave. The music was rock and roll and spilled out onto the garden. The neighbours were all there and even my Boss attended, briefly since he was called away to an emergency at an appropriate moment!

Sometime amongst all this hilarity Mike had finally left us. One day he arrived home somewhat abstracted asking for advice. He had fallen in love and wondered what to do. I was happy to advise and as a result he had left to set up his own establishment in Lusaka.

I had more or less stopped writing to my parents, until one day I received a letter from my father admonishing me and saying, in situ, 'Winifred holds the purse strings now'. I could visualise her standing at his elbow dictating. It took me a few days to couch a reply, adding that beneficiaries names were bandied backward and forward like so many shuttlecocks. His reply was obviously written without her knowledge, and I kept that letter of warmth and love for many years.

Peter was perhaps two years old when a taxi bumped to a stop on our rocky anthill driveway. Out popped Winifred. My nightmare was realised. Where the hell had she come from? My first word was not even hello, but rather a whole sentence, dragged from the depths of heaven knows where, as I blurted out with a gush of air "Where did you come from?" Deja vu!

Her reply shocked me almost more than her appearance, "Your brother sent me."

It transpired that Antony and his family had transferred from Fort Jameson in our far north-east to Livingstone, down by the Victoria Falls. A position as Manager at the prestigious Boat Club had arisen and Antony had put forth my father as an applicant for the position, and actually secured an interview for him. My brother had then purchased an air ticket for my father. Imagine their total shock when they arrived at Livingstone Airport to meet Daddy. Instead, there stood Winifred, the Dragon. It's a picture I have the greatest difficulty visualising. I cannot even imagine it on the cinema screen – Winifred in the doorway of the aircraft, scanning the African landscape, clutching her fur coat, and scowling down from the steps; or perhaps the faces of Antony and Tina, registering absolute shock. Go back in imagination to my father's face when she had conceived the idea of somehow using his ticket and making it her own. How did she manage it? The mind boggles! It seems it took only two weeks for the rot to set in, then my dear brother bought her another ticket and set her on the plane for Ndola, the town closest to Kitwe with an airport, and here she was, taxi and all, which had to be paid for. No one thought to tell us. Of such things are dreams made, or perhaps nightmares.

I was petrified. John was thunderstruck. Everyone else saw the funny side.

I knew without any doubt, that she would not fit in with anyone she met. Poor Mum, John's mother, was immediately squashed; Cliff, my dearly loved little 'grandfather', ignored; Marie, my best friend, asked if she, Marie, had coloured blood, the list is pretty endless. John remained stoically silent until one night he said, "If your mother doesn't say good morning to me tomorrow she can leave tomorrow night."

And that was that.

Wow, that was something coming from John. I didn't quite know what to do so I simply told her what John had said. She had no money. John felt it was not up to him to fork out for her return ticket. My brother had sent her, and it was up to him to send her back again. At her request I took her to the British

Consular Representative not at all sure what she had in mind. I soon found out. He said she couldn't expect the British Government to assist in her return to England. She countered with if they would not pay perhaps she should throw a rock through the shiny Consular windows and then they could deport her. He then advised me – not her, me – to contact my brother again. Fortunately we now possessed a telephone and after calls had been made by John to my brother, and my brother to John, the Consul to my brother and back again, my brother finally sent an air ticket to the Consul for delivery to me. John and I took her back to Ndola and made sure she was aboard the right flight for England. End of that story. Looking back I sometimes find it very odd that none of her dreadful misdemeanours were ever mentioned again either by her, or by my father.

John had acquired the habit of calling in at the only Newsagents in town to read the magazines, for free, and thus became friendly with Roy Homan, the Manager, and his wife, Natalie. Shortly after our friendship had developed they transferred to Chingola, another Copperbelt town, but we continued to see them regularly. Natalie was a shorthand typist and I expressed a desire to know how she made any sense of the little squiggles which made up the dictation. Willingly she explained. I was so fascinated she gave me her little blue book of Pitmans and from this I taught myself shorthand. I loved it. Having gleaned all I could from the little blue book I enrolled for a few private lessons and then officially took the examination gaining 130wpm. However, these words were quite useless without typing skills so John bought a secondhand ribbon Remington and on this I learnt to type.

While all this learning was going on Peter had reached the age of three and a bit and we decided it was time for him to join in with other children to a greater degree. We entered him into the

Infant Class of the only private school available. It was a multiracial Convent School catering for both sexes which we thought would be the best thing for Peter since he was an only child, and this would give him the opportunity to mix with other children the same age. It turned out to be very rewarding. I recall the teacher of his class was one Sister Alphonsena, and when we made a play on her name Peter became fiercely loyal in her defence. A year or so later in the Junior School, the Mother Superior sent for us both to appear before her. John and I, in trepidation, did so, wondering what dreadful misdemeanor he had committed. It was to complain that he spent his classroom hours making paper aeroplanes to skim across the room, only completing his work at the eleventh hour after several reprimands, and it had therefore been decided to put him up a year ahead of himself hoping thereby to encourage him to work harder! It didn't help all that much except he made fewer aeroplanes, and still managed to pass.

19

I do not know whether there are Gods,
But there ought to be.

Diognes the Cynic
412 – 323 BC.

It was inevitable that my father should suffer several heart attacks. The first was a bad one, and this was followed by two smaller ones. John, dear man, decided I should travel over to see him, taking the grandson he had not yet met. Peter was just shy of his fourth birthday. We flew out of Ndola Airport, I almost unwillingly, but pleased to be seeing my father again. He and Winifred met us at Gatwick Airport and we drove down to Bexhill on Sea where they lived. It was cold and damp and as we passed through various villages I remarked that it must be a holiday as none of the shops were open, to be told it was still only 8 o'clock in the morning and shops in that part of the world were more civilised and only opened their doors at 9am.

My father had taken a job with a car company based in Hastings, a short distance along the coast and they lived in a company flat. This was an apartment few will have seen or even envisaged! It was actually above garages which had originally been horse stables and was one of a kind around a cobbled courtyard, with the buildings above being the housing for the grooms and such. The stables themselves had been converted into a working garage for servicing cars. The entrance to the flat was through a stone archway then up a stone staircase, which Winifred had stained bright red while the banister railing was painted a royal blue. At the top were two doors facing each other, one each side of the staircase. These were painted royal blue too, and each door had a bright brass letter box right in the centre. The effect of this on what would have been a dreary entrance was astonishing A lick of paint here and there turned what would have been a dull entrance into one of cheerful welcome. I wondered later, when I was gazing out of the bedroom window, what history might tell of the warm smell of horses and the clop of iron shoes on cobbled stones. Now it was the stink of oil and the honk of horn. Winifred, for all her faults, was adept at making a silk purse out of a sow's ear as I have said before and that entrance was no exception.

We entered the door on the right, which led into two interleading rooms: the first was the kitchen/dining area which boasted not only table and chairs but a sleeping couch against one wall; and the second was the lounge with a very pretty lounge suite across which lay the cloths, purloined by Winifred, that I had embroidered years previously for my 'hope chest'. There was no shortage of beds with another single against one of the walls. The second front door immediately facing the first, entered into a mirror set of the opposite two rooms, these sparsely furnished, the first with a single bed, the second with a double bed and a dressing table. There was a third door which led into a tiny area housing a bath. The hot water, servicing the two flats, was provided by inserting coins into a meter which later in my stay I was continually feeding. For some peculiar reason the water was always cold when I needed the bath for Peter. This then, was the domain of the Part family.

Also included was my father's dog, a small Manchester Terrier who accompanied my father to work on most days. Winifred had covered the entire dark wooden panelled walls with plain paper which she had then painted white. It was an incredible piece of ingenuity and resulted in light, airy, pretty rooms. Peter and I slept in the double bed, Daddy in the single in the adjoining bedroom where he always slept anyway, and Winifred slept in the lounge, where she usually slept too, it seems.

The day following our arrival I asked advice on which Bank I should use in which to deposit the money John had given me for use in an emergency should Northern Rhodesia blow up like the Congo. Our first day therefore was spent without too much excitement while a suitable Bank was found and the money deposited. Silly me!

After that, with some relief, we enjoyed a couple of glorious days driving around the countryside, looking at Battle Abbey, the field in front of it where the Hastings Battle was fought, and various other historical points of interest which seemed to abound in that coastal area of Sussex. My father appeared to have recovered quite well from the heart attacks although he had to be careful. He had been prescribed tablets, one of which he was advised to place under his tongue should he anticipate a further attack.

No sooner had my father returned to work than Winifred worked herself up into one of her rages. This time Peter was the target as she screamed at him to take his feet off the floor she had just washed. He scrambled up onto the couch where I was sitting, only to be further admonished for putting them on the couch. I said that the poor little devil couldn't do right for doing wrong, diverting the shouting to me. That brought on the tempest. Peter cried, Winifred stormed, and I gathered up my son and retired to the other flat, closing the doors en route. Of course, she wept and apologised: she was distraught, they had a Bank overdraft and the Bank had demanded payment. She had a plan: would I be prepared to buy the diamond ring Nanna had left her so that they could pay off the overdraft? I fell for it, drew most of the money out and paid off the overdraft. I now had Nanna's ring. A couple of days later Winifred came into our bedroom almost before I was awake, weeping copiously, and saying Nanna had come to her in a dream and was haunting her. Apparently Nanna, before she had died, had said that if ever she sold the ring Winifred would be haunted. I believed none of this, but allowed Winifred to decide I was an even bigger fool than she had thought. The tale was long and wet with sobs, but I let her continue for as long as I dared before I handed back the ring. I packed a bag and left for Halifax, where John's relations were looking forward to meeting me.

What a difference in atmosphere. We stayed with John's uncle, Mum's brother, and his wife, in a tiny terraced house in Halifax. It might have been small but it was bursting with affection. Relatives from far and near visited us during our week there, all boisterous and happy. Truck drivers and mill workers, they were the cream of England's working class. They took me to pubs on the Yorkshire Moors, and the Local in the Town. I was shown the interesting historical sites and even the gibbet of long ago, still erect. None of them were as daft about history as me, but they were all happy to express interest in anything that would please me. I asked for cold tripe and vinegar and was given a serving dish piled with white tripe which I manfully tried to finish, but couldn't quite. I haven't eaten tripe since! I was given fish and chips which only North country folk really know how to cook, with mushy peas and lots of vinegar. And Yorkshire pudding, a huge portion with onion gravy served before the main meal which was not necessarily a roast, but was the Yorkshire way, and dumplings to die for when we had stews. They were good days, with good people. What a vast contrast. John's first cousin said he was due to take a trip down south and would visit us before we returned to Kitwe. I was a bit horrified wondering what Winifred would make of a great burly truck driver pitching up on the mews doorstep, but thought I would cross that bridge when I came to it and decided it would be quite funny. In the end the visit did not occur. Pity really.

I took a day off from Halifax and took the train over to Leeds to meet up again with my cousin Peter, and his wife and son whom I had never met, in dear Auntie Lily's house. She had packed the place with as many of Winifred's relatives as she could muster. They were such lovely people, I wondered where Winifred came from? Although nothing detrimental had ever been said of her, I do know there had been a time when one of the sisters had not spoken to her for many years. Even darling Auntie Lily had refused to put her up on one of the occasions Winifred had arrived unexpectedly by train. (I was there so I know). It is to my regret that I have lost touch with The Family, as Winifred christened them. It is a shame because I would have liked them to read the true story.

We returned to Bexhill refreshed from the family atmosphere, the same environment I had adopted since my marriage. I felt renewed by the warmth and love that had surrounded me in Halifiax.

Winifred had a couple more attacks but I was prepared for them, and as they were not directed at Peter I was able to counter them. One episode is worth repeating. One evening after I had bathed, I stood at the foot of my father's bed and chatted. We discussed Winifred and her problem, and I asked if it was possible she was suffering from a psychological personality disorder that might be curable. He said he had tried, but of course the old adage that although you could lead a horse to water, you cannot necessarily make it drink, applied to her. At that moment he put his finger to his lips and glanced at the front door. I looked and froze as the letter box lid slowly opened, but before it reached its apex I was off, through the inter-leading door and into bed with Peter with the covers up to my nose. Winifred came through the front door and I could hear her say that she thought she had heard voices. My father replied that it must have been his radio which he had just switched off. Then I felt, rather than saw, her arriving at my bedside. Coward that I was, I feigned sleep, fortunately successfully.

Later that week I found the opportunity to have a further discussion with Daddy. He told me that once he had seen Antony's children, should another heart attack feel imminent he would not place the tablet under his tongue and thus would let Mother Nature take her course. I looked at him sadly, but could offer no advice. I felt inadequate and selfish. To this day I have loved that foolish, gentle father of mine.

The holiday visit came to an end shortly afterwards, and Peter and I returned to our happy home. I felt rather sorry to be leaving my father as I knew it was unlikely that I would ever see him again; but it was a bed of his own making and he had to lie on it.

20

The selfsame well from which our laughter rises,
Is often filled with tears.

Kahil Gibron.
1883 – 1931.

Back home in Nkana-Kitwe life returned quickly to normal. John was none too pleased with me for depositing the money in my father's bank account instead of one in our name. In the next breath he had bundled up some trousers and a jacket he no longer wore and asked me to send them on to my father. This was a typical gesture from one of the good men of the world who happened to be my husband.

The winds of change, as quoted by Harold Macmillan, one time British Prime Minister, were certainly sweeping across Africa, but in Northern Rhodesia they came like a hurricane. We white Africans went to bed one night as members of the British Commonwealth and awoke the next morning to find ourselves abandoned, and the black Africans awoke to find themselves independent. Northern Rhodesia, by an Act of Parliament published 1964 in the United Kingdom, had become Zambia.

How easy! 'Uhuru - Freedom,' They were by no means ready, but the white yoke had been released. Call it what you will. Personally, I called it betrayal. There was little change in our lifestyle, or in theirs come to that. But the future looked a little gloomy. What did change mean in this new era of being free, of not having to depend on someone else for efficiency, being taught, or told, or whatever else that went hand in hand with Freedom? There occurred a series of amusing incidents I witnessed but could do nothing about. For instance: a butcher-boy in his blue and white striped apron standing before me in the Bank was called by the bank cashier to jump the queue and go around behind the counter to sit there while the clerk took a tea break; the stout African lady sitting in the posh lounge of our rather posh hotel, dipping one of her nipples which she had moistened from the tea tray's milk jug, into the sugar bowl prior to inserting same nipple into baby's mouth; and the Postmaster emptying all the tills of cash into a canvas bag. He told me he did so every half hour to ensure that at least some of the money went into the right place. Nothing balanced. I wondered if it did at the Bank? As for Her Majesty's Mail: unless you had a Post Office box you stood no chance of receiving it. Many's the time we collected bundles of mail from where it had been thrown in the bush opposite our house, and delivered it ourselves, until everybody finally purchased a P.O. Box.

In August of 1966 my brother and his family took the trip to Bexhill, as I had done two years earlier, to visit my father and have an English holiday. He and I had not been in touch since the Winifred episode in Kitwe. However, in the following month he sent me a telegram with the news that my father had died. I was distraught, and went alone to the Church of England, and then the Methodist Church, only to find both churches closed and locked to prevent the vandalism that was occurring. So I went home where John was babysitting, and he held me close and found the right words.

Some years later when next my brother and I met, he told me what had transpired. After my brother had visited Bexhill, he and his family departed for the remainder of their holiday. They were contacted by the police and informed that Daddy had died. From his information, and what I have pieced together myself, I am probably nearer to the truth, confirmed by Antony, than anybody else. Winifred had pulled her usual stunt, had a fierce row, and departed to visit her family up North, and Daddy had not 'used his pill' after her departure. The first bit of that sentence is true, the second a fabrication of mine, but in all probability the truth considering what he had promised me. My brother dealt with all the formalities, then bundled Winifred into the hired car, and with our father's ashes in the boot of the car, wrapped in a coat of Tina's (my sister in law), departed for Leeds. To Tina's horror and disgust, Winifred asked them to stop at a shop where Winifred had seen a black nightie she wished to purchase!

Antony then made what I considered to be a mistake – then again, perhaps he had no option for even Antony could not face up squarely. to Winifred. I think Daddy would have preferred his ashes scattered in the English Channel, or over the countryside in any of the southern counties which he had loved, grown up in, and flown over. Instead he was interred with his other son Robert in the Lawnswood cemetery. My little verse for Robert was removed and Daddy's names inscribed in its999 place. This is probably where Winifred's ashes were eventually to be interred, although nobody ever bothered to inform me. I shudder to think that poor Daddy is with her throughout all eternity, but perhaps our souls really do roam free, and his has found solace.

Meanwhile I had put my new found skills to work and found a 'mornings only' position as a secretary to a surgeon. His rooms were on the lower floor of a two storey house, and his home, a beautifully constructed house built so that it straggled over the Kafue River. He was of missionary stock and a very religious man. Once he asked me to prepare the dining table for a dinner party he was giving for President Kaunda and his entourage. I thought it would be a nice gesture to display the flowers in the

Zambian colours, but when I telephoned the Zambian Youth Centre to find out what these colours were they did not know, so I used red and white roses, but the inference was totally lost!

Above our consulting rooms were those of a very popular gynaecologist/obstetrician, and in the fullness of time he offered me a job as his personal secretary. It was a fantastic position which I greatly enjoyed. He had all the latest office equipment, and a Dictaphone, the controls of which slid beneath a golf ball typewriter. He would dictate, and then intersperse his works with pieces of classical music to dull the monotony, he said!

A very sad and tragic act occurred. His consulting room nurse, on her way back from a picnic with her husband and two small sons, was injured by mobs throwing stones at passing motorists. One of the stones cracked her ribs, and although she was rushed to hospital a broken rib had pierced her lungs and her life could not be saved. It was a pretty bad time for all of us.

On the plus side we held a Medical Conference in Kitwe, the first Zambian Medical Conference to which medical men from all over the world were invited. It was part of my job to type the letters of invitation, and to complete the follow-up correspondence, without dictation, which my boss then signed. It was an enormous success, and afterwards even I received letters of thanks from some very eminent people.

Some of our friends had been steadily dribbling down south on a permanent basis, including my friend Julie, Tony, and their three boys. I was partially consoled by her little back dog which she had given me on her departure. Pat and Ken had also departed, as had Joan and her partner Brian, so our little group was fast sinking. Joan had a bad time of it since once they had settled down south, Brian left her for a very much younger woman, whom he married. At one stage it was decided that John should go down and bring her back, but Joan declined and later married again herself. She popped back into my life later.

John had a friend from his earlier days on the Copperbelt, one Piet Vander who had married an English woman, let us call her May. We seldom saw them for May and I were totally different characters, and did not get on particularly well together. However, fate decreed otherwise, and on the last occasion we visited Durban on holiday they were there, and we met. For some time John and I had discussed the possibility of leaving Kitwe and returning to Durban. The idea was further enhanced when a Unilateral Declaration of Independence was adopted by the Prime Minister of Southern Rhodesia, Ian Smith, making Rhodesia an independent sovereign state. This was the first colonial break with Britain since the Americans had done so 200 years earlier. Britain declared it illegal, and called for total sanctions against the land locked, now ex-colonial, country.

The Frestels and the Vanders decided to join forces and purchase a business which the Vanders already had in view. I'm afraid I kept a low profile, for although I would love to return to Durban, if we went anywhere, I was a bit worried about getting so involved with the Vanders. Our holiday continued with nothing written in stone, but the idea had certainly lit a flame. At the end of our holiday we invited our old friends Bob and Lillian together with Julie and Tony out to dinner. During the course of conversation our possible return to Durban was discussed. Lillian asked what I would do with my dogs, and Julie decreed that I would never find accommodation with them as rentals were at a premium in Durban. It had not occurred to me, and I paused for a moment to digest this information. Then I pointed to each of my friends in turn and said that if the worst came to the worst they could have one each, temporarily, considering that Chippy had once been Lillian's and Blackie had belonged to Julie. It was a thought I stored away, just in case.

We returned to the Copperbelt with nothing decided or accomplished, but with a lot of thoughts churning around.

I had made a couple of friends at work who owned the Pathology Laboratory, Ray and Jean Still. We occasionally dined together and I loved to visit them because they had two enormous black dogs. One evening we were there along with John and Marie Hopton, and it was decided to play a board game. However, when I saw what they had chosen I declined, and said I would sit and knit in the lower lounge attached to the dining room where they were to play the game of *Ouija*. I heard their commotion but placidly continued knitting until Ray pulled me from my comfortable chair and insisted I join them saying it would not work because of me. I simply must 'sit in on it' with them even if I didn't play. Ten minutes later I was close to tears. It had been John's turn and he had asked if it was wise to return to return to South Africa and the answer was No, so he asked why? And the answer spelt out 'death'. Whether *Ouija* is a matter of auto-suggestion, self-delusion, telekinesis, telepathy or plain foolishness I do not know, but the entire thing was abhorrent to me and I said so. End of game. I collected a sleeping Peter and we left. John tried to make me laugh, saying he and John Hopton had pushed the glass, but how did their fingers, along with all the other fingers, know which each of the other fingers was spelling, and even if they did, how and why would the owners of the fingers be so cruel? Eventually John calmed me, and I tried to forget the incident. It really was very foolish.

In due course the decision was made and the Vanders and Frestels somehow contrived to buy a fresh produce and dried fruit business we had been inspecting in Durban, with the Vanders preceding us to Durban by about six weeks.

By now we had two cars, our faithful little Beetle and a Volkswagon Variant. We also needed a furniture van somewhat larger than the little blue trunk for the rest of our belongings which, prior to our arrival there, had to be stored in Durban until we found accommodation. Lots to be organised and attended to with little time to think of anything else. Then the day arrived and John, with the Beetle piled high with luggage, and me in the Variant with two dogs and Peter, we left our happy little home. I took one last look and with a very large lump in my throat, we departed for Durban. Our future was uncertain but we had each other, and with Peter and the dogs we were our own little family unit.

Never commit the sin of complacency. I did not know what lay ahead.

21

Home is the sailor home from the sea,
And the hunter home from the hill.
> From Robert Louis Stevenson's Requiem
> 1850-1894.

We could not tarry on the way south because Piet and May Vander had already been running the business for a week and were anxious for our arrival. We headed straight there and arrived just as they were closing at six in the evening. Both of us were pretty exhausted after the three day trip. Peter looked very pale and the dogs jittering to be exercised. May was a very out-going woman, a bit overpowering, knew what she wanted and generally got it, Piet being very quiet and restrained. They had two boys, one the same age as Peter, the other still a baby. They had rented a flat temporarily quite close to the shop. To this we all repaired for the first night where I was immediately put to work chopping vegetables by hand for packing, and eventual sale as soup vegetables. I have never met anyone, before or since, who was quite as capable as May! She exuded confidence which, in a way, did nothing for mine!

The following day I took the dogs and Peter for a walk because both dogs would be much curtailed in the shop until we could get settled. A woman from the flats stopped me and told me if we were to stay in the block of flats I would have to get rid of one of the dogs. I stood my three dependents in a row, Peter being one, and asked her to choose which. I knew there would be problems but didn't expect them to start quite so soon.

The shop was an easy adjustment. It had been bought as a partnership: one third paid by us, one third by the Vanders, and one third on loan from the Bank. We inherited two staff: a lady shop assistant – one Mrs. Dawson – and an Indian called Dick who was a general purpose worker and made up the most beautiful fruit gift baskets.

Although the shop was large and spacious, it was overstaffed with six of us, but we only discovered that much later. May had purchased, on a hire-and-buy scheme, three magnificent electronic weighing scales for each side of the shop, much disapproved of by John who thought them an unnecessary expense, but more of that later too. May and Mrs. Dawson mainly worked in the vegetable side of the shop while my domain was on the dried fruits and cigarette side, and with the vegetables when we were busy. John was the one who went down to the market every morning at 5am buying fresh fruit and vegetables, and sometimes travelling out to local farms to purchase fresh vegetables. Piet was sort of general, a meet and greet man if you like, who helped everyone, everywhere, and occasionally visited the farms with John. May and I balanced the tills each night, and both John and Piet kept the books.

We had purchased the business from an old lady who had run it with her husband until he had died. Their son, Terry Webb, a Director of a large accounting firm was the man who had made all the arrangements to purchase the shop. He paid a large part in the lives of John and myself as we came to know him and his wife, Pat.

We sort of fell into the shop life quite easily although it was hard work with long hours. It was everything else that was fraught with difficulty, accommodation being but one. After their long trip confined in a car, and now tying them up for long periods in the shop, the dogs were stressed. Within a few days Chippy developed what appeared to be constipation. I took him to a local veterinary surgeon hoping she would advise me on the best potion to relieve this, but on examination she said there was a lump in his tubes and she would have to operate. It was to be a big operation and she thought he might not survive. I took him to another vet. who pushed something up one end and something else down another end, and then took him outside to a patch of grass and told me to wait with him there. The wait was not a long one and the desired effect was accomplished! Subdued, I very quickly thereafter began scouring the town for accommodation. I had made this even more difficult because it had to be in the area which was an accepted zone for the school I had chosen, Durban Preparatory School for Boys. John told me to broaden the horizon. I did, and signed a lease for one. I took the lease to John who blew up. I had taken a house in the local coloured area. John phoned the agent and asked him to call in. When he arrived John tore up the lease saying I was simple in the head and not permitted to sign anything. I began again. This time an agent took pity on me, and suggested I telephone a Margaret Massabo who had a town house on the Berea, lived on the ground floor and rented the floor above which was a self-contained flat with a separate entrance. She also owned the property next door which was a geriatric nursing home run by herself, being a nursing sister. As she was also the Chairman of the Durban Animal Anti Cruelty League it was a pretty good bet that she was a dog lover and willing to take my dogs. Right, thought I, and found a quiet spot where I could speak without interruption. We had a great deal in common. She came from a similar part of England as myself and she had a son a year older than Peter. She loved animals as did I. Years later she told me she had decided that I sounded the right sort of person for the flat when I suddenly came up with the statement that I had two small problems. She immediately thought I was going to say my two small problems were two small babies which she did not want. One because baby sounds might disturb the patients next door and two because she did not like babies anyway! When I said in the next breath that I had two small dogs she was so relieved she just said yes without any further thought.

We settled in quite comfortably. Peter went to a Church school just down the road which was the pre-school for Durban Prep. and as I collected both him and the dogs around 2pm each day, everybody was happy.

After we had been in Durban for about two months Mum and Cliff arrived with their caravan, together with Judy, their one remaining dog, now pretty elderly too. John lowered the tyres of the caravan and pushed it into one of Margaret's garages. We all pitched in together for an indefinite period which made my life very much easier. We were back to meat and potato pie suppers which, after a day of fruit and vegetables, was a blessing, the dogs were walked, and Peter collected. My landlady didn't seem to mind but then John had charisma that would charm the most stringent of landladies. Besides, this landlady was pretty charismatic herself, a very beautiful blond who was particularly kind and who eventually became a very dear friend.

The shop was doing reasonably well but we were definitely overstaffed. Six weeks in and John, pouring over the bank statements, suddenly announced that the idea of leaving one third of the business on loan was totally ridiculous as the interest was exorbitant. A meeting was called between the four of us where John suggested we pay off the Bank between us. He was surprised to learn that the Vanders had used their funds to purchase a house.

This was surprising as Piet had worked on the mines without

interruption for some years longer than John, whereas John's service had been interrupted, and he had lost his money in the petrol station. It was a bit of a problem, but the Frestels would pay off the Bank loan anyway, and would therefore own two thirds of the shop. A gentleman's agreement was officially drawn up by Terry Webb whereby it was agreed that to help Piet out, the business would remain on a 50/50 basis. I was asked if I had any objection, and of course, officially, I had not. However, as time passed I had good reason to have an objection. May had taken a full-time secretarial post with one of the factories. I put it to her that she should actually share half her salary with us. She did not agree! I'd really had enough of domineering women, but I held my peace. It was enough that they knew what I thought.

The shop suddenly took off. I was making a 200% profit on my dried and glazed fruit gift presentations. They went out in all shapes and sizes from glassware to basketware. I even had special boxes for overseas gifts which I listed in a little book showing sender and recipient, and had the Post Office stamp. This didn't excuse me from the vegetable side of things, and I did my share that side too. I enjoyed it. Each afternoon May would arrive, go straight to the tills, and ring up to see how much we had taken. Another blight on our relationship, but I smiled on.

Terry Webb kept a maternal eye upon us. He and Pat visited occasionally on a Sunday. During these periods he taught me how to take books through trial balance right up to Income Tax. I hoped, with fleeting visions of my last maths teacher, that I would never have to go that far. He was shocked to learn that we had not bothered to make joint Wills, especially now that we were in a business agreement. He also told me to remember that if anything should happen to John I would contact him before I did anything else, and the same applied to John. Off we went to make our Wills without further delay.

Margaret Massabo and I had become quite friendly. Her husband, a handsome, blonde, blue-eyed Italian from San Remo, was maître d' at one of the big hotel restaurants, and as such was often out most evenings. John and I would take her along with us whenever we went to the cinema. This was quite frequent as John loved his movies and we had built in baby-sitters in Mum and Cliff who loved to stay with Peter. We both found the Hollywood magic, or the British humour and drama, relieved us in one fell swoop from evening conversations and shop worries.

One day John and I went to a photographer to have passport photos taken for submission for South African residency. All three of us had already passed our medicals. On the way, driving, John put his hand on my knee and asked if, with my new bookkeeping accomplishments added to my secretarial skills, I would be able to get a good job if anything should happen to him? I was horrified at the very idea and wondered what had brought this on. I asked what would happen if I died first? And in any case, I argued, it should always be the man who should bring up a son, not a woman. We had a small debate about it which I thought I had won. The subject was squashed.

My old friend, Lucy, told me her parents were vacating the house they were renting, and wondered if we would like to take over their lease. It was about six properties further down the road from where we were living, had three bedrooms and a back garden for dogs. Splendid! Margaret seemed pleased for us, but I think she was even more pleased to have the caravan finally removed from her garage!

Out of the blue Piet dropped a bombshell: he had decided to find permanent employment working for somebody else rather than himself. After he had found employment, when it was all confirmed, he told us. Pretty underhanded, but there it was. He was to begin his job on the 1st October, a date a little out of sight, giving us, he said, time to make a plan of sorts.

It was, without doubt, a very low and rotten blow. My poor John, so trusting of an old friend, who had now stabbed him in the back. We consulted Terry Webb who was shocked. We simply could not afford to buy Piet and May out, and they must have known this. We could perhaps ask the Bank to take over where they had left off. It was not as straightforward as that. Banks did not do business like the Vanders did, but it might be arranged. John and I would be hard pressed to pay off another third at the Bank. Perhaps John should also find a job and I could run the shop, with the excellent Mrs. Dawson and Dick to help. Or we could ask Piet to leave his third share of the shop where it was for a couple of months, which was a reasonable request considering his dismal action. That would at least give us time to figure something out. It was left at that.

John developed a bad cough which he could not dispel. One day he returned from making deliveries looking unwell. I asked Piet to kindly take over some of the lifting of heavy boxes and delivering them, something he had never offered to do, which might relieve John while he was unwell. I made an appointment with the doctor whose rooms were above us, and then insisted John went to see him. Grumbling, John went. When he returned he laughingly said all he had was bronchitis and that there was nothing wrong with his heart. The doctor said he was as strong as an ox and I could feed him his favourite chip sandwiches, starting about now. I didn't believe him!

Exactly two days later, as I was emptying a sack of potatoes into the spud box, I glanced at John who was sitting at our little table behind the counter. He smiled at me and gave me such a look of love my heart gave a great thump. He came and stood beside me at the counter, and began cutting the white paper into the right size for wrapping the vegetables when I heard him say

"Oh" very loudly. As I turned to him he fell sideways, and backwards against the potato box, then to the floor. I screamed "John!" I don't think he heard me. It was too late. He was dead.

22

Behind the veil of tears is a very quiet, secret place.
I know for I have dwelt there.

What happened in the next hour or so is seared on my memory. Initially I flew up to the doctor before anyone else even appeared to notice what had occurred. The doctor was out. I flew back down the stairs, only to be led into the chemist shop adjoining. Mrs. Dawson came to me there and asked if I would like to go in the ambulance with John to the hospital. Yes, of course I wanted to. But no. They would not allow me. Instead a doctor with his adult son who had been in the shop, bundled me into his car along with Mrs. Dawson, and took me to the hospital. Once there I saw the ambulance with the rear door ajar, outside the Emergency Entrance. Mrs. Dawson tried to restrain me but I pushed her away and climbed from the car, and then rushed toward the ambulance to meet a doctor coming out of it. I asked how John was, and he replied "Oh, he's very dead." I don't suppose he knew who I was. Perhaps he thought I was an inquisitive passer-by. I stood befuddled.

Somehow we returned to the shop, but I didn't speak nor hear their talk. There was a puddle on the floor where John had fallen, and I stood looking at it. Then I heard someone say "Clean that up", and I surfaced. I went to the phone and rang Terry Webb just as he had asked me, and then phoned Marie in Johannesburg. (She and her husband John had left Zambia just after we had, and now ran a swimming pool business) I asked them to come down as soon as possible. Incredibly I arrived home, I don't know how. Mum looked at me in astonishment, and I told her John had died. Peter was dressing for Boy Cubs. I told him.

"My wonderful father?" he questioned.

I took him to Cubs, and told them. When I returned home I started to cry. Mum and I together cried. It was just not believable. Our John, gone out of our world. I wanted to see the priest at St James Anglican just up the road. Mum, Cliff and I walked up together. There were others with us, but I don't know who. The priest was there. He did not know me, I was not one of his parishioners. I told him John was agnostic, and that I didn't attend church, but nevertheless I beseeched him to perform John's funeral rites. In front of the altar we knelt, with others standing behind us, and there we were blessed while he held one of Mum's hands, and one of mine. The strength of his hands seemed to flow into mine, and give me courage. After the blessing he said he would conduct the Service for John.

After that I didn't speak very much at all. Cliff collected Peter. May and Piet Vander were there, and Margaret Massabo. At 9 o'clock that evening Marie and John arrived. After my phone call, she told me later, she had packed in fifteen minutes for the pair of them, sorted out her household, collected John from his office, and driven down immediately. Wonderful friends. I was given pills the chemist had provided, and finally it was bedtime. I slept with Peter, and put Marie and John in our room. I awoke the next day feeling guilty that I had slept. Cliff took over. That little man with the enormous heart must have done everything that needed to be done, even collecting John's wedding ring for me. I did nothing. Our friends had to be notified, and my brother too. The house was filled with flowers. I have never seen so many. Someone told me to make a list and begin thank-you notes.

Someone else provided notelets. My friend Julie arrived. She came every day, sometimes with her three boys as company for Peter. Lucy came then, when the shop re-opened, she went off to help there.

My brother arrived on the morning of the funeral. It strikes me now that my brother Antony, in spite of Winifred's unworthy efforts of trying to keep us apart, was somehow always there when I really needed him. The Chapel used by non-conformists was smothered with flowers and full of people. I did not want to go in, and my brother said that was okay if you don't really want to say goodbye. So he led me in. I saw the coffin was open. Then the Father led me to John, with Mum following closely and holding my hand. I could see my John, Peter's wonderful father, lying asleep. I kissed his forehead and it was so very cold, and now finally I accepted that he was really dead. True to his word the Father gave a moving service and spoke beautifully of John. It was as though he had known John well. He addressed me, and said that God opens his portals to all, and I have no reason to doubt those words.

My sister in law, Tina, had remained at the house with Peter, and had organised the funeral wake. She had provided a wonderful feast. The house was packed full with everyone talking at once. I sat in a chair and wondered how anyone could laugh when my John was lying cold.

Marie and John had planned to stay on for a while. Julie, concerned that I was not speaking, had phoned her brother who was CMO at a hospital for the mentally disturbed in Pietermaritzburg, to ask his advice. He said that I was simply in shock and it might take a little while for normal talk to resume, but once it did I would never shut up! One evening she was sitting on the floor at my feet with her arm resting on my knee, when she said it was time she went home to her boys. I didn't want her to go, and knew I had to say something to make her stay. I announced that I would return to the shop the following morning now that a week had passed.

Terry Webb promptly called a meeting at his house. John Hopton accompanied me for moral support, and with the Vanders present, Terry opened the meeting by asking whether I intended to keep the shop. May Vander piped up that it must be immediately sold for whatever we could get. I suddenly came alive and banged loudly on the table making everyone jump several inches, and in a loud voice that even surprised me, said, and I remember each word, "Nonsense, what rubbish. We sell it for as much as possible. My husband, worked long, hard hours, longer than anyone else, and I will not sell it for anything less than we paid, preferably more." Terry stated that it was just what he wanted to hear, and John Hopton later told me that he wanted to applaud!

The Vanders made a couple of inane suggestions, and Piet pointed out that the cash till owed him R70.00 being the float they had originally put in the till. Terry politely pointed out that we were discussing thousands not comparable cents, and with that withdrew his wallet, from which he extracted R70.00 and handed it to Piet. The meeting came to a reasonably amicable end. I felt very much better.

The shop went on the market. One or two interested purchasers wandered through over the next few short weeks, but nobody actually nibbled. Once, May and I were leaning against the counter watching a couple being shown the opposite side of the shop, my side of glaze fruits, when I remarked to May that I hoped they would buy.

"So do I," she said. "My husband lost a bloody good job because of all this."

I turned to her, looked directly into her eyes, and said, "Yes, and I lost a bloody good husband."

In the end I called in upon the man who owned a similar shop a little along the road from us. He and John were in friendly competition, and both had fostered the hopes of eventually owning a whole string of high class shops. I asked him if he would like to make me an offer. He did, and I accepted, consulting the Vanders as a matter of courtesy. The amount was exactly what we had paid, on the proviso that I remove the three fancy scales the Vanders had ordered on an even fancier hire purchase scheme. I had made no profit from the hard work John had put in, but Terry had advised me to take the offer. The Vanders were paid out exactly one third which was more than they deserved, but Piet had, after all, lost a good job!

They, the Vanders, refused to have anything to do with the scales, which finished up, clean and shiny, on my bedroom floor. The scale company refused, initially, to absolve me from the agreement, but I invited the persons responsible for this around to the house, told them of my dilemma, and showed them the scales. They left with them and nothing more was said. Possibly they thought that, in the long run, I was the loser.

Thereafter, with Mum and Cliff beside me, some very good friends, and a wonderful son as John's legacy to me, I began again. So:

> *I walked a mile with Pleasure, she chatted all the way,*
> *But left me none the wiser, for all she had to say.*
> *I walked a mile with Sorrow, and never a word said she,*
> *But oh the things I learnt from her,*
> *when Sorrow walked with me.*

This written by one Robert Browning Hamilton* who does not appear to have written anything else, more's the pity.

23

Lord, what fools these mortals be!
W. Shakespeare.

Three weeks after John's death, and before the shop was sold, Peter went down with chicken pox! Then one evening, as I was lying in bed reading, Chippy, my dog, rose from his bed and wobbled towards Blackie's bed where he began to heave as though about to vomit. I leapt up and collected him in my arms whereupon he threw back his head and howled, then died. I could not believe it. Mum, Cliff and Peter were all asleep. I carried him in my arms up the road to Margaret and Roberto to ask them if Chippy was really dead. Of course, he was.

One day, just before closing the doors of the shop for the last time, I walked out into the Centre only to be stopped by a large hand. Looking up, who should I see but Ray Still at whose house we had played with the *Ouija* board. I had not seen them since, and they had only recently arrived in Durban. We spoke for a few minutes and he said how sorry they both were to learn of the death of John. He asked if I remembered our evening of play. For a medical man I was surprised he took any notice of such foolishness. Yet who was I to question such fallacy, or even if it was a delusion? I was yet to broaden out into even wider fields of idiocy!

Mum and Cliff were making plans to move into the caravan park which had opened almost on the same spot as I had learned to ride bareback on a pony. I found a job doing some sort of bookkeeping. It was a small, tool manufacturing company run by the owner, a quite objectionable man. On the third day of arriving home, tired and worried, Cliff thumped the arm of his chair and told me not to return – no job was worth it. He wasn't going to watch me distress myself. That was the end of my foray into the bookkeeping world, and I returned on the fourth day, braved the owner, and left, without pay. It was not worth pursuing. I found a job as a medical secretary with a leading gynaecologist and was happily reunited with medical terminology and a decent typewriter. A small cloud on the horizon was the fact that I knew Cliff was only waiting until he reached pensionable age before they both returned to England. I had come to rely on them and would miss them terribly.

Time moved inextricably onward. Peter and I went up by train to spend a few days with Marie and John. Peter was now a pupil at Durban Prep. He had a best friend, there, another Terry, who lived with his mother facing the Massabo's, but Margaret Massabo's son, Stefano, had been entered into a private school. However, the three boys were all of an age and were frequently in each other's company. They remained friends, on and off, for many years.

Almost a year went by. Another friend of my Kitwe days, Joan, who had moved to Salisbury long before any of us left, wrote to say she and her fairly new husband Les Church would be visiting Durban on a passenger ship and staying in port for a few days. Would I like to meet the ship and join them while they were in port. I was quite excited. I still had built in baby-sitters even if they were at the caravan park. Down I went to the docks once more, to meet the ship as she arrived, and waved gaily up to Joan and Les. Once aboard they introduced me to a fellow passenger, also from Salisbury, whom they had befriended.

While they were in Durban we all four spent a lot of time

together. Their friend, Arthur, seemed extremely pleasant and reminded me, especially the way he spoke, of my father. The fact that he was twenty-five years older than me left me feeling pretty safe for he was obviously 'enamoured', but I didn't really at the time treat it seriously. Bad mistake. The next thing I knew, after their holiday ended, he returned to Durban for two weeks further holiday, and at the end of that time asked me to marry him. I have absolutely no idea why I accepted. I do not know to this very day what induced me. The continual flow of roses and letters and telephone calls was no deterrent. He returned to Durban again, and a year later we married in the historical Old Fort Chapel. My brother gave me away. Betty, Arthur's eldest daughter, was my bridesmaid – she insisted. She was two years younger than me, was an air hostess, unmarried, and lived with her mother, Nan, in Salisbury, now Harare. Arthur and Nan had been divorced for seven years, and were on amicable terms. There were two other adult children – another daughter, married, and a son who was single.

I think Arthur should be commended for taking on a much younger wife who had a small son and a little black dog to be cared for. To be honest, I had visions of a life of reasonable comfort without too many concerns, and in a way that is exactly what I got. But that age gap was a little too vast. If I had ideas of an older man being less 'physically capable' I was very quickly disillusioned. He was also a pure perfectionist. Perhaps being a surveyor had something to do with that. Meals had to be taken at exact times, to the minute. These had to follow a strict regimentation, fish Fridays, mince Mondays, etc., and homemade vegetable soup every single night. Table manners, which I had always thought to be acceptable, were now imperfect. Beds had to be made with army precision, no ornament moved a centimeter out of place. No television, so I put mine in Peter's bedroom. We had eighty rose trees in the garden, all different, each one squared off within a fraction of the next. No one was allowed to walk on the front lawn which was top-soiled annually. Each blade of grass seemed to know exactly how high to grow! The list could go on indefinitely. It was hard for me to conform, and impossible for Peter, a little boy. Even our servant asked me if the Bwana knew I had a child when he married me? Yet he was kind in a Victorian sort of way; very strict, but quite kind. He put me on a pedestal, but it took effort indeed to retain my balance.

We had been in Salisbury, now Harare, for about a week, when one night after dinner (always partaken at seven o'clock on the dot), I looked for Arthur and found him in bed fast asleep. This was part and parcel of his regular routine, and his first unbroken rule I was to experience. No "Goodnight", just silent disappearance. I didn't mind at all, but was somewhat disgruntled to discover that the physical bit would in future always occur at six o'clock in the morning! He also had a very bad habit of sending me to Coventry every couple of weeks; not speaking for as long as two days then continuing as if the silence had not happened. On the first occasion I was reduced to tears, but soon adjusted, and actually found it amusing, if a little weird.

Arthur insisted I work since I had to provide for Peter to a degree, in fact, for all things. I had a good job with the Rhodesian Medical Council. Peter attended the local Government School but was not very happy there. After days of indecision, on Arthur's insistence, it was decided I should apply to a boarding school. I was against it, and yet I began to think that Peter would probably be far happier. In desperation I approached a lawyer with a view to divorce, but was laughed out of the office. I had only been married six weeks. Then I approached the Department of Education and put my case before them. Living almost next door to a school, it was unlikely a place would be allocated to

Peter, so I felt fairly safe. I was very wrong. The gentleman in the Department not only listened, but advised, and then took the decision out of my hands and found a place for Peter at Hartley Junior School, an hour's train ride away, and where I could easily visit every week. So it was done. Hartley was the same village John and I had found ten years earlier when we slept in the car on our way to the coastal holiday, and found the Hartley Hotel five minutes' drive away, after being woken by the cows.

I saw Joan and Les, my friends who had introduced me to Arthur, quite often. Less frequently they visited us. She was a staunch friend. Her advice, once I asked for it, was to stick it out and make the best of it for, after all, it was 'an interlude in my life,' which was her way of putting it. I knuckled down and settled into quite a reasonable existence, if slightly clock-worked!

Peter also settled down. The first term for him was hard as the teacher was an unpleasant person and something of a bully. But by the second term a new teacher provided Peter with very good grounding. I went down there on his first Sports Day and was standing watching a three-legged race when the man next to me turned and exclaimed, "Patricia, what on earth are you doing here?" It was Dave Midgeley, a friend of one of my earliest boyfriends, Peter Pienaar, previously mentioned.

I told him my son was a boarder.

Dave replied "So is mine. But just weekly. My farm is not far off."

When I pointed Peter out, who was in the middle of a three-legged race, Dave was astonished. "Good heavens. He's tied to my son Alan. They're best friends."

Indeed it was so. Peter had mentioned this boy but I had not made the connection for only the first name was used. After that, and in fact before, Peter spent many a weekend on the farm with the Midgeleys, and on occasion I was invited for Sunday lunch.

Jumping ahead a little, when it was time for the boys to be entered into High School, I didn't know which to choose, or even where to begin. Dave said that they gave you three choices, but if you wanted one school in particular you had to put it under each choice. As far as Dave was concerned, there was only one choice, that being his own old school, Chaplin, in Gwelo. When the time came I did just that, and also Dave gave me a letter of recommendation. It worked. Chaplin happened to be co-ed, and the school that Ian Smith, our then Prime Minister, had attended. By all events I think they were undoubtedly the happiest school years of Peter's life.

Meanwhile my own life marched steadily, if slowly, onward. One of the nicest things about being married to Arthur was that I now had two holidays a year. He spoiled me atrociously when we were on our own! Twice a year he would take me to Beira, in Mozambique, for a few days where we would stay at the beautiful five star Dom Carlos Hotel. I loved it there, not just for the hotel, but being used to the massive surf of the Durban beaches, I could actually float here on the warm, gentle curve of the East African waves. For me, being a non-swimmer, this was a really enjoyable accomplishment.

I enjoyed my first taste of the full, juicy crayfish, crowned on each protruding tentacle by a number of tiny sweet red cherries. The owner of the hotel, once we had come to know him, met us at the airport in his personal car, and drove us to the hotel thereby avoiding the rickety old bus, or the unreliable taxi. For the first and only time in my life, I received a kiss on the hand at each greeting, and learnt that this is not an actual kiss, but a gentle breathing against the skin. Fact!

At Christmas time, after our first dismal festive season, Peter and I would entrain for Durban and take up a booking in one or another of the beachfront hotels. We loved the train ride, long but not boring, and of course, we loved the freedom to do as we wished. Stopping at stations in the middle of Botswana where, with Arthur, we would have been obliged to keep the windows closed with the blinds drawn, but we would hang out of the windows into the dry heat, and bargain with the locals for ridiculous items, or beautifully carved wooden animals. We walked the entire length of the very long train, stopping only to buy fizzy drinks in the dining car, and gorge ourselves in the same car for dinner where we ate anything that didn't look like soup! I didn't miss the crayfish.

When we woke up in Mafeking, the first train stop in South Africa, the train engine had been exchanged for a South African one, and all the staff swopped from Rhodesians to South Africans. This was the first time we experienced polystyrene cups. The cups were handed to us, in our coupe, and contained our early morning coffee. I thought the coffee cold, and the steward had to show me how to remove the lid to reveal the steaming contents.

In Durban, we caught up with all the old friends. Arthur, to give him his due, was always prepared to entertain my friends when he arrived. He would fly in just prior to Christmas Day, and then fly out again just after New Year's Eve. On one of our New Year evenings, when Arthur had retired to bed as always, we met up with the Headmaster of Hartley School, who coincidentally was staying in the same hotel, and saw in the New Year with him and his family. On our second Christmas trip, Peter, (who had his own single room while Arthur was in residence) and I joined other residents in throwing out the toilet rolls seemingly provided by the hotel for this very purpose, from the windows to create streamers to the revelers below. Silly, happy memory things. Then Peter and I would entrain back to Salisbury as it still was, in Rhodesia. Today of course, for those unfamiliar with African history, it is now Harare, in Zimbabwe.

I suppose it could, and should be, considered kind of Arthur to allow us to go off without him, but he wouldn't have enjoyed the things we did. Bearing in mind that it cost him nothing financially, since I paid for train fares and Peter's entire holiday as well as my own when Arthur wasn't there. Arthur paid for himself and for me, but only for the time I spent with him. Once he said he would ask for a separate bill for just Mr. and Mrs. Cole's holiday, but I put my foot down, and said it would make him look like an idiot, and he would just have to calculate the balances himself.

The last holiday Arthur and I took together was a trip to the Inyanga Mountains via Umtali, and as we were travelling by car we took Blackie, my little dog, along with us. I wanted to see the cottage Cecil John Rhodes stayed in during his visits there, and Arthur wanted to spend a few days trout fishing.

One of the pioneers of Rhodesia was a man called Moodie and his grave lies forlorn and lonely between the main winding road and the mountains. I wanted to see that too, just to let him know he was still remembered, if perhaps only by me. The Inyanga Mountains, tall and majestic, divide Rhodesia/Zimbabwe from Mozambique and stretch right down to the tip of the Kruger National Park in South Africa, where they become the Lebomba Mountains, and thence almost to the magnificent Drakensburg.

Arthur would not drive any distance in his own car for reasons I was never told, and I was driving my own Volkswagon Variant. As I was driving along a particular straight stretch of good macadam I noticed ahead a troupe of baboons in the middle of the road. We drove closer and Arthur said, "Do not stop. Do not speed. Keep the window closed and continue driving steadily ahead." I tried not to look at any of them but it was difficult not to notice one of them lying prone in the middle of the road. I hoped he was dead and not injured, but there was nothing we could do with any safety for the animals were extremely angry, showing fangs and gesticulating. I felt like a zombie myself, driving mechanically and stoically until Arthur instructed: "Right. Accelerate". I did. It was very sad but also very frightening. We reported it at the next town.

It was shortly after this that we took the turning directing us to Moodie's grave, and parked alongside what amounted to nothing more than an animal track. We walked along this with waist-high brown grass on each side. Blackie pulled ahead on his leash. All of a sudden the little dog totally collapsed. Initially we thought it might have been a snake, but there was no sign of one. Blackie lay unconscious. I gathered him up and we walked back to the road where there was a stone culvert which afforded some shade. Into this I crawled with Blackie. He came around and opened his eyes but he was very weak. Arthur now had little choice and had to drive, like it or not. We returned to Umtali and found a veterinarian. I thought Blackie might have suffered a heart attack, but the idiot of a vet. gave him a bilharzia injection in case he had been bitten by a mosquito! This only served to induce vomiting and the poor little chap threw up violently into my lap. We repaired to the local hotel and while Arthur ordered tea on the verandah, I contrived to visit the ladies rest room draped in a towel beneath which I cradled my little dog without detection. We cancelled all thoughts of continuing a holiday and returned immediately to Salisbury (Harare). Arthur drove slowly but steadily for about 5 hours while I nursed Blackie whose eyes never left mine. I talked quietly to him all the way and we reached our local veterinarian in time for the evening surgery. The Vet. put the stethoscope in my ears and told me to listen. Blackie's little heart was giving weak intermittent soft beats, and I was told it was time to let him go. I continued to nurse him, talking and looking into his eyes until they finally closed, and the Vet. told me it was over. So was another piece of my life.

Arthur arranged to have a deep hole dug beneath the oak tree in a corner of our garden, and there we laid Blackie. Arthur maintained that a rose tree could be dug up, but no one would disturb an oak tree. He was very wrong. On returning to that part of the world, after it too had gained independence, I hired a taxi for the day. I took flowers to the Warren Hills Cemetery, and found the copper had been stolen from all the memorial plaques. Then I called in at the house. There was no one at home. The rose trees had all gone, and someone had chopped down the oak tree. I returned to the taxi in a flood of tears. The taxi driver put his arm around me and said I should not look backwards. Here I am today, digging up almost everything I can remember, writing it down, and doing just that: looking backward.

There is no doubt that although Arthur was a difficult man to live with, as his previous family would attest, he was extremely kind. We tried doing without a dog, but it was difficult. You expect them to be there and look round before remembering they have gone. You write down dog food on the shopping list, and then scratch it out. But most of all you miss their very presence. Within about a month we decided another dog would help to fill the empty space. Looking at dog pictures we both decided that a Staffordshire Bull Terrier looked most like Blackie. Not at all so! A Staffie is more than twice the size, and the temperament couldn't be more different. Yet a Staffie is what I chose, and Arthur named him Tiger.

One Saturday morning in May, before I had risen, when Tiger was still a puppy and too small to jump upon the bed, Arthur lifted him up to me, and then turned to the window. It was pouring with rain. No rose garden this morning. Arthur turned back to me clutching both hands to his chest, with a face as gray as the day outside. I knew immediately that he was about to have a heart attack. It was an instant thought and before I knew it I was out of bed and helping him into it. He was in great pain and although I immediately phoned the doctor, there was no sign of a doctor or an ambulance for a good twenty minutes. All I could do was remain calm, and keep Arthur calm and quiet. Shockingly, I thought, when the ambulance did arrive, without a doctor, Arthur was made to walk the length of the bedroom passage to the lounge where the stretcher was. It was I, not the men, who found the strength to lift him from the sitting position he had assumed at the foot of the stretcher, into a semi prone one, before the ambulance men wheeled him out of the house to reach the vehicle. The second attack occurred as the stretcher was shifted into the ambulance. I was standing at the foot of the stretcher, and watched as Arthur died before my eyes. Days later I wrote a strong letter to the Medical Council as a result of which, I understand, a more mobile system was introduced. I truly believe that he might have lived had he not been obliged to walk the length of the house to reach the stretcher.

Thus did another period of my life reach its ultimate conclusion.

What to do now? I needed time to think, and knew I must not sink into another quagmire of indecision. This time I must think before acting. I was growing older and wiser, or so I thought. I was forty years old. Decisions had to be made, and there must be no turning back.

Peter was sent home from school for a week, and my dearest friend Joan, who had introduced me to Arthur, spent many hours with me. She talked, I listened. We lit the wood fire two weeks before due date. Arthur would only light it on a certain day each year. But this was a particularly cold spell and I didn't think he would mind! I hauled out a pile of letters from Winifred which I had not read, and one by one we burned them in the wood fire. Joan read a few of them and with her sense of humour made fun of them all.

I had organised a fitting funeral for a man well liked within his little circle. The Presbyterian minister of that particular local church visited at my request, and also went to see Nan, Arthur's ex-wife who obviously knew more about Arthur than I did. At the chapel Nan and her family sat in the front row on the right, and I sat on the left with my son beside me until Joan, who had been seated at the back somewhere, moved up to sit on my other side. There had only been one rose in the entire garden, and that was a Papa Meilon, a deep dark red, which I had cut and placed on the top of the coffin. It was Arthur's favourite rose.

24

You can, because you must.
         Goethe 1749-1832

After the funeral, and once Peter had returned to school, I began to seriously consider what should be my next move. Politically it would perhaps be wise for me, as a single mother and living alone in a country which itself was insecure, to consider making yet another move. I had to think of a future for my son while he was still young enough not to be disturbed by a further change in education. With this in mind, I made an appointment with the Headmaster of Chaplin School fully prepared to take his advice before making a decision I might regret at a later date. He was wise in his advice and I made all my plans accordingly. It was decided that Peter should continue at Chaplin for a further year, so that if it was decided I should leave Rhodesia it would be timed so Peter could begin his new school year at the very beginning of the three year senior matriculation syllabus. It was also decided that he should remain a boarder, provided I transferred to Gwelo so that he could become a weekly student. My immediate future, and Peter's was marked out.

Arthur had left me without any money, but willed the house to me along with a small investment in South Africa, probably wisely believing that I would return there. His previous family benefited from any monies available in Rhodesia, and whatever I might like to give them of his personal items, which I divided up between them. Regretfully I had to sell his car so that I could pay for the expenses incurred by his death. I sold the house, and moved into a government rental property in the next suburb. I was entitled to this, as by now I was working within the Ian Smith government as a researcher delving into the African Chiefs' Totems, Tribal Laws and Customs. Fascinating stuff. I put in for a transfer to the Provincial Commission in Gwelo, the small mining town where Chaplin School was situated, and then sat back to see what would happen. It looked like I was on the move again.

Meanwhile, the lady from whom we had purchased our dog, Tiger, telephoned to enquire if I would like a fully mature female Staffie who had turned out to be a queen. This is a term applied to a bitch who is unlikely, or unable, to have puppies. Being established breeders they were anxious to find a good home for her. I explained that my situation had changed and I was unable to purchase a second dog, but she said that she wanted to give the dog to me because she knew it would be going to a good home. She was presently in season and was kenneled for the duration. From there I could collect her. This all coincided with my transfer being granted, a private rental property in Gwelo obtained, and my move to that fair town imminent. That was how Bess came to join Tiger, together with Arthur's old black cat, in my little car en route for a mining town halfway between Salisbury and Bulawayo. I was a devil for punishment!

I had been in my new abode for about a month when a short school holiday came up, and I decided it was an appropriate time to visit Durban and have Peter sit the entrance test for Durban Boys High, one of the best government schools at that time in South Africa. I had by now definitely decided to return to Durban armed with the knowledge that the outcome of schooling for my son had been determined in the best possible manner. It was a good time too for house searching in Durban bearing in mind that the area had a large part to play in the zoning of students for Durban Boys High, locally known as D.H.S. or Durban High School.

I had remained in contact with Terry and Pat Webb, the people from whom John and I had purchased the shop. In fact, Terry had managed my financial affairs, small though they were, from the time of John's death. I say 'managed' but perhaps 'advised' would be a better word. He had, for instance, been against my purchasing a small simplex to house Arthur, Peter and myself, and had been quite worried that I would over-ride his advice had I been able to convince Arthur to up sticks. Now that I had made yet another earth-shattering decision, his knowledge and know-how was invaluable. He put me under the wing of a highly respected agent, and a small selection of properties was made available for inspection. Only one of these fell within the time frame for there were still several months to go. This was a delightful house on the edge of the Berea, between my two friends Margaret and Joy, appropriately zoned for D.H.S., freehold, with an enclosed garden suitable for energetic dogs. Terry had ensured the money from the shop had been well cared for, and Arthur had left me a little in South African shares. I was by no means rich but there was enough to buy the property. Terry suggested I return to Rhodesia as soon as our holiday was over, and told me he would take care of the details. All I had to worry about was packing up and moving south.

I ought to have known better. No sooner had I returned to the hotel than a message came through that Bess, my so-called queen Staffie, had been covered by Tiger, and was probably pregnant. Impossible. She had only recently finished a season. I have since learnt that dogs, rather like humans, will come into season if distressed or over-excited. I was told that, quite often in the dog world, a female will not mate with a male if she doesn't like the dog. Bess, it seemed, liked Tiger, or did then! She had undergone two seasons in less than three months. With hindsight, I should have had her aborted, but the idea did not come to me until much too late.

The due date arrived. I was given compassionate leave and watched her produce six beautiful puppies. An expensive experience as it was necessary for me to create a kennel name and register them all with the Kennel Club of South Africa in Capetown. An added expense was Tiger, jealous of the attention being given to others, had set about finding something to attract my attention. I went in search of the scrunching sound coming from the lounge to find him busily nibbling away at my top denture which I had left on the dressing table the night before. Quite disgusting, but extremely funny. I gathered up all the bits of teeth, soaked them in disinfectant, and stuck them all back together again. I was only missing one little bit which he had probably swallowed. Of course, they didn't fit me. The dentist I presented myself to on the way to work, roared with laughter and said it was not an unusual occurrence. What was unusual was that I had stuck them back together. Nobody ever did that.

I spent the following two days at the office neither speaking nor smiling no matter how much they tried to make me laugh, until the teeth were returned to me, and gave me another twenty years or so of gnawing. I only sold one of the puppies, to a family who came all the way up from Bulawayo to fetch him. Definitely the best of the litter, I called him Bruiser because that he certainly was. They kept the name. The others I gave away to carefully selected homes, together with the Registration Certificates.

We prepared to depart for Durban, and in due course we were on our way once again.

25

*There are very few mistakes in life
that cannot be corrected – if you've got the courage.*

I had bribed the furniture van's driver with the gift of Marie's old Hoover washing machine, which she had so kindly given me all those years before, if he arrived at the front gate of the house Terry had successfully negotiated, for me, by 8 o'clock on the morning of 1st December. Peter and I, with the dogs, took our time, making three night stops – where dogs were permitted – which I had planned and booked ahead. We descended on friends for the final night, leaving the dogs to sleep in the car, so that we were able to meet the van on time.

Sure enough, the African driver arrived ten minutes later, a very large grin on his face. He had changed crews at the border crossing, and was not at all impressed with the local crew members, which we found amusing. However, we were obliged to sit in a row on the pavement with our feet in the gutter waiting for the owner, whom we had agreed to meet there, to depart from the now empty house and hand over the keys. This he did as the church clock down the road struck 12 noon. It had not occurred to me that, by law, I could not take possession until midday on the day of the transfer. He, the previous owner, definitely stuck to the letter of the law, which confirmed my opinion that there's 'nowt so funny as folk'!

We lived happily in that little house for eight years. Life was about as normal as life could be for a widow bringing up a young boy, and grooming him for manhood. I had been blessed with an intelligent youngster who fortunately was very much like his father in character. His only real disappointment in the school change was that he had not been chosen for the rugby team, and was only a reserve. Instead he took up gymnastics, did pretty well, and joined the Durban Gymnastic Club. In his final year at school, when his coach at the club wanted him to put in six hours practice daily in the hope of good things, I had to put my foot down and say matriculation was more important. In any case, Peter had only one dream, and that was to fly aeroplanes. Even when his father had been alive, flying had been his only love, so much so that I recall John saying that if Peter wanted to be a pilot there was nothing to stand in his way except that he must do it properly. I tried once to dissuade him, to no avail. In Arthur's day Peter would cycle to the aero club, and once cadged a flight on a glider, to my horror. In Durban it was no different. When his friends were surfing the curling waves off the golden beaches, Peter was as often as not, working in the office of the Durban Wings Club earning enough money to pay for his flying lessons. In fact he obtained his Private Pilot's Licence before he was old enough to take his Driver's Licence!

As for me, after one or two false starts, I found a job at the Lion Match Company which was just down the road. I was employed in the Human Resources Department, known as Personnel, who paid everyone. I only worked during the mornings because I liked to be at home when Peter returned from school. However, once he entered the wide, wild world, I extended my hours to full-time, and by doing so became a member of the pension scheme.

We were in constant touch with Marie and John Hopton from our Kitwe days and often visited them in Johannesburg, and they us in Durban. My old Durban friends were all close by, and now

I had added two of the greatest friends in my life, Margaret Massabo, previously mentioned, and Joy Bell a new neighbour of Margaret's. These last two, and myself, became known to our other friends and acquaintances as the Golden Girls, a skit on the sitcom of that name, because we did almost everything together. Each Saturday night we spent alternating between one house for dinner and the next, with the fourth Saturday as a restaurant treat. Margaret's husband, Roberto, had succumbed to a fatal heart attack while I had been in Rhodesia, and Joy had been widowed before I met her. We all three had the occasional odd male friend but nothing ever came of any of them. I made two more dear friends with whom I worked: Pearle Ham, my boss, and Margaret Haskins, my colleague. Both had a great influence on my life. Sometimes my old Rhodesian friends from Kitwe, or from Salisbury, would come and stay for a few days. They were all now scattered throughout various areas of Southern Africa, and having Durban as a place to visit was something of a treat for those who did not live by the sea. I kept in touch with quite a few until they either left the continent of Africa forever, or passed on to different climes.

It seemed to me that nothing ever stayed the same. My dear friend Julie, whom I had met again in Kitwe, had departed for Canada. Bob and Lillian were no longer around because Bob had died. Lillian became something of a recluse, and eventually took her own life by quaffing two bottles of red wine and a bottle of sleeping pills. Little Lucy, whose bridesmaid I had been, was another old friend. (I lost touch with her for a period in later years, but recently on visiting Durban I did some investigating and telephoned her. I did not say who I was but she guessed immediately. We spent an entire day together and never stopped talking. I remain in contact.)

One day, out of the blue, I received a visit from the authorities in the form of two gentlemen who issued me with a warning. It seems a neighbour had complained about my dogs barking in the mornings. They informed me that there had been two complaints from the same person. The men were very kind and pleasant, but they had to do their jobs. Should a third complaint be made, they would impound the animals without further warning. I wondered what would happen if I complained about the two screaming boys who played daily in the pool behind my back fence!

It was time to employ an African maid for the mornings only so that she would ensure the dogs, though allowed to bark because they were dogs, would not do so quite so frequently or so loudly! She would be my dog sitter so I would have to find someone that actually liked dogs. In those days there was an official employment agency with long lists of people looking for work, and down to this I went, with Tiger, the male bull terrier in the car on the back seat. I was offered four hopefuls all swearing their love of dogs, and led all four to my parked car. Tiger sat, pink tongue lolling, waiting patiently for me. As I opened the driver's door I called across to my aspiring applicants that they could open the passenger door. Holding Tiger, who was now very excited, by his collar, I got in myself. I watched as three of the applicants, shouting and gesticulating as only Africans can, disappeared en route back to the office. The fourth calmly opened the door and climbed in, albeit gingerly. I was still in control of Tiger, with some difficulty as he was in the back seat, but he took an instant liking to the woman, roughly pushed off her "dook" (a cotton headdress) and slobbered all over her in his anxiety to sit on her lap. I had found a dog sitting treasure.

I was having a little problem with my Staffies. Bess had taken a dislike to Tiger and fought him constantly. During the last fight her eye-tooth became lodged in his dewlap and his shrieks of pain were dreadful to hear. I had to hold the two heads together with my knees so that I could ease her tooth out. After that I found an excellent home for her, better than mine, after widely advertising and turning down several applications.

I acquired a stray cat that Peter brought home from school, but she disappeared one evening and we searched the neighbourhood for hours but could not find her. The next morning we found her dead body right by our front gate. She had either crawled home, or someone had dumped her. The Vet. thought she had been hit by a vehicle. Later I bought a sable Burmese kitten from a friend at work. After this kitten had lived with us for a few weeks, she thought she was a dog! How intelligent they are. One evening we heard a great screech of brakes. Peter fled out of the front gate only to return to pick up a spade. I was devastated. The lady who had hit her was very distressed. She said it was unavoidable and offered to replace her, but I couldn't face a third attempt. Dogs you can keep in, cats not.

I settled for a miniature Pomeranian. Why I felt the need to have a third dog I simply do not know. But they all got along very well together and it was quite safe to leave them alone while I was at work. I forgot to mention earlier that I had kept the last of the puppies and called her Elsa.

My life, which should have been boring with the constant everyday things one had to continually do, was anything but. Instead it was full of twists and turns, of ups and downs – some of my own making, some just destiny.

26

Select a pup and your money will buy,
Love unflinching that cannot lie.
But when the dog that lived at your single will
And its whimper of welcome is stilled, how still,
Then brothers and sisters I bid you beware'
Of giving your heart to a dog to tear.
              With thanks to Rudyard Kipling.

I decided to make alterations to my house and turn it into two attached cottages. It was really too big for me now that Peter was older and likely to leave home once his schooling was complete. No encouragement to further his education to a facility for higher learning was likely to be considered by him. His only desire was to become a pilot.

The idea of turning my house into two cottages was a good one. I could rent one side and live in the other. The plan went ahead and I employed what later could only be described as a backyard builder, and the alteration began. It should have been simple.

From where did I get the idea that anything in my life could possibly be simple?

During the period I was at work I was obliged to lock the dogs in one of the rooms that was not being affected. One day the builder phoned me while I was at work and told me that there had been a dog fight in this room, and he thought my little Pom was dead. I'm ashamed to say I went a little mad, pummeled my boss on his chest with my fists. and told him that everything I loved was taken away from me. Peter had been called away to his army training – it being compulsory at that time – and I was totally alone. My bruised boss went off to see Margaret Massabo, my close friend, and the two of them, who now had my keys, went off to see the damage. It was considerable. Margaret telephoned me and told me to call upon her before I went home, and indeed I had to in order to collect my keys. She was able to explain that my poor little dog was dead, but she had removed all trace of her. I could blame neither Tiger or Elsa, because they would only have done what came naturally to them, and in their excitement had overdone it. The blame was due entirely to my stupidity. The African builders with their shouts, and general builders noise would have excited all three dogs. The outcome should have been obvious to me.

There were no further incidents, unless you count the builder who, instead of building, used my shower and walked right through the glass door! The new sewerage ditches collapsed inwards after heavy rains, before the inspectors had chance to look at them. Not the builders fault, but it added for the delays and extra expense. So much for my foray into the building world.

In due course the place was complete and I was delighted to advertise the rental available which read something like 'Dogs allowed. Only pet lovers need apply.' As a result of this I accepted a young couple who brought with them a small puppy who grew into a bull mastiff of gigantic proportions.

The years passed rapidly enough. In the fullness of time, Peter left school and applied to the South African Air Force where he hoped to complete his two year compulsory military training. He had long since obtained his private pilot's licence, but this did not appear to have any bearing, and his application for the Air Force was ignored. Instead he was commanded to report to an army light infantry contingent and entrained for points north and Potchefstroom, a small town not far from Johannesburg in the Transvaal. He was chosen for the Army Officers Training Course, but he refused the offer because he was hoping to hear from the Air Force. After some months the signal was unearthed from wherever it had lain, and he was transferred accordingly.

Meanwhile, adjusting to a life without my son was difficult, and I found myself counting the days between his home visits. These were rare indeed, especially during the training period, but eventually, once he had obtained a car, dilapidated though it was, he was able to visit more frequently, nearly always with several other trainee pilots in tow. Having decreased the size of my house, this became a difficulty, overcome by the number of sleeping bags placed in a row across the lounge floor. I never knew how many bodies I would have to step over on a Saturday morning.

The three hundred odd applicants to the training course were, over the weeks, whittled down to twenty-four, and it was a proud moment indeed when I witnessed the Chief of Air Force pin the wings on not only my son's chest, but on the chests of several other young men whom I had come to know.

My worries had only just begun. Peter, along with many others, was posted to trouble spots, flying single engine spotter aircraft, which hovered over these areas until the more substantial jets arrived. More than one young pilot lost his life one way or another. I attended two military funerals from his unit, one of them on my own. On this latter occasion it was a graveside service and I couldn't help but stifle a sob when I saw the coffin containing a young man whose nickname was Sunshine, disappearing with his formal ceremonial sword and cap gleaming atop the coffin. A woman beside me put her arm across my shoulder and told me to be brave. I was happy when Peter transferred from fixed wing to helicopters and moveable blades. Then, of course, my worry was what would happen if the blades stopped spinning!

I could write extensively about The Adventures of Peter, and that would be another story, but one such escapade comes immediately to mind. He and a friend decided to put their motor bikes (oh yes, he had one!) to good use, and travel from Capetown to Johannesburg, a distance of 1,397 kilometers. They made it as far as the Roadhouse, just south of Johannesburg, from where they were both rescued by the sons of Marie and John Hopton, muscles cramped with pain, exhausted and dirty. Marie deposited them in hot baths, fed them, and sent them to bed.

I still had two of my dogs, Tiger and Elsa. Peter sometimes took Tiger surfing when the time allowed. On one such occasion, Tiger, now wearing the new-fangled flea collar, came home soaked and salty, and we hosed him down with fresh water. Later that night I was woken by his antics. He was having his first epileptic seizure and was to suffer from these for the rest of his life. The vet. told us that we should not have allowed the collar to become wet, which instruction was given with the collar when first purchased, but I had not read the fine print. This had caused a serious reaction in insecticide poisoning, and damaged that part of the brain from which stems epilepsy. He was under continual human medication. I would hold him down during fits by lying on top of him until the vet. warned me of the danger of doing this, and instructed me to cover him with a blanket, and only then restrain him. A sad state of affairs, but like a human being he quickly recovered and was quite happy and normal in between time.

Letters continued to arrive from Winifred. Occasionally I read one. They all harped upon the same theme: what she had done for someone else's children, and how she deserved better. Most

I disregarded. Once, Peter collected the mail and tore up the blue airmail letter before I had chance to be distressed.

One day he suggested I ought to try and find my real mother. I pondered this, and decided it was as good idea. All I needed to do was contact the same lawyers I had been instructed to visit when we were running the fish and chip shop in Eastborne, and were in need of money to pay my father's back income tax. I did so, and within a very short space of time was given the address of Eileen Lamb, living in Fowey, Cornwall, as a widow in much reduced circumstances to what she had once been accustomed. Bingo! Thus began a deluge of letters, like a love affair between a long lost mother and her daughter.

At about the same time I heard that dear old Mum, Peter's grandmother, who had long been widowed, was living in Halifax, Yorkshire. She had taken an overdose of pills and was hospitalised. It was time for me to take action.

Gathering together all my financial resources, and planning everything down to the last detail, I booked an airfare to London. I employed an elderly lady to live in my house and dog sit, and departed happily for England's green and pleasant pastures in the Spring. I worried about Mum, but had kept in touch with the hospital who informed me that she had returned home to her council flat, where she was checked occasionally by the caretaker.

Winifred, my stepmother, was also living in Yorkshire, ensconced in a private flat as a sitting-tenant in Bridlington, the town where I had spent some of my disrupted early teenage years. She had been attacked by a number of teenage boys, and robbed of her purse, apparently wadded with pounds sterling! She was a leukaemia sufferer and had acquired a male live-in sub-tenant, who saw to her needs. She was, in general, a mess. The owner of the flat wanted her out, but she could not legally be evicted.

Eileen, my real mother, awaited my arrival with, I suspect,

some trepidation

    All said, what had I let myself in for? I found out soon enough.

27

This only is denied to God:
The power to change the past.
> *Remembered by Aristotle 322BC*
> *But attributed to Agathon 400BC*

I decided before I faced these three dilemmas, or perhaps three 'mothers' is more appropriate, I would take a ten day spell in London and look at all the historic places I longed to visit, from the tiny square where the last rapier duel in London was fought, to the scale where all George III's children were weighed. So was I. I kept notes which I still read and take pleasure in to this day. I wrote a note to Winifred saying I would visit her for two days on such and such a date. It took me a few moments with my hand in the mouth of the red post box before I could bring myself to drop the letter, and therefore commit myself. Finally it was done.

Dear Mum, my husband's mother who was more like a mother to me than either of my own, was living in a Council flat in Halifax where she was neglecting herself. I made arrangements to transfer her to a local government home for the aged where she could have an independent little flat with all the facilities including a small kitchen. The great advantage was that there was constant daily care. Menus were delivered each morning whereby a meal could be taken daily in the dining room if required. I moved her myself, packing everything up, and taking even the carpet to her new abode. Before she moved we took a couple of days off and caught the bus over to York where we stayed in a little boarding house right outside one of the Gates in the City walls, so we couldn't possibly have found anywhere nearer the oldest part of the City. Mum was pretty bored after a while, but was happy for me to drop her every hour or so in a nearby café where she could indulge her fancy for sweet delicacies, while I loped around the Shambles, or tore around the top of the walls, or seeped up history in tiny churches looking almost exactly as they had three or four hundred years earlier. The Cathedral we explored together. It was all quite an experience for her and I know she enjoyed it.

During the time I stayed with Mum I took the promised trip by bus to see Winifred in Bridlington. I did not stay with her, but asked the taxi driver at the bus station to take me to a pleasant private hotel quite near to where she lived. My heart was in my mouth – well perhaps not, but it was certainly beating loudly – when I knocked on the door of her first floor flat which displayed a card stating Mrs. Winifred Part, Private. She ought to have added 'Beware all ye who enter here'. I could hear voices so I was aware that she had visitors which I thought was a good thing as they might smooth the initial greeting. It was a man who turned out to be the lodger who saw to her needs, whatever they were. He was in his mid-sixties and a nice enough man, sleeping in the adjoining back bedroom. Her bed was in the living room facing the television. Unlike John's mother, Mum, Winifred, although accepting the government pension, had refused to go into a council flat, deeming it beneath her. I have since had the thought that she was also more than likely to be in receipt of a Royal Air Force Pension. Even so, while I was there, she was happy to accept the few notes I had in my purse. The lodger, whose name eludes me, left us and we spent the remainder of the day talking pleasantly enough.

The following day, after rising early, I spent an hour on a memory walk before I returned again to her flat. The lodger and she were engaged in loud words to which I listened with some amusement until I rose from my chair and prepared to depart saying I had better things to do than listen to inane squabbles. The squabbles ended abruptly, the lodger departed, and I was left alone with Winifred. (It strikes me, as I write this now. that I should have spoken to her with such forcefulness many years earlier, had I not been so terrified of her. Perhaps I would not now be ironing other peoples' shirts in order to eke out my pension.) She spoke to me of her illness and how she was carted off to hospital in Driffield, a town some miles distance, there to undergo blood transfusions to cope with the leukemia, but did not add that this was all done under the National Health Scheme. I have no doubt she made herself unpleasant there, for she told me, braggingly, that when she had to share a room she twisted the television set toward her bed so that the other lady could not share the pleasure.

The lodger returned and I regret I cannot remember his name because he was very pleasant to me. He very kindly took me in his car for a short drive around Bridlington, and at my request, to the old convent school where I had learnt to be a lady, if nothing else. The school proper had been transferred to another area and the house turned into a home for retired nuns. I was invited for tea with one of the older nuns who knew some of the ladies who had taught me. They were all dead, but this little modern nun had memories of them. Although we had tea my visit had to be brief since I was to meet the lodger at the local ancient pub. Needless to say, I didn't enlighten the nun, although no doubt she would have been amused by my reticence! This was the pub, I learned, from which Winifred had been banned for life. On my return to Winifred, I didn't enlighten her either!

Unknowingly, I was about to be enlightened myself, with the second of Winifred's Cardinal Sins even worse than the first.

The following day, toward the end of my visit I casually asked what had happened to the Fillingham Williams Trust Fund that my brother and I had ceded to her all those many years earlier.

"I spent it," she replied without so much as a blush, which shocked me into silence. Trust Funds cannot actually be broken, but the secondary beneficiaries can cede it, and the Title sold, probably to a money lender, who then must wait for the original beneficiary to die. Both my brother and I, although we knew her faults, never for a moment imagined that she would ever dispose of it, except by willing it back to us. I wonder if she ever told her family, or anybody else, what she had done. Certainly she was no longer the unpaid nursemaid of her favourite refrain, but one of the highest paid in the history of nursemaids! With the proceeds she had paid a visit to the south of France, the Casino, and Monaco. She had also visited friends in Canada where she had planned to live. Surprise, surprise, it did not work out with the friends, and she returned to England with her tail between her legs, and probably out of Funds. (Ours!) That is not how she told the story, but it gives me pleasure to tell it my way!

Eileen, our mother, who received an annual income from the Trust until the day she died, knew what had happened, yet never once reproached us. In the end we really only had ourselves to blame.

As I took my farewell, which indeed it was, I experienced a strange sensation: I actually felt sorry for her.

On the bus, returning to Halifax and my dear other Mum, I watched through the window the sunset reflecting shades of pink, orange and lilac across the darkening sky. The silver of the clouds slowly turned into night, and I prayed for the woman I had left behind. Departing from Halifax was sad too, for I knew I would not see John's mother again. She did not need prayers, for she was a good and gentle person who had given me more than love, and indeed she did indeed pass quietly away within twelve months of our sad goodbye.

On my way down to Cornwall I dropped off in London for an extra day because I had promised Winifred I would visit the Royal Air Force Benevolent people, which address she had given me, to see if they could accommodate her, as the widow of a retired permanent air force Wing Commander, in more salubrious surroundings than she was presently enjoying. It was explained to me that she had given them no end of trouble with continual letters and demands. They had offered her accommodation in the sergeants and other ranks establishments, which she had rudely refused. They said they could hardly put her with other officers' widows, and sorry as they were, they knew I would understand. I did. I was also ashamed.

At last I was on my way to meet my blood mother, waiting patiently at a bus stop conveniently situated next to a pub on the edge of Dartmoor. This was Mama who had not seen me for over forty years. We were strangers to each other, apart from the letters we had recently exchanged. She had arrived ahead of me by some thirty minutes. When I alighted from the bus in what appeared to be the middle of nowhere, there was no one in sight. I headed toward the lights of the pub, and met my mother halfway. We hugged in the centre of the road. It was dark so my vision of her was limited, unlike the scent which was not my favourite – whisky. Perhaps, thought I, she had fortified herself with a dram or two at the pub. I don't know what I expected, but it certainly wasn't this. This was no simple, sweet old lady like dear old Mum left behind in Halifax. Nor was she a brassy, faded blonde like Winifred in Bridlington. This was a competent woman who, when she spoke, sounded like the Queen of

England. I hoped I would come to like her, but my initial reaction was disappointment. My Halifax Mum had said I was expecting too much. Perhaps Mama's opinion of me was similar. We travelled in the back of the taxi to Fowey, making stilted, polite conversation in front of the taxi driver, whom I was aware could hear every awkward sentence that passed. We were both relieved to finally arrive at our destination.

The accommodation was a very comfortable one bedroom apartment in a rather superior Council block perched on the top of the hill above the town of Fowey, on the banks of the River Fowey. For a person who had once owned several houses scattered across the southern counties of England, she had dropped dramatically down the ladder. But she was comfortable, happy, and still in receipt of the allowance she received from the Fillingham Williams Trust Fund. That was at least something that could not be taken from her. With this, and perhaps with other income from her second husband, she lived a pleasant albeit unproductive life in this beautiful area of Cornwall. That she missed, and had dearly loved that husband, was evident by the marks on the wall in the flat from the tyres of his wheelchair, which she refused to have cleaned.

Of course I could not have visited an area more suited to my idea of history, surrounded as Fowey is with historical events dating back almost as far as it is possible to delve. I could explore with ever increasing interest, the old churches and ancient meadows seeped in history of bygone years. Even the Cornish fabled knight, Tristan, a medieval lover, held some sway. A Stone of Tristan, in a field near Fowey, is a granite pillar immortalising him, and can be spied by clambering up a tall Cornish hedgerow and peering between the brambles at the top. Mama knew where all these secret treasures were, and although not particularly interested herself, was happy to indulge me. Oh what bliss, not to be scorned! There was but one car for hire in Fowey, and Mama had managed to obtain it as a gift for me for the duration of my visit.

We drove to almost every National Trust House in Cornwall, and many of the churches; walked the causeway to Michaels Mount, and visited Lizard's Point, the true southernmost point of England, not Land's End as many believe. By this time I had discovered the green gin bottle in the kitchen cupboard which went down 15 mm's or so, along with the orange juice every morning. I just wish she could have told me instead of trying to hide it, then I could have ensured she did not have to get distressed every time we didn't find a pub in time for the next shot. After all, she was doing a lot for me to keep me happy!

Once, when I could not enter a particular church I wanted to see, she enquired from the local pub where she could find the vicar. Receiving the information she popped out of the pub, walked along the road passed a house or two, knocked on his door, requested the key and permission to enter the church, leaving me nursing a warm lemonade blissfully unaware of her doings. Neither the key nor the permission were forthcoming, but at least she tried. On another occasion, while visiting a well-known National Trust House, she nipped over the guard ropes, and seated herself at the Duchess' dressing table pretending to powder her nose. I'm afraid I pretended too: not to know her! We visited Jamaica Inn, the pub on Bodmin Moor, made famous by du Maurier's book of that name, which Mama and her second husband had run at the time before his illness and subsequent death. We had hoped to return to Fowey across Bodmin Moor, but the mists came down and I was too afraid to drive across, so, much to Mama's dismay, I drove the long way around adding a considerable number of kilometres to the next drink.

To reach Boddinick on the other side of the river, we had to take the ferry. This in itself was quite an experience for me as the ferry was in the process of departing. I was directed to drive over a downward sloping concrete ramp, already awash with water, through about six inches of river, and up the boat's ramp to dry safety. We visited some friends whose little cottage near the quay fascinated me. It was so very, very old you had to walk uphill in several of these rooms in order to reach the opposite side of them. Presumably the cottage had settled over the years.

From the river we had a wonderful view of the house Daphne du Maurier called home at that time. Although this paragraph might appear to be irrelevant here, I am including it because it has a great bearing on my story, particularly later, when writing of my visit to Arnhem. Author of many Cornish novels, she had previously leased, from the Rashleigh family, their house Menabilly, west of Fowey. It had been the seat of the Rashleigh family since the sixteenth century, but the family had temporarily moved away. Daphne, Lady Browning, was married to Lt. Gen. Frederick Browning who had been the Commander of the First Allied Airborne Army during Operation Market Garden of *A Bridge Too Far* fame, the phrase used in relation to Arnhem Bridge in the Netherlands, (see a later Chapter), and she had rented the house, living there from 1943 to 1969. I mention this here because Menabilly is used several times in her novels, notably perhaps in *Rebecca*. Because of my interest in anything historical, Mama introduced me to a woman whose grandfather had been a coachman to the Rashleigh family. A relative of this woman was a builder who had been doing some repair work to the roof of Menabilly. He very kindly gave me two handmade six inch iron roofing nails which were very, very old. They became treasured possessions.

My brother Antony, and I had arranged that Mama, who had purchased her own ticket, would return with me to South Africa for a six week holiday, three weeks with me, and three with my brother who was then living in Pietermaritzburg in the Natal Midlands. My time was drawing to a close and Mama, true to form, booked a taxi from the man from whom she had hired the car, which took us from Fowey to Plymouth where we were to catch the Heathrow Bus. On arrival in Plymouth she disappeared, presumably to visit the powder room, as I sat on the bench and waited patiently. Five minutes before departure time she reappeared and it occurred to me that this was typical of Mama. She might keep you waiting but she would never let you down – except, of course, for that dreadful faux pas she had made all those years before.

As she climbed aboard I took her carry-on bag which rattled suspiciously of bottles, as indeed they were: little miniatures of various alcoholic beverages with which to fortify the trip. Hence the disappearance at Plymouth. Mama had booked us into the Coach Inn at Heathrow for the night, hoping it would be historical for my enjoyment, but of course it wasn't. Again, the thought was to be commended.

We changed planes in Johannesburg for the final lap of our journey to Durban. At Johannesburg, Marie Hopton, my old friend from Kitwe, had made the hour trip to the big city, together with her sister, especially to meet Mama during our sixty minute stop over. When I asked Marie later what her impression was, she replied that it was difficult to learn about anyone when they will not remove their sunglasses! Unbeknown to me, prior to leaving Cornwall, Mama had, whilst I was bathing, telephoned Antony and made arrangements with him to meet us at Durban airport. She had not enlightened me so I was surprised to find Antony meeting us. Peter was there too, along with one of his pilot friends. It had been decided, without my knowledge, that Mama would travel back to Pietermaritzburg with my brother instead of the initial plan of staying with me first. Therefore, after a brief trip to my small home and a warm welcome from my two Staffordshires, Mama was whisked away by my brother. Imagine my astonishment when he telephoned a week later to tell me they had invited her to live permanently with them. I foresaw disaster. By the time they had themselves discovered this, it was too late to turn back.

Poor Mama. For all her faults, deserting us, and letting her heart rule her head, she tried very hard to make my holiday with her a happy one. Although I did not manage a closeness with her, I nevertheless have very happy memories of the time we spent together in Cornwall, and could but wonder at what a good mother she might have been.

Some years later, Antony and Tina had moved to Westville, an inland suburb of Durban, and Antony informed me that they had found it convenient to accommodate Mama in a Durban Retirement Home. Shortly thereafter, one night, she had fallen to her death from an upstairs bedroom window. This was determined an accident. On meeting Antony outside the Home where the memorial service was to be held, he handed me an envelope. Once inside, seated at the back, I opened the envelope and found several old black and white photographs. The first one I looked at was of my father. I thought it was fitting that he was here, at the funeral memorial, with me.

28

And I wonder do I dare, do I dare defy the universe?
In a minute there is time for decisions and revisions
Which a minute can reverse.

T. S. Eliot
1888 - 1959

Thus did I continue my journey, alone, making one massive mistake after another, never learning my lesson. Always jumping in up to my eyebrows, drowning, and hoping someone would arrive to pull me out of the quick sands of my own making. Someone once told me I was like a yo-yo, spinning down and then up again, then down and up, never quite unravelling, but also never quite accomplishing anything worthwhile.

However, before the next calamity occurred there came a joyful interlude. Peter, when he came home for odd periods, always managed a girlfriend or two. Some he brought home, some I never met. Two I was particularly fond of, but nothing ever materialised until one day he telephoned from the Transvaal and asked me to phone a girl, Susan, and ask her out for the following Friday evening. I told him to phone her himself, but with queues of young men waiting to use the telephone, made doubly difficult because Susan herself was receiving the call in the hall of the Young Women's Residence, it was not easy to arrange a first date with any degree of success. It was left to me! It didn't however, stop there: if she said Yes, then would she like to go out for the Saturday night as well? Since I was doing the asking, it seemed worthwhile to kill two birds with one stone! The end, or rather the beginning, of that story is that they announced their engagement on her 21st birthday, and were married a year or so later. They moved, temporarily to Johannesburg, and began their married life together, but that is their story, not mine.

Then I sold my house.

Although it sold for almost twice as much as I had originally paid, I had unwittingly sold it for considerably less than it was worth, but fortunately for my peace of mind, I did not discover this until some years later when it was resold for considerably more!

Peter and Susan had returned to Amanzimtoti, just south of Durban, close to Susan's family, which is where I bought, off-site, into a Retirement Village. I had sold my Durban house before the Village was finished, so had to find other accommodation, and went to board in a private hotel near to my employment. My two remaining Staffordshires, Elsa and Tiger, were literally palmed off onto Peter and Sue, difficult for them for they had a German Shepherd my Staffies did not care for. However, Peter and Sue did their best and accommodated my dogs in a tiny area, better than kennels but not what they had been used to. This might have all turned out to be not such a bad thing except for two disasters. One, the Village, which looked so good on paper, underwent several setbacks, and the builders themselves declared insolvent just prior to completion. The second was my beloved Tiger, who had long suffered from epilepsy, became impossibly ill, never recovering from one attack before the next was upon him. Upon his demise, which hurt more than I can say, Elsa was left alone, in her tiny accommodation, without me.

I could not take her with me, my life in such a turmoil, nor could I leave her where she was. She would not have stayed with anyone else being far too dependent on me. After agonising for many days I reached a decision I have regretted to this very day. I cannot write the words. I cannot understand how I came to do it, and I will never forgive myself. I am ashamed that I put myself first. Many years have gone by, but I don't think a day passes without my thoughts turning to Elsa. She was just a dog, but she was my dog, and I killed her. There are no other words for it, even if it was not me that pressed the plunger. May God forgive me for I cannot forgive myself.

Shortly afterwards I became a grandmother for the first time when Jennifer was born, the first of my two granddaughters, and life began to brighten up.

Yet it would seem that Robert Burns was right when he wrote that the best laid plans of mice and men, often go awry.

29

There is no armour against fate.
James Shirley
1596 – 1666

He was a charming, well-spoken man about three years younger than me and fate would decree that I should share his table at the private hotel. Very knowledgeable, I found him quite easy to talk to. It seemed we had a shared interest in history, and struck up an immediate friendship. He told me he was a plumber and worked for his brother-in-law. In no time we gathered a few fellow guests around us, and spent long evenings in convivial company talking far into the night. Inevitably we grew closer, and before I realised what had happened, he whisked me off to the new Sun City Resort in the Northern Transvaal for a luxurious week in the five star casino hotel with its enormous wild game park next door, edging Botswana. It struck me as extremely odd that a mere plumber should have such expensive tastes that could be realised. He seemed well able to afford it, so I held my peace and enjoyed the sudden bonus of enviable living. This was definitely my cup of tea, and I was not going to give it a miss for the sake of convention. After all, I was not hurting anybody. It was only later that I realised I was hurting myself, but by then it was much too late. Let us call him Simon.

I thought I might have found love again! How naïve could one be? On returning to earth, and the little hotel in Durban, we moved in together and everyone there thought this a great idea. I was living the dream, but it really was a fool's paradise, as I was yet to discover

One Saturday morning a huge rugby match was held in Durban which half a dozen of our friends decided to attend. As we were dressing in the early morning I took a swig of water from Simon's glass, and promptly choked. It was pure Vodka. Actually, it was South African Cane, but better known elsewhere, as similar to vodka. The aftermath argument should have served as a warning, and I ought to have extricated myself from the relationship there and then, but I did not. The excuse Simon gave me was the excitement of the match and everybody got plastered anyway. After months with him I still had not discovered his secret which was probably pretty obvious to anyone not quite as simple as me.

Poor Simon. He was a gentle person, perhaps too much so, with the kindest heart. I learnt that he was the offspring of one of the wealthiest and finest of families, much loved by them all. He had recently divorced, and it was said to have been a mutual decision. The family, once I had met them, took me to their hearts, and warmly welcomed me within their protected circle, but neither they, nor I, were able to save Simon.

The truth was that Simon was an alcoholic. This home truth was never fully accepted by the family, except perhaps by the younger generation, but they were not living with him, I was. We spent, on and off, the following ten years together. Over those years I learnt a great deal about this horrible disease, about which I had previously known nothing. No one, once afflicted, ever truly recovers. It is usually an addiction suffered by the gentlest of people. Being so kind, and almost simple, is perhaps why recovery is so difficult,

We were both interested in modern and ancient history,

particularly military history. There was plenty of that in South Africa, right on our doorstep. I took a short leave and away we went to explore the lands where the Anglo Zulu War, and other local wars, were fought.

On the banks of the Tugela River which separates the border between Natal and Zululand, stood the Ultimatum Tree. This beautiful historical tree was totally destroyed by vandals at the beginning of this century and is now but a rotting stump, but I am writing about the mid 1980's, and it was still there when I photographed it, before the rot set in. It was beneath this lovely old tree in January 1879, that the British presented the Zulus with a document which the Zulus refused to sign. Their refusal began the Anglo Zulu War, so it was from this tree that Simon and I began our little history tour. I was in my element. One of the bloodiest battles ever fought by the British Army, resplendent in their bright red uniforms, was the battle of Isandhlwana. It was the biggest mess-up, to be polite, of indecision and lack of communication that had ever occurred in British military history. Briefly, 22,000 Zulu Impi slaughtered 1200 soldiers. It was followed by the bravery shown at Rourkes Drift where some of the survivors had thought to find sanctuary in the mission station there. I could write more in much greater detail, but this has been done by those far more qualified than I. After many more such bloody battles where the British were outnumbered by the Zulu tribe, and so many lives were lost, the War ended with the defeat of Cetswayo at Ulundi. Victory after the defeat at Isandhlwana, and bitter sweet it must have been.

One must not forget that it was the Dutch Boers, or Afrikaners as they have become known, those intrepid farmers were the first to forge this land into a civilised nation, long before the Anglo Zulu War. Many of them lost their lives doing so. In 1838 Piet Retief, and seventy of his settlers, were invited to dine by Dingaan, King of the Zulus, who then set his Impi upon them as they were eating, and killed off the lot! The Zulu tribe had their origins in the Valley of the Kings, Umfolozi, where Dingaan's great kraal stood. Dingaan who had murdered his half-brother, Shaka, was the fiercest and cruelest of all the Kings. Shaka was that great man who had moulded the Zulu nation together in the first place. Many of the beehive huts of Dingaan's kraal have been rebuilt for a tourist attraction, but I actually stood on the original floor of one beehive hut I found, which was not yet fully demolished. Grey straw, mouldy with time, and chewed by long dead insects, trailed down from crumbling walls of sunbaked mud, the colour of red sand. I hesitate to write that I ran in horror when I thought I was being pursued, an angry dark spirit at my heels. No doubt it was only a small black chicken! Quite a lot of blood has stained the rolling green hills of beautiful Natal before it finally became a part of the Rainbow Nation.

Simon and I spent the following ten years together, on and off. They were years of conflict, misery, and excitement, some tempered with sheer joy. When sober, he was a good partner, and I was very fond of him. When not in his cups he was thoughtful and generous, and surprisingly considerate in bed. Keeping him sober for anything longer than a month or two, was not possible. He was never physically violent, but had an extremely wicked tongue which he used as a lash in a continuous torrent of abuse. One never quite knew when the drinking bouts would begin. They lasted anything as short as a day and a night to an entire week. They usually finished abruptly followed by sorrowful bouts of contrition and empty promises of sobriety.

I managed to sell my retirement cottage to a company that had purchased the entire village, and I didn't lose too much in the transaction. I was glad to be rid of it for it had caused me nothing but one big headache. Simon purchased a holiday cottage not far from Durban, which I often visited, and I took a flat nearer my work which he visited, even more frequently. It was decided that we would purchase a trailer, and fill it with camping equipment. With this we set off one day on an adventure.

It is here that the story of my life is filled with memories that I shall always treasure. It is an episode that few will have had the opportunity to enjoy. Of course, you have to be a history idiot, like me, to appreciate it.

We decided we wanted to follow the route the British soldiers took during the Boer War from when they disembarked at Port Elizabeth to when Kimberley was relieved. No mean task since, apart from those mounted, they walked all the way, most of it under fire. It was at this stage in my life that I got into the habit of dropping flowers, or flower petals, on any British War Graves I found, on a battlefield, or in a memorial park. Sometimes on Boer Graves as well. It is a habit I have maintained to this day.

In 1899 President Kruger of the Transvaal issued an ultimatum declaring war unless the British withdrew from certain borders in South Africa. A bold threat, this redoubtable man took on the might of the British Empire. Let's face it, he had remarkable success. In comparison to the British Army he had a mere handful of Boer farmers willing to fight for what they thought was theirs by right. These tough, honest men had already been pushed far to the north, away from the green lush lands of the Cape, where the mountains dominated like sleeping giants. They had forged a new country and called it the Orange Free State. It was riddled with diamonds.

Over the Vaal River to the north another new country flourished. This one yielded something men had sought for over the centuries: gold. This country was named, prosaically, the Transvaal.

This journey was an exciting and rewarding experience for me if only because Simon managed to stay sober until, like the troops, we relieved Kimberley! One day I would be a British trooper, lying prone in the thorny scrub of the Little Karoo before the heights of Magersfontein with the Boer troops above on the top of the hills, where they lay safe in the first of the trenches ever used in wartime battle. The sentry Boers could see for miles around – a perfect hiding place for men, horses and ammunition. The British were sitting, or rather lying, targets. Often these troops were of the Scottish Regiments, and wore kilts. Lying there, utterly exposed to the enemy, for there was no cover, only thorn bushes and scrub, they suffered from severe sunburn not only to the backs of their necks, but also to the backs of their knees. At one stage, the British casualties were so great it took two months to rebuild morale. The Boers were farmers, not soldiers, and rode sturdy horses with strong legs across miles of stunted bushlands. They, under their great commanders like de le Rey, Joubert, and Botha, perched atop every available hill and took on the might of the British Empire, not just the English. They must have known they could not win, but they very nearly did. All credit to them.

The next day I took on the British Empire too, on the top of another mountain peering down at the brave British walking into a fusillade of bullets. Eventually we arrived at the Modder River, and I lay concealed by bushes, firing from a long make-believe rifle in the form of a stick, a Scottish make-believe stick of the Western Highlanders Regiment, firing at the Boers, safe in yet more trenches on the other side. No two ways about it, Simon had to remain sober to contend with this suspiciously certifiable female contender for the VC!

It was not the easiest thing to cross a river, for the Boers had laid barbed wire entanglements beneath the water which cruelly trapped both horse and man, but the end was in sight. One of the

Boer generals, Cronje, was camped on the riverside at a small place called Wolveskraal, near Paardeberg. Here he was finally exposed to the full force of the British. He surrendered, which marked the beginning of the end of the war. However, Kimberley had been finally relieved by British forces approaching from a different direction. Simon and I had reached our objective too – Kimberley.

I found a few relics on the battlefields of Paardeberg: what looked like a bully beef tin with a bullet hole right through it, an old bent tin plate, and numerous small pieces of smooth coloured glass, and a few small broken bottles. I took them to a new museum that was just about to be opened in a small hamlet not far from the area, but I cannot for the life of me remember the name of the little village, but very possibly it was actually Woveskraal. There, where hardly any English was spoken, I was allowed to touch the very flag used by Cronje, now grey and tattered, its colours long faded, before it was placed under sealed glass. Not surprisingly English-speaking people, even though they might be South Africans, were not exactly warmly welcomed in these sacred Afrikaner settlements. A pity really, because they are a nation of whom I am particularly fond.

Finally we reached Kimberley, and settled down in one of the best camping parks I ever came across: the Kimberley Caravan Park, with tents permitted, so it was not necessary for our tent to be pitched in a different area to that of the caravans. There were sparkingly clean facilities beyond which was soft green grass backing onto the blue soil from the diamond diggings where I was told you just might find a diamond!

In this pretty city Cecil John Rhodes had bunkered down, and his place of residence still stood in almost regal splendour. Here he entertained the British generals, including Kitchener, a leader not well liked by his men. Oh, he got the job done, but at what expense? Unlike Buller, the other side of the country, who fought valiantly to relieve Ladysmith, tried to do so without too much loss of his beloved men, and who received little recognition from anybody else. Buller, who had received the Victoria Cross for bravery under fire during the Zulu Wars was virtually ignored. After several setbacks he was victorious in the Battle of the Tugela Heights, those hills around Ladysmith which Winston Churchill* called "the hills of whispering death". Thomas Packenham,* in his book *The Boer War* paid high tribute to Buller saying the man had the toughest job in the entire war. I was privileged at a later date to find Buller's memorial in the ancient Parish Church of the Holy Cross in the market town of Crediton, Devon. There is an equestrian statue of him in Exeter; and in Winchester a memorial reads 'a great leader – beloved of his men' so, in spite of Lord Roberts using him as a scapegoat, his people remembered him. I had to write this little piece because I too admire his memory.

We had managed this fantastic trip without personal incident, but Kimberley was to be Simon's downfall. He managed to get magnificently drunk on the eve of St. Valentine's Day which we celebrated in one of the original old hotels. It was four days before I could sober him up sufficiently to move on.

Life could not of course be a series of summer holidays. I was my own woman, so to speak, and to a greater extent paid my own way. I was working full-time – for the same company – now that Peter was married, and there was no need for me to be at home in the afternoon.

As far as I could gather, Simon was still working for his brother and brother-in-law as a general handyman. He was pretty much his own boss and seemed to come and go as he pleased. A couple of times he did not work at all. These were occasions when he suffered most, as did I, when he found consolation in the bottle rather than me. It was during one of these lapses that I approached the family and tried to explain his problem. They were obviously not sure whether to believe me or not. I especially asked that they ensure work for him as keeping him busy seemed to keep him out of trouble.

The Cane alcohol he drank looked like water and had no odour. Simon was adept at appearing to be sober when in actual fact he was definitely not. He kept glasses of Cane hidden in the most unlikely places, or so he thought. Much loved by his family, it was unlikely that much notice would be taken of me so, for the moment, life moved on.

We continued to enjoy little holiday trips, perhaps to the Drakensberg Mountains towering over neighbouring Lesotho, or up to the Mpumulanga which borders the Kruger National Park in Jock of the Bushveld country, where it is breathtakingly beautiful.

One trip was particularly memorable for me. I had taken annual leave and flew down to meet Simon who was on his way back from Capetown, pulling the trailer behind him. We took what is known as the Garden Route, which I had never seen. We began from Port Agulhas, that being the most southerly point of all Africa, then to Mossel Bay where the first post box used by the passing exploring sailors who dropped and collected their letters can still be seen in the natural rock formation – just a hole in the rock. On we drove to Knysna, a seaside Garden of Eden, home of the forest elephant, the pansy shell, the loerie bird, the sea horse, and the visiting whales. Beautiful, lovely Knysna, an earthly paradise and one of my most favourite places.

Our next stop was Plettenburg Bay to see the frolicking whales. Of course, whales don't actually frolic, but they are a magnificent sight to see. A bugle was blown by an ancient Cape coloured man every time whales were in the area. We pitched the tent as near the edge of the cliffs as we could be in the caravan park, just for the view. Not such a good plan since during the night a gale force wind blew up. Simon had by now passed out in the bell tent which was firmly attached to the ground, but still it wobbled and squashed up in the most amazing shapes, yet remained, incredibly, in place. I had by now decamped to the car and watched with some amusement tempered with the fear that the whole thing, including the occupant, would disappear over the edge of the cliff. By the time Simon awoke the following day he had missed the entire storm. I left him to do his own thing while I went exploring.

We went inland from there to Grahamstown, an historic university town. The caravan park was nestled prettily between large hills which attracted the violent lightning from a vicious thunderstorm while we were there. Simon had fallen asleep in an empty bath in the ablution block, and as it was in the male block I had left him there. He couldn't come to much harm and was not much of a nuisance to anyone there! I was alone in the little tent in the middle of the night, and was actually rather frightened during the fierce storm.

The following day Simon was repentant and sober, but I decided it was time to head for home. I would go and Simon could follow or not, as he pleased. Of course he pleased! Away we went, together, and foolishly decided to take a short cut through the Transkei in order to reach the coast again, at the mouth of the Umzimkula River which is the boundary of Southern Natal.

Pulling a trailer with a sedan car along dirt roads is not such a great idea. We met potholes that lay in wait at the bottom of even bigger potholes, but finally we reached the Wild Coast, not far from Port Edward. There we decided we had earned a rest, and booked into the Casino Hotel for two days before our final stretch home. Worthy of note is that in that particular part of Southern Natal there is a stretch of ground not far from the sea where King Shaka and his Zulu Impi fought a tremendous battle against a Pondoland tribe. So much blood was spilt that the soil is stained red to this day!

Quite often during these trips Simon would let me down, and become paralytic with all that implies. Once I had extricated myself from the car in the middle of nowhere, northwest of Johannesburg, because he was so drunk he could hardly drive, and wouldn't let me take the wheel. I really cannot understand how he managed to get away with it over the years. A man, who had been following us, very kindly stopped, identified himself, and gave me a lift to the nearest petrol station from where I telephoned Marie and John Hopton. Marie came to collect me, a good two hour drive, and took me home. Where Simon disappeared to I neither knew nor cared, but he guessed where I was for he finished up on the door step, sober, all spic and span, three or four days later, contrite as usual, with one black eye and a yellowing bruise where his kidneys were. He never explained, and I didn't ask. This was quite a frightening and dangerous thing to happen. If I was to continue our association I had to be entirely self-sufficient. On all our future trips together I drove my own car and we met at our destinations.

Why, might you ask, did I not leave him? If anyone is aware of alcoholism they will understand. The disease appears to affect the nicest of people who, when sober, are truly repentant and make promises to avoid temptation, which they are totally unable to keep.

In some desperation I eventually joined the Al Anon Support Group. It is a difficult life when someone of whom you are fond is busily ruining not only his or her life, but the lives of several other people with whom they are in immediate contact. At Al

Anon you share this experience with equals because all our lives are affected by another person's drinking. Al Anon gives advice on how to live with someone who has yet to seek help, or is already a practising alcoholic, for they are never truly cured. This did not go down well with Simon who verbally and loudly condemned my decision. However, in the fullness of time, Simon too made the effort to overcome his illness, and joined Alcoholics Anonymous. You cannot force someone to make this decision. They are responsible for their own lives. Regrettably, his choice was not a permanent one. He frequently fell by the roadside through sheer stubbornness. But each attempt he made would bring several months of sobriety before the sword fell once more.

It was during one of his sober sessions that Peter and Susan decided to take a trip to Australia and realise a long awaited holiday. The two girls were just old enough to leave for a couple of weeks or so, and Sue had close family there. I was concerned. My first thought on hearing of their plan was 'Dear Lord, I hope they're not 'packing for Perth',' a phrase heard too often in those days. But no, Margo and I were assured they were going for a holiday and a 'look-see', another familiar phrase.

Simon was enjoying a healthy period, and as a result, so was I. It was decided that we would look after the house, the girls, and the dog, not necessarily in that order. Simon was now attending the local Alcoholics Anonymous Group, and we also both attended the Baptist Church, a strong supporter of the A.A. Peter and Sue had built their house on land given to them by Sue's mother, Margo, and as it immediately adjoined Margo, we had another Granny we could call on if needed. In any case, needed or not, she was a pleasure to have close by. For me it was a delightful period of enjoying life as it should be. All too soon they returned.

Life returned to normal, and Simon fell off the wagon again.

I had been partnered with Simon for about five years when I finally decided that I would leave, on pension, from the company who had employed me for fifteen years, and actually moved in with Simon officially. This was no doubt another of my impulsive moments. It might well bring misery, but it was certainly a godsend for Simon. He was a controlled asthmatic and suffered a dreadful attack one evening when he was totally drunk. He collapsed at my feet. Cutting another tale much shorter, I managed to get him into hospital, via ambulance, and was fortunate to literally bump into a heart surgeon who was just departing for his house. This kind man took over, and saved Simon's life. Once during the three hours I waited in the hospital foyer, the surgeon came out and asked me if this man was worth saving! How very strange.

I never got to the bottom of that remark and frankly I didn't want to, either then or now. The outcome was that Simon stayed sober for almost a year. What joy. And the family believed me.

About a year after that Simon had hip replacement surgery. It was my shoulder he leant upon when learning to walk again. Neither of these episodes cured the alcoholic disease from which he suffered. They merely delayed the bouts which always, inevitably, recurred.

From time to time I tried to make a run for it. Often I pitched up at one or another of my close friends and tried to make a clean break. Simon always found me, and sorrowfully would beg my forgiveness. I always returned. Finally it was my son, Peter, who all but made the break for me:

"Mom," he said, "you have a choice. I cannot bring your granddaughters to visit you if there is the slightest chance that Simon is drunk, or seemingly so."

There it was: Hobson's Choice. I left Simon, not temporarily this time, but forever.

30

He who knows others is wise,
He who knows himself is enlightened.
From The Seven Sages of Greece.
6 century BC.

I was offered a small flat which had become vacant, in a block owned by my daughter-in-law Susan's family. In effect, it belonged to my daughter-in-law. The rent was reasonable and an added bonus was its closeness to my small family. I settled in quite comfortably and life began to take on a completely different hue. Gone were the hours of concern, of difficult decisions, of not quite knowing where to turn, or whom to turn to.

I missed Simon, of course, but we remained friends. He visited me sometimes, but was never allowed to spend the night, which fact was practically written into my lease. In any case, I was afraid that the affair would begin again. I need not have worried for within a very short time, a week actually, Simon had begun a relationship with another lady he had met on one of his local shopping trips. I had met her on the local shopping bus and was aware that he had taken her to the movies when I was not present. I heard no more from his family who had tried so unsuccessfully to marry us off, but had never truly believed he had a chronic problem.

Out of the blue, I received a beautifully written letter from Winifred's lodger with the details of Winifred's death in hospital.

Her niece, Shirley, to whom I had presented a floral horseshoe on her wedding day all those years earlier, had made all the final arrangements. She had also disposed of the contents of Winifred's flat and personal possessions, some of which had belonged to me. I replied to the man who had so kindly written and thanked him for all he had done for Winifred. He had included Shirley's address and I wrote a letter of thanks to her too. She did not reply.

To supplement my small pension I began to look after animals whose owners intended to go on vacation. Because this entailed actually living in their houses I could save a good deal more on expenses. It was a very successful venture, and my customers booked me well in advance, one family even changing their holiday dates to fit in with me. I had no animals of my own, and came to love those I cared for, even sending the dogs cards at Christmas time. My circle of acquaintances grew because of house sitting, both dogs and cats, and others. I even once looked after a South American crow, lonely in its huge cage, and desperate for freedom. I felt sorry for it so confined. It should have been soaring over the mountains, catching the wind currents, not clutching a round piece of wood. I wondered what pleasure the owner had watching it in the unhappy confinement. The owner, obviously wealthy, lived in a magnificent house, and complained about my fee saying that it was a lot for just one bird. I simply said that I charged the same be it dog, cat, rat, parrot or crow. I never did a recall but could not help but wonder what happened to it. The cats I cared for always gave me a headache. Mainly because it is impossible to constrain them, I was constantly afraid they would finish up spattered across the black tarmac of any adjoining road, as had happened to my own Burmese.

My granddaughters, Jennifer and Kirsty, were growing up

quickly, as children are apt to do. Jennifer christened me Mimi which was a nickname I liked, and which I carry to this day – very useful when my daughter-in-law, Susan, did not like to call me Mum, and I didn't like her to call me by my first name. Mimi suited very well. The girls did all the usual things fortunate little girls do, and both of us Grannies were in constant demand collecting or delivering to either school, or ballet, or swimming, or tennis, or parties. Susan held down a full-time job as one of the necessities of today's life style, so we were very fortunate to have the pleasure of seeing as much of them as we did. Margo, the other Grannie, also taught them both to play the piano until they were old enough to begin examinations. Today it is a pleasure to hear the classical result.

 I took every opportunity to visit my dearest friends Marie and John Hopton, in Johannesburg. Over the years Marie's migraines, from which she had suffered since childhood, had developed into unimaginable periods of pure pain A visiting American professor had been consulted some years previously, and it was decided that Marie, at her request, undergo his latest trial operation. It was very involved, with minute pellets being inserted, via the groin, into the base of the back of the neck where they lodged, thereby stemming the flow of blood. There was a 50/50 chance of survival, but if successful, promised Marie a further fifteen years of migraine free life. It had been a great success, and she was now in her seventeenth year of being migraine free. The promise had been kept, but now her time was up. Marie and her husband John, were my son's godparents just as I was the godmother of their daughter. She was like the sister I never had, and I think we were as close as siblings could be. It was incumbent upon me, and indeed my greatest pleasure, especially considering what they had done for me after my own John's death, to visit, and do what I could to make Marie's few remaining years as happy as I could.

She died in hospital, with her large, happy family around her, and with me as her dearest friend. My son Peter, came up from Durban to attend the funeral, and to take me back for my return trip home.

Her death would have been something of a closure except John, her husband, who had never been ill in his life, and almost as close to me as Marie was, died too of a heart attack before the end of that miserable year, following Marie by just six months. I could not attend the funeral because I was house-sitting for people who were overseas. Instead I wrote a poem for them both which their only daughter, Julie, very kindly printed and framed. Their deaths put me in mind of a doggerel I once read:

She first deceased,
He for a little tried
To live without her,
Liked it not,
And died.

Meanwhile in the back of my mind there hovered a seed that I had never allowed to flourish. In recent weeks the rains had come, and gone again, and now the sun shone, the seeds germinated, took root, and an idea formed in my head which would not be stilled: I telephoned Jan, my first love.

31

Now is the way clear, now the meaning plain.
Temptation shall not come in this kind again.
　　　　　from Murder in the Cathedral,
　　　　　T.S. Eliot, 1888-1965.

Over the years Jan and I had kept in touch. Whenever we thought there was something momentous to report, a birth, a death, a marriage, a glorious sunset (!) we would make contact by letter. Our letters were innocuous, and harmless. I had always handed them to John, Peter's father, when he was alive should he so wish to read them.

It will come as no surprise that I had decided it was time to once again make contact. It had taken Jan a further ten years to marry, and produce one son who was, by this time in his early twenties. Jan's life had taken a totally different turn, leaving the sea, and joining his elderly father in the diamond business, and opening his own jewellery shop.

It was time we met once again. I knew I was safe with Jan since he would never in a million years jeopardise his marriage. I was not so sure of myself, but hoped I would be able to simply rekindle a relationship that had always been, and always would be, a very large part of my life, without disrupting the smooth waters in which we had sailed. I contacted Jan by telephone from my son's house.

I sallied forth, all sails to the wind – forgive the cliché – and landed in Amsterdam. I had given this trip very careful consideration, and told Jan I would telephone once I had settled within a week or so, not wanting to descend immediately upon them. The very first thing I did upon landing on Dutch soil was to purchase a ticket, at tremendous cost to my small purse, that allowed me unlimited travel by train, or bus, throughout the Netherlands for twenty-one days. Costly or not, it was an absolute godsend. I found the trains fast and furious, and always on time to the very second, which astonished me. The buses went to all the places the trains didn't, but you had to be sure when to take a Citiliner, and when to take a town bus. These had a tendency to go up and down, and all around the same roads in the same town, which if nothing else, gave you a clear idea of the town. I used both, extensively.

I had made a very short list of several B&B's, or Pensions as they are called on the Continent, and the first of these was in Bilthoven, a satellite town near Utrecht.

Amsterdam, unless you are loaded, is like all big cities, very expensive, and is but a short train ride from Utrecht. My very first day I travelled by train from Amsterdam to Utrecht. My first views were of sunflowers by the thousands, not as I might have thought, of tulips, and of a huge Shell Petrol Station, Makro, and mealies (corn) growing in dead straight manicured rows. I began to think I was still in South Africa, but the rows were too tidy.

I changed trains in Utrecht and went on to Bilthoven, a mere twelve or so kilometres further, a pretty town full of large mansions, and lots of trees. There I booked into a very clean and comfortable Pension and settled down to enjoy a good night's sleep. The next day in Utrecht I explored the Dom, and got lost along the cobbled streets. I wandered amongst bent and twisted ancient houses steeped in a history kept a secret from me, a stranger, but nevertheless, no less appealing.

The following day I returned to Amsterdam and saw all the

things I wanted to see, from the Jewish ghetto to the wailing tower and a great deal more in between, including the pelicans who pecked their own breasts to draw blood in order to feed their young. They are actually stone statues built above a portico and are based on a legend.

I walked along the 'ladies street' where the shades were down, and the road was up, (Sunday?)! Because of the way the city is built, the farther out you go from the hub the further the walk around the rim. In the end I caught a tram. My expensive ticket was a key to healthy feet! There was so much to see. In the end, one row of canal houses looked very much like any other.

It was already my third day when I once again entrained, this time for Haarlem, not far from Amsterdam. I wanted to visit the Corrie Ten Boom House, less well-known than Anne Frank's but even more poignant and thick with sorrow. During the war the Ten Boom family hid the underground resistance workers, students, and Jews, and smuggled them out of the country along the resistance routes. The family were finally betrayed and caught. I crawled into, and stood in a cupboard which looked like the bedroom wall. In this cupboard six such refugees hid, and stood shoulder to shoulder for two days without food or water, with a large pot for human waste while the Gestapo searched the house. They were finally released by other resistance workers. It was an experience I cannot forget. The entire family died in concentration camps with the exception of Corrie who survived, and spent the remainder of her life preaching the gospel.

On the train one day from Utrecht I met a passenger who lived in Utrecht but worked in den Haag (The Hague), who, in a rush, had caught the express train to Amsterdam by mistake – rather funny because he told me this before he realised I wasn't Dutch. Na hebt hij het langzamer spreekt en ik hebt het begrijpt! Loosely translated means I had understood his speech. He had to change again in the big city which made him rather late for work! I went there myself the following day, but did not make the same mistake.

I must mention that normally when I tried to speak Dutch all I received in reply was a very polite "Pardon". Everyone spoke English almost better than I did, but they were all pleased that I did at least try. I only came across one woman guest in a hotel who listened to me trying to make a booking, and told me to stop speaking excruciating Dutch and speak English to the booking clerk whom, she said, spoke perfect English. The clerk later apologised.

It was time for me to move on and I left Utrecht and its easy access to that area, and travelled down to Nijmegen. It was also time for me to telephone Jan.

They lived in the village, or small town, of Wijchen, which was almost, but not quite, a suburb of Nijmegen. I was invited to lunch for the following Sunday and although Jan offered to collect me I elected to travel by train because they were so fast and frequent. He met me at the Wijchen station and I remember it was raining. He was standing outside at the end of the platform, and held aloft a large black umbrella which got in the way when we hugged a hello, which made us laugh so the ice, had there been any, was broken.

At their lovely apartment above the shop, which was a little extended, so that it was above the next shop too, I met Anneke for the first time. She is ten years younger than me, and her welcome was warm and friendly. I had found a dozen golden tulips for her, orange because it's the Dutch colours, and tulips for the Netherlands. I tried to think what it was like for her to welcome me so kindly into her life. She is a typical Dutch woman who had stood behind Jan through all their troubles. I asked Jan if I was intruding on their relaxing Sunday together, and he replied, "No. We are together all the time." The only time they are apart is when he cycles in the early morning. They work, eat, sleep, live, dream, always together. Do you fuse, and become as one? I really don't know because it never happened to me. I don't suppose it does happen to many. Jan said he just goes for a cycle if he feels like a change.

Anneke understood a little English, but Jan had to do a lot of translating because my Dutch was much worse. Between us we sorted through the lies Winifred had told me all those years ago which had ultimately destroyed a life together. Anneke was horrified, and said in Dutch "U moeder was n hek." Your mother was a witch – an understatement.

She suggested that Jan should book a table at the local Chinese restaurant for supper, and must take me home afterwards as the trains at night could be dangerous. She also told me that the following weekend they would be at their holiday cottage near Vlissingen. If I could be there at the right time they could pick me up, and show me around that part of the Netherlands. What can you say about such kindness? What would I have done had I been in her shoes?

Jan took me down to show me the shop, and cleaned my rings for me. He ordered a Zeeuse ring for my granddaughter, a ring peculiar to that part of Holland, Zeeland. It's a traditional ring worn on the small finger, and is made of solid silver with a solid silver centre giving the impression of a stone in twisted silver, very pretty. In due course I gave it to Jennifer, but she never wore it, and of course it turned black. (Recently Jennifer very kindly returned it to me. I cleaned it up, but did not wear it either. Now it's black again.)

It was a wonderful day, and evening, always remembered. Emotions fully charged, but not released.

Returning to Nijmegen I discovered that my landlady's mother owned two pensions in Maastricht. Although not on my list I went down and spent two wonderful days in a beautiful city abounding in history which I could so easily have missed. I also met the mother: a very glamorous and exquisite woman of sixty-eight years who had travelled to South Africa and intended to visit again. I was almost sorry to leave at the end of the two days I had allowed myself. But my time was limited.

The following day on my return to Nijmegen I found myself walking behind the English veterans of the "Market Garden Parade" on the very day commemorating the 52nd Anniversary of the airborne landings near Arnhem well behind enemy lines. I did so with great delight tempered with a good deal of pride. The aim of this operation was to capture the bridge across the Rhine River at Arnhem.

Ignorant of the time of this anniversary, I had spotted two elderly beribboned gentlemen, and stopped them to ask why they were there.

"For't Market Garden," said one.

I was invited to walk with them to the Market Square, where there were perhaps fifty more such veterans, Poles included. There were many ribbons and medals displayed across many chests: German campaigns, Battle of Britain, even Palestine ribbons.

"Go and see Jonkersbosch Cemetery," said one, "me Captain's buried there."

It was already on my list, as were others, many of which I visited.

There was a Dutch Airforce Band to do homage, and we all joined hands and sang "You'll Never Walk Alone." We watched them all march to the ancient Town Hall, and someone said "They're out of line."

Then I said, "They were in line when it mattered."

"That they were," was the reply.

I went by bus to Arnhem to see the Bridge that was too far, and had crossed it before I realised. Of course it is totally rebuilt. But I visited the Airborne Division Museum Headquarters at the Hotel Hartenstein in Oosterbeek, a suburb of Arnhem in the hills above the city. These headquarters had been occupied first by the Germans then by the British, then again by the Germans, and finally by the Allied Forces.

I walked the long walk from the Hartenstein HQ which the British and Polish troops stumbled down, in retreat, in the middle of a black and filthy night, led by a leading rope and little else, to the river. I saw the old church which still bears the ammunition scars. Then I climbed up another hill, and yet another, to the Arnhem Cemetery, mostly filled with airmen, and paratroopers, and the dead of war.

A great bond was forged between the incredibly brave civilians of the Dutch Resistance, the 1st Polish Independent Parachute Division and the British Airborne Troops, and their struggle to liberate Holland is commemorated annually.

I dropped many flower petals throughout the Netherlands on many war graves, particularly Polish and British. I've seen row upon row of white tombstones almost as though they are on parade, and visited quite a number of such cemeteries all over Holland – all beautifully kept and cared for by the Dutch. God bless them.

Jan did indeed collect me from my Pension in Vlissinghen the following weekend. Anneke had elected to remain at home where Jan was to take me after he had driven me around, because she had invited Jan's parents to visit, and I could then meet them. I have never been able to decide whether Anneke was being foolish, clever, or just plain nice. I think it was her nature, and she was, quite simply, a good person. Jan, like me, had been fortunate in his marriage.

He drove me all over Zeeland that day, and we talked and talked and talked. We went across the Delta Project, and visited the Veere Yacht Harbour to look at a totally wooden yacht Jan used to own. Once, when he and Anneke were broke, he sold it for f45,000, and it had just been resold for f550,000! We saw some beautiful villages and walked around Zerikzee, said to be the best preserved village in Holland. It had been submerged beneath the waters several times.

We drove across the Zeeland Bridge which is 5 kilometres long – a magnificent engineering feat to rival the Afsluit Dam that keeps the North Sea out. Finally we returned to Jan and Anneke's cottage. We all sat chatting, or rather they chatted and I sat and listened! I apologised to Jan's mother for not being able to converse in Dutch, and she replied in English that I was doing very well. Jan said he did not know she could speak any English, but he had forgotten that she had taken lessons when they thought that he and I were to marry. She had practised whenever occasion rose ever since. He wondered why she had never practised with him, but neither of us asked her.

My farewells were said once again. I had long since got used to hiding any emotion I had in regard to Jan. After all, I had years of experience behind me.

On the long train ride north to Assen, which I decided would be my next base, I reflected as I looked out of the windows at the countryside how everything in Holland was neat, and clean, and orderly. The old-fashioned windmills were fast disappearing, being replaced by modern ones with sails like aeroplane propellers. They stand in neat but fluid lines. The few remaining were as picturesque as ever. One of these still stands on the quayside at Vlissingen, and this was used as a beacon for Liberation Forces of WW2 passing up the Scheldt in the darkness, the relief of Antwerp in their sights.

Holland was not, as I had first thought, totally flat. Granted there are polders, land claimed from the sea, and even some flourishing villages lying below sea level. But to the north, and to the west where Germany lies, were plenty of hills. I saw horses eating apples straight from the trees, masses of roses blooming in very straight rows, lines and lines of furrows all very straight ready for vegetables or perhaps millions of tulips, and green meadows filled with fat white sheep, and of course the sleek, black and white cows of Friesland which was about as far north as I could go.

There are beautiful hilly villages, like Groesbeek, nestling amongst woods and meadows. I actually climbed a hill to see what was on the other side. I met a man in the magnificent Liberation Museum there, who showed me how to operate an explanatory computerised wall plaque. He said he came from somewhere right next to the German border and did a lot of diving into the Isselmeer where fallen aeroplanes still lay. I asked him how he felt living right on the border during the war, as surely they would be almost as much German. He was adamant in his reply and said 'no, pure Dutch, finish'.

Later I visited the ancient village of Oudewater where I was weighed to ensure I was not a witch. The entire village had remained unchanged for centuries.

Soon I had to leave this friendly, pretty country, and return to my chosen home. What memories I could take with me:

I had watched small girls rope skipping in their clogs on the cobblestones.

I had been issued with a Passport at Leeuwarden in Friesland, where I was informed only the Frieslanders were Dutch, the rest were foreigners!

I had seen the sun breathing through the church windows at

Goude.

I had crawled through the Caves of Maastricht.

I had stood on the quay at Delfzuil on the Dollard Coast, and looked at Germany.

I had perched on the very end of the pier at Vollendam and eaten eels out of a paper bag.

I had walked 2 kilometres across the Afsluit Dam, which is 20 kilometres long, and caught a bus for the remaining 18 kilometres!

I had stood on the top of the West Kappelle dike at high tide where the sea looks higher than the houses behind me, which is not surprising because it is.

Maybe God did make the world, but the Dutch made Holland.

I had done what I had set out to do. Nevertheless, I had laid no ghosts, only resurrected them. It was time to go home, and face whatever now lay in store.

32

It is a part of probability
That many improbable things will happen.
Aristotle 322BC

The fool's paradise that I had come to live in and enjoy did not last terribly long. It seemed but a short time later that Peter, my son, decided that their previous visit to Australia had been about as far from the 'look and see' trip they had intended as it's possible to imagine, and become instead a 'look and go'. By the time I became aware of the undercurrents their plans were in the far advanced stage.

The day came when I watched two little blonde ponytails bobbing along and disappearing around a corner in the Departure Lounge of Durban Airport. Margo, the other Granny, had her niece beside her while I stood on the other side of this young woman whom I hardly knew. She put her arm around me and told me to be brave. I was becoming accustomed to being brave.

Other than weeping copiously, which I did not want to do in public, and fleeing the scene, I really did not know quite what to do next. I did flee to my car, and drove to a shopping centre large enough to hide myself in. Even there I was thwarted for, when passing one of the open-air cafes a woman bounded out.

"Patricia, are you ill? You look terrible," she said.

It was one of my dog-sitting customers. She insisted I have a cup of tea and I, of course, unloaded my unhappiness. When I had finished she made me promise to call at the nearest Travel

Agent and book an Australian holiday ticket for the following year, then at least I would have something to look forward to. It was as good a medication as any more professional advice might have been, although of course, it came to nothing.

Peter, to his credit, had tried to soften the obvious blow I had tried so hard to conceal, by suggesting I return to England. Since I was a citizen, it would not be a problem. I had been horrified for it seemed so far from Australia. He had meant to work there, in order to raise enough money for my 'entrance fee' into Australia in due course. The waiting time for Australia in those days was about fifteen years. This was the road I decided to take.

Like a dog with a bone I worried at this idea for days. I bought The Lady Magazine which was well known for advertising numerous and various jobs in England to the positive and the brave. I decided that with my experience I was both.

I found a number of positions available for carers, people who were willing to work for agencies who found the jobs for you. Caring was a live-in, all-found occupation which required total dedication to the person, in some cases, persons, who needed assistance in their own home. I was sure I could do this. Fortunately for me, Margo, my son's mother-in-law, was able to introduce me to an associate who had already travelled this path, who gave me several good tips but was not greatly optimistic. There was much more to Caring than I had imagined, and she painted a pretty dark picture to the whole scheme. Firstly I would have to find an agency that would give me a training session after which I would be bound to that agency for several months. Secondly I would encounter a lot more complications than I had envisioned: the patient might be bed-ridden and I would need to learn how to operate a lifting machine, or perhaps the person was well advanced in dementia and I would need the patience of Jove; or I might need to deal with two people, husband and wife, all of whom were waiting impatiently for God. I was not to be deterred.

My mind made up, I wrote to agency after agency in the British Isles, nearly all of whom replied. Finally I settled on one who advised I contact their recruitment man in Capetown, of all places. They told me they seldom employed anyone over the age of sixty. I talked and talked and talked some more and eventually they were persuaded.

The result of this somewhat hasty plan was that, after subleasing my flat, I travelled to the chosen Agency somewhere in Essex, and presented myself along with several other hopefuls. We were all subjected to a grueling Caring Course which lasted for three full days during which time we all found our own accommodation. Finally, we were presented with certificates and each sent to a listed client. Thereafter all Carers are obliged to update their knowledge by short correspondence courses which they must pass before continuing. It seemed to be a profitable organisation as I counted eight young women manning the computers containing the client/patients particulars, and the particulars of ourselves. Somehow or other they married you up, but it was bit of a hit and miss operation. It resulted in my very first assignment starting the following day with my being sent to an elderly lady who could only move her right arm and her head.

To get her out of bed using a lifting machine was rather like a ship's crane lifting a canvas bag of precious eggs from the ship's hold to a waiting vehicle on the quayside. My waiting vehicle was a wheelchair into which she had to be deposited undamaged. Still very new and a little afraid, I had to appear calm and capable so as not to distress her. However, the more times I did it the more professional I became of course.

Performing ablutions, both top and bottom, required a similar lifting technique which I do not remember being taught. It was more a matter of good common sense. I had the impression she quite enjoyed it as it gave her something more to do than just sitting in a wheelchair. There was nothing much wrong with the lady's mind and she would laugh happily when I had her swinging over the commode without pain or embarrassment. Her daughter, a doctor, came for lunch on my second day, and I heard her say to her mother, "Well, she can certainly cook." Praise indeed.

The Agency could not have sent me to a more difficult job for my first assignment. Surely it could not have been a test. Most agencies would only send you for two weeks to a client, and then you had to be sent to the next. I think this was to avoid Will contesting and the like, but you could return to a client, or they themselves could request you after a suitable break. I very nearly threw the whole experience in when my Agency asked me to remain there indefinitely after a full three weeks. However, with somewhat grim determination, I stuck to my guns and was eventually transferred to a darling lady of ninety-nine summers. She was an absolute love. The only thing wrong with her was her age. I was with her when the dreadful 9/11 disaster occurred, and we watched it together on television in total horror. She was in great distress as she had a great nephew working in one of the buildings, and she needed my close attention and loving care. I grew very fond of her, and was transferred back to her at her request.

I left the Agency when they wanted me to return to my first assignment. They said I had no choice in the matter, but I had not signed a contract and I simply chose to disagree with their telephonist.

My second Agency, called Country Cousins, had a home base is Horsham, Sussex, and I stayed with this Agency for three seasons, returning to South Africa after each five month session. Longer than that, with taxes involved, didn't seem economically viable. I loved Horsham. It was my father's youthful hunting ground as it was close to his school, Christ's Hospital, the ancient school founded by Henry VIII which I had once visited years earlier with my father. In Horsham I rented with a marvelous lady who rented me B&B accommodation for a minimal sum provided I made up all the beds each morning during my short stays between assignments. These were many and varied. Some good, some atrocious, but none as difficult as that first poor paralysed lady.

I sat correspondence courses which kept me updated, and worked continually with just three or four days between cases. I could fill a book with some of the persuasions and antics I encountered. The most difficult were always the married couples – they ganged up against their carer, probably because their family insisted on a carer when they actually considered themselves capable.

One couple, both wheelchair bound, insisted on removing their teeth at the dinner table, picking at the morsels of food lodged thereupon, and leaving the dentures on the table for me to remove and clean, of course.

Another couple had wheelchairs next to their beds upstairs, with another two chairs waiting at the bottom of the staircase. There was a chair lift for their use when they came down in the late afternoon. They consumed a breakfast, and a full lunch served on individual trays, while they remained in bed, and then complained when the food was only moderately warm after I had lugged the trays up the stairs adroitly maneuvering around the lift chair. The lady herself on one occasion, when I was taking up a bonus cup of tea lay prone in bed with her hands neatly crossed over her chest, eyes closed, presumably feigning death. I had been warned by the previous carer that this might happen so I simply turned on my heel, and went back downstairs taking the tea with me.

Of course, not all couples were difficult or ungrateful for the care they received, albeit it was being paid for. One couple, who lived on the edge of Dartmoor, where carers did not necessarily wish to go, were quite the nicest of all my clients. I was requested to continue my assignment there for a further three weeks. They had a marvellous black, oil cooking stove which, I was told, frightened all carers, but upon which I cooked probably some of my best meals ever. I took them once to a Meet of the local fox-hunting group where I was given my first taste from the loving-cup, and I asked permission to go and play with the hounds, which I was given, amazingly. I heard eventually that they had left the little cottage attached to their son's farm, and been moved into a retirement home in the local village. I knew this was something they did not want to do and was sad for them.

Of the many singles I cared for the most memorable was a little lady who lived in Esher, near Hampton Court. I cared for her and her dog, over a period of almost three months, at a special request from her family. Towards the end she suffered a severe stroke from which she never recovered. Losing her was like losing a member of my family which is perhaps another reason why a carer should not stay too long in one place.

Another single I came to love was a totally blind lady. She loved to be pushed to the park, even in the rain, and we would sally forth, she clutching aloft her umbrella, blocking my view, while I pushed the chair and precariously balanced my own umbrella.

All my single gentlemen were delightful, even the old doctor who had been one of the medical men on the notorious Burma Road in Malaya during WW 2, who insisted I read aloud again and again the chapter in a book in which he had been mentioned, until I knew it by heart.

During the period of time I spent in England amassing a fortune, a very small fortune, but to me a fortune none the less, I paid a flying visit to my family in Australia. Peter had kept me informed of the rules and regulations for entering Australia as a mother applying for a permanent visa, and when I heard that Susan's family were all there for Christmas, I thought I would join them for the New Year. I broke my journey in Brisbane where I visited an Immigration lawyer, filled out the forms required, and then continued on, and joined my small family in Mackay. Unfortunately my timing to visit them could not have been worse. After ten days I changed my return ticket to England for an earlier date, departed, unhappily, to continue my work in London, and put on hold any future plans of emigrating to Australia.

Shortly before I had completed my assignments I received a phone call from a Durban friend, Joy, mentioned earlier in this tale, who said she had some sad news. My previous companion, Simon, had died. I was shocked, astonished and dismayed.

"How?" was my query.

She replied that it was too sad to relate, but I told her not to be ridiculous, and I would find out anyway, so she could at least put me out of my misery.

"He hanged himself," she replied.

It did not, of course, put me out of any misery.

Eventually my three stints in England came to an end in as many years, and I finally returned to my home base in Durban, South Africa.

Here my friends, in my absence, and with my wholehearted approval, had taken a flat for me on the top of the local shopping centre at the base of the Berea, within walking distance of where I had lived in my own little house twenty years earlier.

33

One crowded hour of glorious life
Is worth an age without a name.
               Thomas O. Mordaunt
               1730 – 1809.

I settled into my new accommodation with as much happiness as I could muster in the absence of my family. I found local employment in Durban, within walking distance of my flat, as manageress of a small cosmetic company. There I retreated, nursed my mental wounds, and prepared to allow myself thinking and planning time. I had some very close friends, a comfortable if uninspiring lifestyle, and a library in the same block!

All went reasonably well until three things occurred, almost simultaneously, that crashed together like a reverberating clap of thunder, and created a catalyst that re-shaped my life once again.

The first was pretty insignificant for the times. Visiting the bank to deposit the funds for the shop I was managing, I found myself blocked off by a police cordon. A robbery had just taken place within the bank, and the area was hot with heavies, guns at the ready.

A few days later, descending in the lift that serviced the residential complex in order to collect my car from the basement, I almost stumbled into a body lying prone, inches from my foot. Only the shout of an enormous African policeman nearby prevented me from stepping upon the still man's face – not that he would have felt anything for he was very dead, if not quite cold. There had been another robbery, this time in the shopping centre above which I lived. Two other robbers were inside the centre but these were alive, and looking rather white from fear! The African Police Force had done their duty.

The final insult to my already tottering equilibrium was when I visited a very close friend. She was entertaining a house guest from Johannesburg and invited me to morning tea. My friend lived in a rather lovely complex of duplex homes that had the added advantage of visitors parking inside the secure estate. Regrettably, I couldn't fit my car in on that day because our mutual friend's car occupied the space. Without too much concern I parked alongside the pavement on the road, outside the front gate. I was not worried as my steering wheel was attached to the passenger seat base with a twenty-five millimeter thick linked chain to deter thieves. Need I add the dismay I felt when on opening the garden gate once my visit ended, I found an empty space where my car should have been. Before I had even reached the police station to make my report the car would have been in Swaziland. The poor police were not terribly interested, they were far too busy chasing other robbers.

This then was the catalyst that finally drove me to seek greener pastures, stained a less bloodied pink than those I enjoyed. The obvious road for me to travel this time was that which my small family had taken three years earlier.

I began by approaching the same agents in Brisbane, Australia, who had previously handled my application, which I was surprised to discover they still held on file. I underwent the stringent medical needed, and finally set about meeting all the rules and regulations needed to be accepted in that fair and fabulous country.

I had thought to end my little history epistle around about

here, but found my final few days were too amusing to ignore, especially the following.

Being unwilling to hire a car I had no private vehicle at my disposal, and had to put all my plans into place by using public transport. This, in itself, was quite amusing. Unlike the fantastic public transport system of Perth, where one can get from A to B quite easily by bus or train, Durban was different. The best way to travel, in fact the only way to travel within the precincts of the city, and environs, was by African Taxi. These were hysterically funny – at least, I found them so – and are worth a paragraph or two.

They are actually Kombi type vehicles, seating perhaps ten to twelve people but squashing in another half a dozen or so, totally against the law but overlooked because the police are too busy catching other criminals! They are hailed by standing in the road when you see one coming, and raising one hand. Depending on what your hand did, depended upon whether the bus stopped or not. A shake might mean you wanted a trip to the city, a thumb wiggled meant a trip to the next shopping centre, and so on. All these signals are known by the Africans, but only a few signs are known by others. Occasionally a taxi would halt at a designated stop which is the way I preferred to alight. My very first time was uncomfortable: the bus was filled to capacity with laughing, shouting African ladies who squeezed up to make room for me. They all immediately fell silent, but just for a second or two while they got used to the idea of this interloper. Then the noise began again with even more hilarity than before! The vehicle went its usual breakneck speed and swayed from side to side. I was slightly in awe of the driver, and had to admire him! I used this method of transport many times, each time with greater bravado.

Finally, after pages and pages of application, stringent medical certificates, passport updates, general questionnaires successfully completed, with, most importantly, sufficient funds in the bank, I was granted an Australian Visa which enabled me to enter the country legally, and happily, within a required stated time. I didn't wait.

34

Footfalls echo in the memory,
Down the passage we did not take
Towards the door we never opened.
Time past, and time future,
What might have been, and what has been
Point to one end, which is always present.
Fragments from Burnt Norton
T.S. Eliot. 1888 – 1965.

The Ending.

In those days the Durban Airport was situated by the sea in the southern suburbs, and I had flown from there on many occasions. I was aware of various landmarks which I could see from my window seat on the aeroplane as I departed en route for Australia. Looking down, my last view of Durban several hundred feet below was of the enormous block of flats that clung seemingly precariously to the edge of those small hills known as The Berea, below which nestled my little house of long ago, and silently, I cried.

I was leaving the land I loved so much, that had succoured me, and given me hope. I had much to be thankful for, and much to regret. On reflection I decided that my life, blessedly healthy, was very similar to the life of others. I was not alone, nor was I unique. It had been full of opposites: I'd walked in shadows and been swamped with despair; I had danced with delight, and shared the sheer joy of living. I was leaving a great deal of it behind, but I was travelling on once more, this time to a new life, a new tomorrow.

35

Reflections

In those early hours where no dawn breaks
I long for sleep, and the darkened thoughts within my mind,
Beat a hasty rhythm, a metronome of chances missed,
A dream that cannot be recaptured, yet still is there.
A harrowing road of time that passed too soon,
And left the hours behind, hours of sad regret.

My thoughts are tossed and thrown about,
Then reassembled to haunt the coming day.
So have the moments gone throughout the years;
The hopes and loves too tight to hold,
But clenched in a fist of make believe.
This saddens me, and in the night I fear my heart will break.

Suddenly, as dawn comes, a nightingale
Trills his beauteous song, a magic sound,
Surpassed by none, and as I listen,
My mind is reawakened, and I know
That although the past is today's memory,
Tomorrow is today's dream.

The ivy leaves rustle beneath my window,
I hear the cru-crool of a dove which alights on my sill,
And eyes me hopefully.
From the church comes the hymn of a boy,
Who longs to run free in the meadow, the meadow
Where buttercups sway in gentle confusion.

I hear the laughter of children at play,
I smell newly baked bread, and mown grass,
And warm puppies in a bundle of milky contentment.
Then my troubled mind is stilled,
As the tangled threads of life unravel
To a new day, a new tomorrow.

36

A Backward Look: Grandfathers.

Paternal Grandfather Frank Quarrell Part, born 1881.
An odd choice of name which began even further back to my great, great grandfather, Joseph, born 1806, who married Mary Quarrell, and added her surname to their children. It lasted for only two generations my own grandfather being Frank Quarrell Part. (He fared better than his elder brother who was christened Sultan Quarrell Part!) It seemed that battleships played a large part in the naming of my family: I have Rodney as a middle name, after my father Rodney Frank, and both Sultan and Rodney were not only admirals but battleships too. That was all very fine, then, but after all I am a woman, and I don't think they had women admirals, or women battleships either come to that!

During the First World War between 1914-1918 the greatest sea battle fought between Great Britain and Germany was the Battle of Jutland, off the coast of Denmark, in the North Sea between the 31st May and 1st June 1916. In this disastrous encounter between two great navies, *HMS Black Prince* had fallen far behind the British Fleet during a particularly pitch black and stormy night. As dawn began to break she was caught beneath the powerful beams of several enemy searchlights from a bevy of battleships who raked her from prow to stern. She lay, a helpless wreck, without having fired a single shot. As she drifted down the German line unable to defend herself, the enemy ships fired continually upon her until with an enormous explosion, she blew up. All 857 souls on board were lost as she sank to the bottom of the sea. Their bodies were never recovered. Petty Officer Frank Quarrell Part, Engine Room Armourer 1st, was one of them.

The wreck of *HMS Black Prince* is a Protected Place under the Protection of Military Remains Act. My paternal Grandfather is listed on the Royal Navy Memorials in Portsmouth, and in Gosport, as "Killed in Action 31st May 1916".

I write this as my personal memorial to him, and add, slightly altered by myself:

We fell under the folds of the waves, and a memorial
Was raised over us by our country,
Not unjustly, for we lost lovely youth
Facing the rough cloud of war.

The Part Family Tree

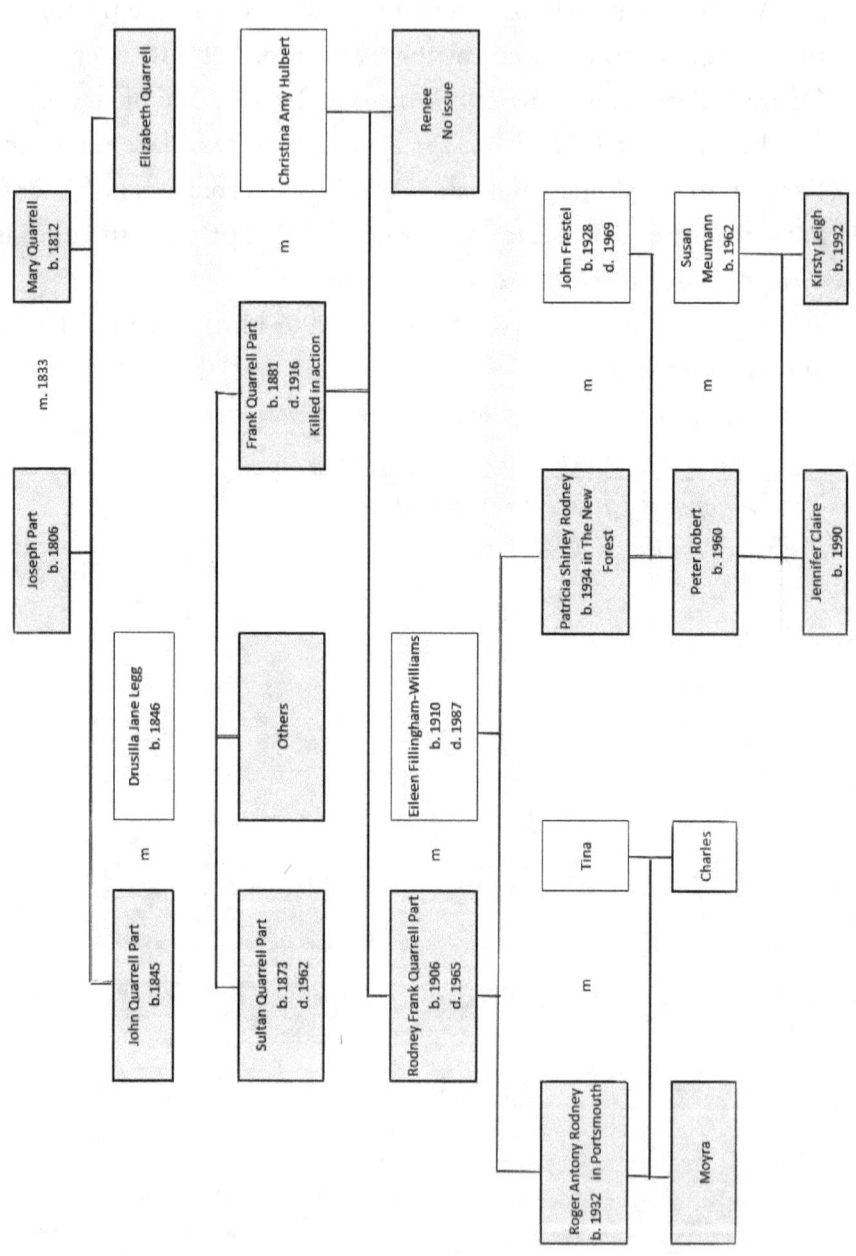

My maternal Grandfather was Harold Fillingham-Williams. I went back quite a long way because I needed to know where the Fillingham had come from. George Fillingham, born 1797, married a Millicent Mary Taylor. They produced only one daughter who married a Charles Williams. She retained her father's name by adding Fillingham to Williams, which act often occurred when no son had been born, in order to continue the male name. So it continued through the years until Harold, the last of nine children, was born in 1872. He married Belle Gillies and they had two children one of whom was my mother, Eileen Fillingham-Williams, born 1910 in Kingston on Thames.

Grandfather Harold became a solicitor, and worked his entire life as secretary to Member of Parliament Lord Glenconner, Sir Edward Tennant, who was Lord Lieutenant of Peebles, travelling extensively with him.

What he did during the First World War undoubtedly fell under the official secrets act, and therefore he enjoyed reserved occupation status. He continued in the service of the aforementioned and died in Ringwood, New Forest, in 1927 at the relatively young age of 55 years. Belle, my grandmother, died in 1932, so neither of them knew anything of their grandchildren.

I have followed the historical facts of my grandparents, rather than their actual memory.

Fillingham Williams Family Tree

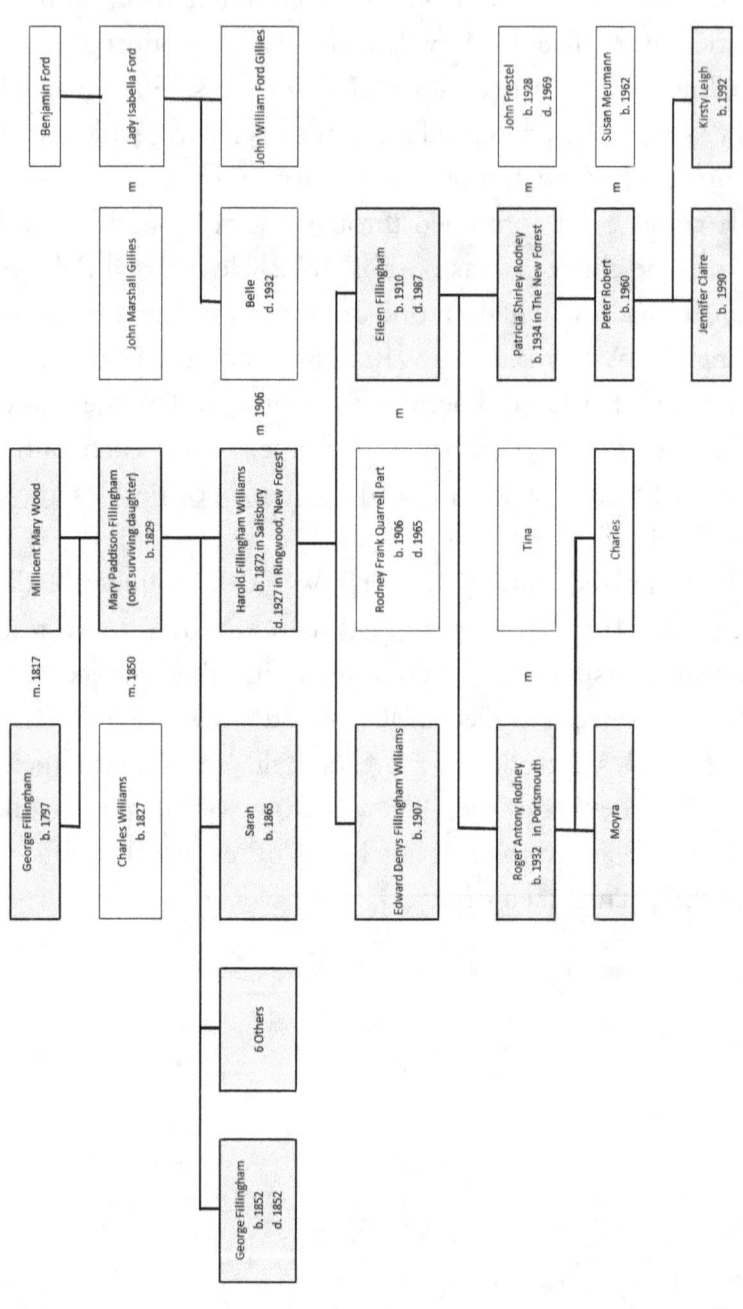

To all those who have faithfully ploughed through these pages, adieu and thank you. Love life and live well.

Tricia Frestel,
also known as
Patricia Cole,
Perth, W.A.

Reference		Page
Charles Dickens	"ineddicated"	8
Douglas Bader	*Reach for the Sky*	8
Pilot Officer Magee	The surly bonds of earth	8
John Milton	They Also Serve	9
Rudyard Kipling	The great grey green Limpopo River, and the Kolokolo bird	168 169
Grantley Dick Reid	*Childbirth Without Fear.*	175
Eve Boswell	*Pickin' a Chicken*	189
Robert B. Hamilton	I walked a mile with pleasure	224
Lt. Gen. Frederick Browning	*A Bridge Too Far*	266
Thomas Packenham	*The Boer War*	280
Winston Churchill	The Hills of Whispering Death & other quotes.	280
T.S. Eliot	Fragment from Burnt Norton & other quotes.	318
www.Wikipeadiea	'The Black Prince' Battle of Jutland	323

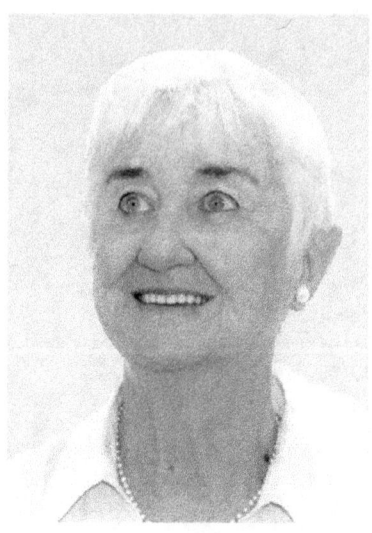

ABOUT THE AUTHOR

Tricia Cole makes no claim to fame for her small contributions to the literary world. Always a 'scribbler', she is a member of three writing groups and has written several poems, some appearing in minor publications. For several years she wrote and edited the bi-annual Animal Anti Cruelty League Magazine in Durban, South Africa.

This book was written because she needed to write her story down, and dedicates it to her granddaughters and their children's children ad-infinitum. She also hopes it will show how life is precious and only given once. It should be lived well and not wasted.

Tricia is currently writing her next book, a compilation of short works, called *A Volume of English Titbits*.

www.ingramcontent.com/pod-product-compliance
Lightning Source LLC
Chambersburg PA
CBHW071224080526
44587CB00013BA/1485